THE ORIGINS OF THE AMERICAN BUSINESS CORPORATION, 1784–1855

Contributions in Legal Studies
Series Editor: *Paul L. Murphy*

Inferior Courts, Superior Justice: A History of the Justices of the Peace
on the Northwest Frontier, 1853–1889
John R. Wunder

Antitrust and the Oil Monopoly: The Standard Oil Cases, 1890–1911
Bruce Bringhurst

They Have No Rights: Dred Scott's Struggle for Freedom
Walter Ehrlich

Popular Influence Upon Public Policy: Petitioning in Eighteenth-Century
Virginia
Raymond C. Bailey

Fathers to Daughters: The Legal Foundations of Female Emancipation
Peggy A. Rabkin

In Honor of Justice Douglas: A Symposium on Individual Freedom and the
Government
Robert H. Keller, Jr., editor

A Constitutional History of Habeas Corpus
William F. Duker

The American Codification Movement: A Study of Antebellum
Legal Reform
Charles M. Cook

Crime and Punishment in Revolutionary Paris
Antoinette Wills

American Legal Culture, 1908–1940
John W. Johnson

Governmental Secrecy and the Founding Fathers:
A Study in Constitutional Controls
Daniel N. Hoffman

THE ORIGINS OF THE AMERICAN BUSINESS CORPORATION, 1784-1855

Broadening the Concept of Public Service During Industrialization

RONALD E. SEAVOY

Contributions in Legal Studies, Number 19

GREENWOOD PRESS

Westport, Connecticut   London, England

Library of Congress Cataloging in Publication Data

Seavoy, Ronald E.
   The origins of the American business corporation, 1784-1855.

   (Contributions in legal studies, ISSN 0147-1074;
no. 19)
   Bibliography: p.
   Includes index.
   1. Incorporation—New York (State)—History.
2. Incorporation—United States—History. 3. Corpora-
tions—New York (State)—History. 4. Corporations—
United States—History. I. Title. II. Series.
KFN5348.S4   346.73'066   81-1017
ISBN 0-313-22885-X (lib. bdg) 347.30666   AACR2

Library of Congress Catalog Card Number: 81-1017
ISBN: 0-313-22885-X
ISSN: 0147-1074

First published in 1982

Greenwood Press
A division of Congressional Information Service, Inc.
88 Post Road West
Westport, Connecticut 06881

Printed in the United States of America

10 9 8 7 6 5 4 3 2 1

Contents

Tables

Preface

This book examines a major factor that contributed to the rapid industrialization of the United States: the role good laws played in accelerating the transformation of one state from rural under-development to the threshold of an urban industrial society within seventy years. A key legal innovation was the passage of general incorporation laws that encouraged the creation of business corporations. In the United States, these laws grew out of the wide-spread colonial use of the corporate device to organize religious congregations, units of local government, and occasionally a local internal improvement project. New York was studied because it was one of the earliest states to industrialize and because it showed exceptional energy in exploiting the commercial opportunities of large interstate markets.

The first class of business corporation to undertake interstate business on a large scale was banks, and as Joseph A. Schumpeter observed, it was the enormous creation of bank credit that fueled the economic transformation of the United States. The second major class of corporation that accelerated economic growth was railroads because, by 1855, they were on the verge of becoming the most efficient means of long-distance, all-weather overland transportation. Business corporations, particularly banks and railroads, were promoted by individuals operating almost en-tirely under state laws because, after the destruction of the second Bank of the United States, the national government used only a small portion of its power (the best known are the tariff and land grants after 1850) to mobilize and allocate resources to socially desirable investments. Therefore, the best way to see how new technologies and enlarged markets were exploited (from 1825 to 1855) is to focus on one state, and preferably one of the most industrially advanced states. To do otherwise would lead to a serious distortion in understanding the policies desired by pioneer corporate entrepreneurs because it was the energy of these businessmen that was a leading factor in creating the nation's industrial base and laying the foundation for the national market.

The business corporation had, by 1840, become a device that allowed popular participation in the profitable exploitation of larger markets and advanced technology. The policy that guided its use during the Jacksonian era was laissez faire, which was best implemented by the passage of general incorporation statutes for business enterprises. The economic, social, and political issues connected with the passage of these laws form the vehicle that helps explain the relationship of law to the economic transformation of the United States.

This study makes two major assumptions, which have guided the use of source materials: first, that the American political system, and particularly that of New York, was highly responsive to the needs of major interest groups and to the aspirations of its citizens because fundamental changes in economic policy were achieved without resort to violence. Second, the legal record (statutes, legislative documents, court opinions, and constitutional conventions) and especially the legislative record supply the best indication of what the people wanted because, during the period of this study, the preponderance of political power resided in democratically elected state legislatures. The political stability that allowed these orderly changes to take place was rooted in the social and religious heritage of the nation and New York, as profoundly modified by the winning of national independence and the achievement of national political stability under the Constitution of 1787.

THE ORIGINS OF THE AMERICAN BUSINESS CORPORATION, 1784–1855

Introduction

This study traces the development of the American business corporation by focusing on the origins of general incorporation statutes in New York and on the policy considerations that prompted most states to adopt such statutes by 1855. General incorporation statutes allowed the self-incorporation of private asssociations at the option of the promoters, without any political intermediary. Soon after the end of the Revolutionary War, the New York legislature passed general incorporation statutes for several classes of benevolent public service organizations. The one for religious congregations was the most prominent because it implementated a policy of denominational equality by offering the advantages of incorporation to all religious congregations without discrimination.

In colonial North America, there had been few counterparts of the municipal and ecclesiastical organizations that existed in England. The colonial organizations were not recognized as corporations under common law, and in order to possess corporate privileges, they had to be incorporated by statute law. During the colonial period, all major classes of organizations were incorporated, and all of the legal devices to create corporations were used. Numerous municipalities (cities, villages, and towns) were chartered by colonial assemblies, as were some prominent educational and charitable institutions, plus a few large business corporations like the Proprietors of the Long Wharf of Boston.

Massachusetts was the leading colonial government in creating corporations. The Massachusetts General Court passed a general regulatory statute for towns as early as 1635 and modified it in 1670, 1692, and 1694. In 1713, the legislature passed a de facto general incorporation statute for persons who held land in an undivided parcel. These persons were usually the heirs of the oldest settlers in a town. They claimed that the town's common land was the personal property of the earliest settlers who had received the land as a grant from the assembly to help bear the heavy expenses of initial settlement, such as clearing roads, building wharves, and erecting a meeting house. The commonly held lands that were not sold to later settlers remained as the private property of these initial settlers and their descendants. In 1735, another de facto general incorporation statute was passed for the owners of wharves and water-powered mills (grist, saw, fulling, forge), and for the types of internal improvement and community service enterprises owned by several persons. Incorporation was a means of dividing ownership by shares without physically dividing the property, and it was also a way of assessing taxes to pay for necessary public improvements like fencing, ditching, and highway maintenance. In 1755, an explicit general incorporation statute was passed for dissenting religious congregations (mainly Baptist).

In the early national period, the advantages of incorporation were eagerly sought by business promoters (especially those with a New England heritage), and the New York legislature readily granted incorporation to businesses that had not existed in the colonial economy. Incorporation of business enterprises offered several advantages: it helped protect the collective ownership of real property; it facilitated the mobilization of capital; it offered a means of limiting risks in speculative enterprises; and it allowed easy access to the courts. For practically the whole period covered by this study, business corporations in New York were limited to the few classes of enterprises that did not compete with single proprietors or partnership businesses. For new types of enterprises, like turnpikes and banks, the corporation was the usual form of organization. The new classes of incorporated businesses were usually fairly large-scale and they often had a high risk factor; and very frequently they required the grant of special powers from the state before they could begin operations. Furthermore, incorporation provided a means of centralized management that large-scale enterprises required, and it was a flexible instrument of organization that could be applied to a large variety of businesses.

The earliest method of creating a corporation was by granting an individual charter. This mode of creation assumed that corporations were legally privileged organizations that had to be closely scrutinized by the legislature because their purposes had to be made consistent with public welfare.

The second stage of corporation creation was the passage of general incorporation statutes for benevolent organizations, beginning with religious congregations. The principle of religious equality was a legacy of the Revolution, and soon after peace was restored the New York legislature passed general incorporation statutes for religious congregations and then for academies and libraries. Thereafter, whenever a class of benevolent organizations was recognized as being essentially nonpolitical and noncontroversial, general incorporation laws were readily passed. Most states had these laws by the end of the eighteenth century.

The third stage of corporation creation was the enactment of general regulatory statutes, which listed all of the powers and limitations possessed by one class of corporation; but these statutes still required that the legislature pass an individual charter for each company. This mode of incorporation was mainly used for franchise corporations that constructed internal improvements. One of the vital needs of all eighteenth-century communities was improved transportation. The Massachusetts colonial legislature had passed laws that encouraged building wharves, and after independence the New York legislature encouraged the building of turnpikes by passing charters of incorporation whenever applied for. The general regulatory statute of 1807 systematized this process.

Franchise corporations such as turnpikes required special powers, like eminent domain, limited liability, and the right to collect a public toll, before they could begin operations; therefore, they needed individual consideration. Individual consideration ensured that a public hearing would be held to ascertain if the improvement was needed and desired, and in the case of turnpikes, that it would actually follow the route described in the petition for incorporation. All of this information had to be a matter of public record before a franchise was granted.

Most franchise and benevolent corporations had equal social utility. It was relatively immaterial whether the services performed by one of these corporations was for private profit or was benevolent. A turnpike and church building were both visible and useful public improvements and all communities needed them. A turnpike was a business corporation that was undertaken for private profit, but because, in the eyes of the community, it performed a vital public service (as important as religious instruction), the state legislatures during the early national period gave equal encouragement to both forms of corporations as a matter of public policy: one by a general incorporation statute and the other by a general regulatory statute coupled with the pro forma passage of all charters.

The fourth stage of corporation creation was reached when general incorporation statutes were passed for franchise and non-franchise businesses. They were most frequently passed in New York in the 1840s and 1850s when steam technology was successfully applied to railroads and increasingly used as stationary power plants for manufactories. At the same time, markets grew very rapidly, thereby creating a popular demand for a cheap legal means of encouraging the exploitation of these new conditions. General incorporation laws fulfilled this demand. The reasoning behind their passage was the same as behind the general incorporation law for religious congregations: they equalized the opportunity to secure the legal advantages of incorporation and encouraged the formation of organizations that performed public services. However, the process of recognizing and defining the public service function of some classes of business corporations often involved a great deal of political controversy. More importantly, general incorporation laws equalized the opportunity for entrepreneurs to secure corporate business profits by which some of them would get rich, which had the effect of democratizing entrepreneurship during the early stages of industrial growth. They also equalized the opportunity for different sections of the state to undertake local improvement projects with their own resources without having to bargain politically for the privilege.

The fifth stage of corporation creation took place long after 1855. It was achieved when general incorporation codes were passed that allowed incorporation for virtually any legitimate purpose. A code extended the privilege of self-incorporation to all classes of businesss for profit and to most classes of benevolent associations. A general incorporation code could not be adopted, however, until public opinion allowed the general incorporation of those business enterprises that were traditionally organized as single proprietorships or partnerships, such as retail and wholesale merchants.

In this whole development, there were many overlappings, so that these categories were not consecutive for any one class of corporation in any one state. Nevertheless, these five stages of corporation creation describe the transfer of the public service function from benevolent corporations (primarily religious congregations and academies) to internal improvement corporations (turnpikes and bridges) to business corporations that exploited an anonymous market (manufactories). This final transfer took place during a time of rapid technological innovation and attendant expansion in the size of regional markets, which inspired many men to organize because they saw the possiblity of becoming rich in a short period of time.[1]

NOTES

1. Ronald E. Seavoy, "The Public Service Origins of the American Business Corporation," *Business History Review*, Vol. 52, 1978, 30–40, 59–60. James W. Hurst, *The Legitimacy of the Business Corporation in the Laws of the United States, 1780–1970*, 13–57. Simeon E. Baldwin, *Modern Political Institutions*, 174–175, 184–187. Simeon E. Baldwin, "American Business Corporations before 1789," *American Historical Review*, Vol. 8, 1903, 450–453. Roy H. Akagi, *The Town Proprietors of the New England Colonies, 1620–1770*, 3–5, 55–57, 67–68, 85–88, 124–129.

1

The Earliest Corporations: Benevolent Public Service Organizations and Municipalities

TRUSTEES OF RELIGIOUS CONGREGATIONS

Under colonial law, the Anglican denomination was established in the southern counties of New York, but there was complete toleration for all other denominations except Roman Catholicism. The established denomination was attended by only about 10 percent of the population, but because it was closely linked to the colonial government, it was distrusted and disliked by non-Anglicans.

Article 35 of the New York Constitution of 1777 disestablished the Anglican denomination; the 38th Article guaranteed the equality of all Christian denominations, including Roman Catholicism; and the 39th Article was designed to enforce the radical separation of all religious denominations from the state by prohibiting clergymen from holding public office and thus interfering in politics.[1] These provisions could not be enforced until political stability was restored. This occurred after the Treaty of Paris was signed (September 1783) and the last British troops were evacuated from New York City (November 1783).

At the first peacetime session of the legislature, held in New York City in January 1784, a general incorporation statute was passed for the trustees of all religious congregations. It implemented the articles of the Constitution that guaranteed religious equality and radically separated all religious denominations from the state, two principles that were direct legacies of the Revolution.[2] The statute provided an equal opportunity for all religious denominations to secure the legal advantages of corporate ownership of their real property. It is noteworthy that the first enactment of a general incorporation law in New York made these advantages equally available by excluding partisan politics from the incorporation procedure.[3]

The statute allowed all religious congregations to elect a board of trustees of from six to nine men who would be a corporation for the limited purposes of taking charge of the congregation's temporalities and defending the attached rights at law. Incorporation was secured when a copy of the certificate of election was placed on file with the county clerk. It was a simple and cheap legal process that was designed for the needs of a dispersed population living on the land.

The incorporated board of trustees was a different body from the governing board of each congregation. A congregation's government remained in the hands of a board of vestry, deacons, or elders, depending on the denomination. This trustee arrangement was modeled on that of the recently disestablished Church of England as it had existed in New York. Since this form of government was not wholly acceptable to the Dutch Reformed churches, the act was amended in 1788 to allow them to elect trustees according to their own usage, and in 1795 the legislature gave similar relief to the reorganized Protestant Episcopal Church.[4]

The great value of incorporation was that the trustees of a congregation could receive bequests and legacies, and that the lands and buildings and other property owned by a congregation was secured by a corporate title that could be defended at law in the name of the congregation. Under common law, an unincorporated company could not legally possess property in its own name; its property had to be held in trust; and it could not defend its property at law in its collective capacity. The common law had long bestowed these advantages on English municipalities, and American lawyers were very familiar with them.

A mortmain clause, limiting the amount of land a congregation could own, was added to prevent the accumulation of real property in immobile corporate hands. Thereafter, some form of mortmain restriction was placed in almost all charters of benevolent societies. This was a legal carry-over from England where mortmain clauses were designed to prevent the accumulation of land in the hands of churches and other charitable organizations. Their purpose in New York was to facilitate an equality of opportunity for individuals to own land. In order to enforce this policy, all congregations had to submit a triennial financial report to the Chancellor or local judge. If this report was omitted, the congregation's incorporated status lapsed. The triennial report proved completely inapplicable to rural congregations that had no endowments, and in 1798, those congregations that had failed to file triennial reports and were legally dissolved were authorized to re-incorporate without penalty if they filed reports within three years. The law became a dead letter soon afterwards, not receiving much attention until 1850, when the arrears of triennial reports were forgiven and further reports were required only from those congregations with annual investment incomes in excess of $6,000.[5]

When, in the 1790s, several states repealed all of the English statutes from the colonial period that had remained in force, one of the repealed statutes was the 1601 statute defining charitable uses (trusts). Its repeal seemed to make it impossible to bequeath property for charitable use if a state did not enact trust legislation or incorporation statutes for religious and charitable societies. Chief Justice John Marshall confirmed this interpretation in 1819, but since most New York religious and charitable organizations were incorporated, his opinion had little significance. However, it did not entirely prevent disgruntled heirs from litigating vaguely worded wills that did not make a distinction between trusts and corporations. A New York case of 1853, *Williams* v. *Williams*, made it plain that a bequest had to go to an incorporated charity to be valid. "The provisions of the revised statutes respecting trusts . . . were devised to restrain the natural propensity of mankind to perpetuate their estates in their families and among the descendants of themselves . . . a propensity which the laws of the mother country have allowed to an extent which could not be tolerated in a purely representative government. . . . I think those provisions were not designed to affect conveyances of testamentary gifts to religious or charitable corporations . . . " because "the provision for creating religious corporations recognizes the duty of the government to provide facilities for the voluntary establishment of public worship. A legally organized system for protecting and preserving gifts and donations to aid Christian charity would fall within the same principles, and would be equally unobjectionable."[6]

The 1784 statute worked very well to achieve this goal. It generated little controversy except among Roman Catholics, whose bishops had great difficulty in asserting hierarchic control over the trustees of local congregations because the boards of trustees held title to the church buildings. The most frequent source of disagreement was local congregations insisting on choosing their own priests. This difficulty was of little public concern until large-scale Roman Catholic emigration started in the 1830s and turned into a flood with the famine in Ireland (1845) and the failure of the German Revolution (1848).

In the final two years of this study, two important additions were made to the state's ecclesiastical laws. In 1854, a general incorporation statute was passed for congregations having rent-free pews, or in the terminology of the time, for free churches. They were to be organized under the rules of the general incorporation statute for charitable societies passed in 1848, and not under the statute authorizing the formation of religious congregations.

The second law, passed in 1855 under Know-Nothing influence, attempted to check Roman Catholic influence in the politics of New York. The statute *required* that the real property of all religious congregations be owned by a board of locally elected trustees. Its purpose was to limit the power of Roman Catholic bishops by placing the ownership of a congregation's church and other buildings in the hands of the lay leaders of each congregation, thus allowing a board of trustees to disagree with policies or teaching proclaimed by a bishop without being deprived of their places of worship on charges of insubordination or heresy. The law was repealed in 1863 during the Civil War, and a highly favorable law was passed that allowed clergymen and their nominees to form the majority of all boards of trustees of local congregations.[7]

EDUCATIONAL INSTITUTIONS

Ten colleges were established in English-speaking North America before the Revolution and all of them were incorporated. Some, like Dartmouth and King's College in New York City, were incorporated by the English Crown, but others were chartered by colonial governments, as in the case of Harvard and Yale. A major reason for incorporating colleges and other schools was to allow them to hold real property and receive gifts from colonial governments and private benefactors.[8] Most colleges were thoroughly disrupted by the war and needed state aid to resume the training of political and religious leaders. Furthermore, after the Revolution, mass literacy became a highly desired social goal, for both religious and secular reasons.

The religious motivation for mass literacy was the belief that all Christians should be able to read the Bible because the Bible was the whole source of religious truth, and more broadly, the desire to expose all persons to the beneficial influence of religious morality as a means of achieving a stable and healthy society. The numerous Protestant Christian denominations did not oppose this policy, and most strongly supported it. They made a direct identification of their common Protestant Christian heritage with the republican (and democratic) mission of the new nation. This is especially true of the New England settlers who streamed into upper New York immediately after the Revolution. They brought with them an intense desire to perpetuate near universal male literacy that had already been achieved in the towns they left.[9]

The secular motivation for mass literacy was the necessity of reading and understanding the written constitutions and laws of the nation, in order to produce virtuous republican citizens. Republican virtue had many ingredients, but some of the most important were religious toleration (including toleration of secularism), the melting of immigrants into American culture, and preparing the ordinary citizen for practical careers in agriculture, commerce, and technology, whereby they were enabled to become small property holders who understood their responsibilities as republican citizens.[10]

In his first peacetime message, in 1784, Governor George Clinton said there was "scarce anything more worthy of your attention than the revival and encouragement of seminaries of learning." The legislature confirmed all the privileges of King's College, changed its name to Columbia College, and vested its government in a new and enlarged governing body, the Regents of the University of the

State of New York.[11] The statute incorporated the Regents and granted them limited supervisory authority over the secondary and primary educational institutions of the state. They could found schools and colleges in any part of the state and confer on them the power to grant degrees, diplomas, or certificates in the name of the University. The power of visitation was reserved to the Regents, and they could also prescribe how the schools should be governed. No religious test oath was required for any appointments made by the Regents, nor was the statute to be interpreted to prevent the foundation of private colleges outside the jurisdiction of the Regents. In effect, the Regents were erected into a state commission of education mainly concerned with supervising the quality of secondary education, although most academies were primary schools as well.

The statute was very unpopular because the Board of Regents was dominated by the friends of Columbia College who advanced Columbia's interests and ignored the rest of the state. An even greater source of opposition was the Regents' control over the endowment funds of all schools under its jurisdiction. Local residents strongly believed these funds should be controlled by local boards of trustees; consequently, Alexander Hamilton, John Jay, James Duane, and others drafted a new statute in 1787 that was acceptable to local interests. Local administration was restored to schools by allowing each one to elect its own board of trustees. As in the case of religious congregations, the board of trustees of each school was erected into a corporation, provided the Board of Regents approved. In other words, the legislature delegated the power of incorporation to the Board of Regents. Academies were to be incorporated upon the application of their founders or benefactors, and the Regents were to examine each petition for incorporation to see whether the school's endowment would yield a sufficient income for it to become an effective teaching institution. If incorporation was allowed, the charter was to be filed with the Secretary of State. The power of the Regents to incorporate academies and colleges was the state's second general incorporation statute.[12] The precedent for incorporating the Regents of the University was probably the colonial statute of 1768 that incorporated the New York Chamber of Commerce for the purpose of "promoting and encouraging commerce, supporting industry, adjusting disputes . . . and procuring such laws and regulations as may be found necessary for the benefit of trade in general.[13]

Under the 1787 statute, the Regents became an effective statewide regulatory agency. The Regents were required to make at least one annual visit to all schools under their jurisdiction in order to inspect their curriculum and discipline, but the visitation usually took the form of receiving an annual report rather than a physical inspection. The right of visitation served as a reserve power allowing the Regents enough discretion to enforce uniform academic standards if they chose. This power was made explicit in 1813 when a reserve clause was inserted in the revised statutes that allowed the legislature "at any time or times hereafter, to alter and amend the charter of any academy."[14] In fact, however, it was the money from the Literature Fund that gave the Regents some measure of control over the state's academies. The monies of the Literature Fund came from the sale of one lot (400 acres) in all newly surveyed townships. The monies from this sale were invested and the income placed in the hands of the Regents for distribution to the incorporated academies of the state.[15]

The 1787 statute also empowered the Regents to test all students under their jurisdiction and enter them in Columbia College or any other college under their authority if they were found competent. Out of this provision has grown the present-day Regents' Examination as a prerequisite of graduation for all high school students of New York who have completed four years of schooling. The law further provided that whenever an academy advanced enough in scholarship or endowment, it could re-incorporate as a college.

The general incorporation statute for schools, academies, and colleges implemented two principles: the equality of opportunity for all religious denominations to provide educational facilities for the children of their members, and the opportunity of every community to support secondary education according to its resources. From the beginning of independence, New York encouraged secondary and higher education as a public function. It did not matter whether the leadership or monetary resources came from private or public sources.

Primary education received very early encouragement, but

immediately after the Revolution, the state did not have the fiscal resources to establish a statewide tax-supported system. The same statute that established the Literature Fund also directed the Commissioners of the Land Office to reserve one lot in every newly surveyed township to be sold and the money used to help pioneer settlers establish a public or gospel school. In 1795, following Massachusetts' lead, the legislature enacted a compulsory primary education statute, in which nothing was said about the length of instruction per year, although it was specified that instruction had to be in the English language.[16] The Regents had been recommending compulsory primary education from their first report to the legislature.

The 1795 statute appropriated state money for five years for the aid of common schools. It was to be distributed to county treasurers who were to apportion it among the several townships on the basis of the number of taxable inhabitants. Each township had to levy a tax that matched half the amount of the state funds it received, and it had to elect an education commission of from three to seven persons. The intent of the law was to create a uniform common school system throughout the state on the model of the Massachusetts system. Particularly, this was intended for New York City. The New York City common council did not fully follow the intent. They used their funds to subsidize existing free charity schools rather than establish a new system of publicly supported common schools.[17]

The state's appropriation ended in 1800 and was not renewed in spite of repeated pleas by Governors John Jay and George Clinton. A permanent common school system was not organized until 1816, although a long-range commitment toward its establishment was made in 1805 when the legislature appropriated 500,000 acres of state land to the newly established Common School Fund and incorporated the Free School Society of New York City.

The capital from the sale of land appropriated to the Common School Fund was employed in two principal ways. Up until 1814, substantial funds were invested in bank stock, which the legislature required newly chartered banks to set aside for purchase by the state or the Common School Fund, so that by 1819, up to 25 percent of the income of the Common School Fund came from bank stock. The second source of income for the Fund was loans made by the Comptroller at 6 percent interest for as long as three years. Lenders had to mortgage to the state improved New York real estate having at least double the value of the loan, exclusive of buildings on it. The income of this fund was to accumulate until it yielded an annual income of $50,000, which was then to be distributed to the common school districts of the state. The Fund's income did not reach $50,000 until 1816. In an effort to increase the income of the School Fund and to put the education statute in operation as soon as possible, a tax on bank shares was proposed in 1811 but it was rejected.[18]

In anticipation of the Common School Fund's income reaching $50,000, a compulsory primary education statute was passed in 1812 and applied to New York City the following year, but the War of 1812 prevented it from going into operation.[19] Under this statute, local school districts had to levy a tax to match the funds contributed by the state, and the office of Superintendent of Common Schools was created to supervise the whole system.[20]

Each township had to elect a three-man Commission of Common Schools to supervise the laying out of local school districts, and each school district within the township was to elect a board of trustees, but neither the township school commission nor the school district trustees were erected into corporations to hold title to the district's real property. This was a major deficiency that was noted in the first report of the Superintendent of Common Schools (1814). This report recommended that the trustees of each school district should be incorporated and each board of county supervisors granted the power to force townships to divide themselves into school districts. It was not until 1815 that both the township Common School Commission and the trustees of the several districts within each township were defined as corporations with limited powers to own property and defend it in the courts. These amendments made the formation of common school districts a process of general incorporation, and by 1823 there were over 7,300 in the state.[21]

In 1821, the general incorporation privilege was extended to the trustees of Lancaster and Bell type schools (where the older students tutored younger students). Governor DeWitt Clinton had urged the passage of such a statute in 1820.[22] The statute further provided that any incorporated Lancaster or Bell school could become a tax-supported district school under the provisions of the common school statute, if the board of trustees of the local school district approved. Governor Clinton strongly supported the monitorial system of teaching because it promised mass secondary education at a low cost. Only a few of these schools were organized, and at the time of Clinton's death in 1828, the movement was practically extinct.[23]

From 1787 to 1817, the Regents incorporated forty academies. From that date to 1853, the Regents shared incorporation with the legislature, but not without the legislature questioning the Regents' power under the two-thirds clause of the Constitution adopted in 1821. The two-thirds clause required all charters of incorporation to be passed by a two-thirds majority of all elected legislators. On the face of it, the two-thirds clause would seem to exclude the Regents from continuing to incorporate schools. In 1825, the legislature requested the Regents to submit a list of academies they had incorporated since 1821 and to explain how they interpreted the power of incorporation delegated to them under the 1787 statute in light of the two-thirds clause of the 1821 Constitution.

The Regents said that the two-thirds clause applied only to the legislature. Furthermore, they quoted from Article 7, Section 14, of the Constitution, which said, "Nothing contained in this constitution shall affect any charters or grants made by the state or by persons acting under its authority." The Regents said that this clause confirmed their powers of incorporation delegated to them by the act of 1787. The Regents' opinion was referred to the Committee on Literature, which did not concur. The Committee believed that the power of incorporation delegated to the Regents had been abrogated by the 1821 Constitution. It drew up a bill that would have legalized the charters the Regents had granted after 1821 and provide that all future petitions for incorporation would be presented to the Regents for their inspection before the legislature acted. This bill was read twice but not passed because it raised too many embarrassing constitutional questions in regard to the banking policy the Regency was then pursuing.[24]

The Regents continued to incorporate academies and colleges, and by 1854, they had chartered 137 and the legislature 177. The first major change in policy after 1825 occurred in 1851 when a general incorporation statute was passed for proprietary academies and high schools.[25] This statute took incorporation of proprietary high schools completely out of the hands of the Regents and caused them to ask for a clarification of the state's policy. In response, the 1853 session excluded the legislature from school incorporation as part of a general policy of providing general incorporation statutes for all classes of corporations. This policy had been clearly indicated by provisions in the Constitution of 1846.[26]

The 1853 legislative session passed two additional statutes dealing with education. One authorized the general incorporation of medical colleges, if adequately endowed, and the other facilitated the consolidation of adjoining school districts to form one that had a large enough tax base to support a public high school. This reform had been suggested ten years earlier by the Secretary of State in his capacity as Superintendent of Common Schools.[27] He had complained of too many small school districts, but consolidation at that time would have presented a vast legal problem if each consolidation had had to be reincorporated by a special act of the legislature. This might have been the court's interpretation of the two-thirds clause of the 1821 Constitution because in 1843 the controversy over the constitutionality of a general incorporation statute for banks was at its height.[28] To get some idea of the confusion that might have resulted, in 1843 New York had at least 10,000 school districts, and by 1850 there were over 11,000. This statute laid down the procedure for consolidating school districts which, in effect, was a general incorporation law.

The school district consolidation statute closely followed a Massachusetts statute of 1838. A consolidated district was also authorized to take over any existing academy if the academy's board of trustees unanimously approved of it becoming tax-supported. Any high schools established by a consolidated district was subject to visitation by the Regents. This action marked a shift in policy by the state. In the past, the state had relied on privately supported secondary schools. By 1870, this statute, as amended, had resulted in the establishment of a system of tax-supported public high schools that had largely supplanted private academies.[29]

LIBRARIES

New York's third general incorporation statute was for public libraries. It was passed in 1796 as a sequel to the primary education statute of 1795. Libraries had been frequently incorporated in other colonies before the Revolution, especially in Pennsylvania, and their public service contributions were well known.[30] The libraries were public in the sense that private citizens were encouraged to invest their capital in lending libraries open to the public. Like the general incorporation statutes for religious congregations, academies, and colleges, the election of library trustees had to be acknowledged before a state judge before the articles of incorporation could be filed with the county clerk.

The library general incorporation statute remained practically unchanged for the period of this study. An 1835 supplement allowed the inhabitants of each school district to tax themselves $20 the first year, and $10 each subsequent year, to support a district library to aid teaching in the primary schools.[31] For the most part, this tax authorization was unused. In 1838, the first "loan" from the federal surplus came into the possession of the states, and Governor William L. Marcy recommended that New York's share be devoted to aiding education by matching any funds raised by local school districts to support a library. The legislature obliged by earmarking $55,000 annually for three years from the income from the "loan." In 1839, the next logical step was taken, of allowing school district trustees to be library trustees and allowing adjoining school districts to combine their libraries.[32]

In 1853, another general incorporation statute was passed for proprietary joint-stock circulating and reference library corporations.[33] Unlike several New England states, New York did not have a general incorporation statute for lyceums. They were classed as literary institutes or libraries, and if the promoters of a particular lyceum declined to use the general incorporation statute for libraries, they petitioned the legislature for a special charter.

CHARITABLE AND BENEVOLENT SOCIETIES

The first charitable society recognized as a corporation in New York was the Society for the Relief of the Widows and Children of the Protestant Episcopal Church in the State of New York. It was similar to a mutual insurance company, chartered in Pennsylvania, which had received legal recognition of its corporate status in New York and New Jersey.[34] It was organized to provide support for the dependents of deceased Episcopal clergymen; however, Pennsylvania proved too distant to service their needs, so one was chartered in New York. Thereafter, until a general incorporation statute was passed in 1848, the trustees of all charitable societies were incorporated by special charters, numbering approximately 350.

There were two exceptions to this policy, but neither statute appears to have been used. In 1811, the charter for the Albany Bible Society contained a provision allowing any five or more persons to associate themselves on the model of its charter, provided they filed articles of agreement with the Secretary of State, and the 1817 charter for the Auxiliary New York Bible and Common Prayer Book Society had a provision allowing general incorporation for any number of similar societies. In 1820, a general incorporation statute was introduced in the New York Senate for charitable socieites, except schools, which came under the jurisdiction of the Regents.[35] The statute was not passed, nor was it re-introduced in 1821; so that when the Constitution of 1821 was adopted, with its two-thirds clause, charitable organizations could be incorporated only by special acts. Until a general incorporation statute for them was passed in 1848, all such charters appear to have been granted whenever petitioned for.

MUNICIPALITIES

The legislature placed the erection of new townships and counties on a regular basis in 1788, but these municipalities were not specifically designated corporations. The statute aimed at breaking the political power of the Hudson River manors by facilitating their division into townships and, at the same time, encouraging western settlement by providing a framework of local government. The legislature also passed a poor law vesting support of township paupers in the hands of two Overseers of the Poor. In none of these general organizational statutes were the governing bodies designated corporations because they did not need to own real property to perform their public duties. In the 1801 compilation of laws, the two compilers, James Kent and Jacob Radcliff, specifically authorized county supervisors to hold property for public use, but counties were still not designated corporations.[36] It was assumed that common law made them corporations for purposes directly connected with their public functions, but this was an ambiguous assumption at best. This ambiguity led to litigation, which dragged through the courts until 1826.

In 1791, a land speculator donated a lot in Cooperstown to the people of the County of Otsego as a site for a courthouse and jail. The county supervisors took possession of the lot and erected the buildings. By an act of the legislature in 1806, the supervisors were authorized to sell the land and buildings, which was done. An ejectment suit was brought against the purchaser on the grounds that the people of the county had no power to own any land; therefore, the county's title was faulty and the sale was void.[37]

The attorney for the plaintiff argued that the only persons capable of holding land or of conveying it were natural persons or corporations. The benefactor's deed to the people of Otsego County was void because there were no identifiable persons or corporation named in the deed. The people of the county, collectively, were not a corporation and the supervisors of the county were not named in the deed; and even if they were, it is very doubtful if the legislature considered them a corporation. The court accepted this interpretation and held that the people of Otsego County were not a corporate body known to New York law. The 1801 statute did not apply because it authorized conveyance of land only to county supervisors. To be valid, the title had to name a corporation or persons who could possess in their own right or as trustees.

In a similar case, judged at almost the same time, the facts were nearly identical except that the land on which the courthouse and jail were built was conveyed in trust to the county supervisors.[38] The same benefactor donated additional land in trust on which to erect a church and a school for the use of the inhabitants of the county seat. The court recognized the validity of the county's title to the land on which the courthouse was built because it was properly conveyed to the County Board of Supervisors. The court admitted that the supervisors were a corporation for special purposes under the 1788 statute, but it was doubtful if they could have held land until after the passage of the 1801 statute. The court went on to say that the supervisors could not hold land in trust for use by the village. They could only hold land for use by the county because the Board could not hold land for purposes foreign to its function.

This opinion was confirmed and expanded six years later when townships were recognized as corporations for limited purposes under the 1788 statute.[39] One of the limited corporate powers they possessed was to improve their common lands, which meant that the residents of a township possessed *sub-modo* corporate powers for specific purposes. In 1820, the same reasoning was applied to the township office of Overseers of the Poor.[40] This office was also declared to be a *sub-modo* corporation to an extent necessary to perform its public trust, even when the legislature had not expressly designated it a corporation. This opinion was reconfirmed in 1823 and 1826.[41] The *sub-modo* corporate status of these public commissions gave them a legal standing equal to that of the trustees of townships and district schools and was in conformity with the common law that gave towns and parishes sufficient corporate powers to perform their local duties. Finally, the revisers of the statutes in 1828 expressly declared all townships and counties to be corporations known by the names they possessed.[42]

LOAN OFFICERS AND COMMISSIONS

During the financial stringencies following the Revolution, two of the most critical needs of New York citizens were a sound paper currency and a reliable source of credit for city merchants. Two methods were used by the New York legislature to supply these needs: incorporating money banks in the cities and incorporating county loan offices, or rural land banks. A land bank was first used to supply New York with a paper currency in 1737 when the legislature incorporated loan officers for each city and county. County loan officers issued mortgage certificates in relatively small denominations on improved agricultural land. These certificates then circulated as a local currency.[43] New York's first money bank was organized in 1784, at the same time trade resumed with England, but it was not incorporated until 1791.

The New York legislature incorporated loan officers in 1786, 1792, and 1808. In statutes of 1786 and 1792, each county agent was individually incorporated because he was authorized to make mortgages and engage in lawsuits to defend the mortgaged lands in his possession. Under the 1808 statute, however, the county loan commissioners were united in a single corporation.

A county loan officer became incorporated when the county judge or county supervisors met and elected a county resident who could post bonds of sufficient value acceptable to them. Upon accepting the job, the single person became a corporation, an arrangement that was identical with an ecclesiastical corporation sole. In this instance, the legislature clearly saw that a loan officer required incorporation in order to deal with the problems arising from the disposal of foreclosed mortgages on real property. The common law covered similar situations faced by municipal and ecclesiastical organizations by defining them as corporations, but the loan office was unknown to the common law and, therefore, required explicit statute definition to be a corporation.[44]

MEDICAL SOCIETIES

The general incorporation device was used at an early date in an attempt to achieve a uniform standard of medical training. The state first regulated the practice of medicine in 1792, but only in New York City.[45] No person was to practice physic or surgery in the city unless he had been apprenticed to a reputable physician for at least two years and graduated from a college in the United States; or, if not a graduate, had served a three-year apprenticeship. After fulfilling these requirements, the M.D. candidate could not practice until he had been examined by a board consisting of two city or state officials plus three practicing physicians or surgeons who would issue a certificate of examination if he was found competent.[46]

If a person practiced without a certificate, he was not entitled to collect fees through legal action, and he could be sued for practicing without a license. The statute did not apply to a person with medical degrees from colleges in the United States having authority to confer medical degrees. This mode of licensing proved cumbersome even in the compact boundaries of New York City, and was replaced in 1797 by a more decentralized licensing system that applied to the whole state.[47]

This also proved difficult to enforce and in 1806 the whole regulatory structure was reconstituted on a more decentralized and enforceable basis by the passage of a general incorporation statute for county medical societies. The idea of district regulation was borrowed from an 1803 Massachusetts statute, which was probably based on New Jersey's plan of 1790.[48] The supervisory powers of the state medical society were broadly patterned after powers granted to the Regents of the University and the rules adopted by the state Supreme Court that specified the legal training needed by lawyers who practiced before it.

County medical societies annually elected a three- to five-man Board of Censors to examine candidates for a medical diploma; however, before a candidate presented himself for examination, he had to complete three years of medical study. The New York Medical Society consisted of one representative from each county society. Its Board of Censors retained a concurrent examining power with the county boards. At a later date, boards of censors were organized in each senatorial district for the benefit of those counties that failed to organize medical societies. Finally, unlicensed doctors were prohibited from using the courts to collect debts owed them for medical services, and they were subjected to a fine if convicted of practicing without a license.

The New York Medical Society was reluctant to set a high penalty for unlicensed physicians because, as the 1810 report stated, heavy penalties would probably cause the public to believe that the legislature was persecuting practitioners who lacked formal training and who could not afford the time and expense to get it. Public sympathy might act to increase the number of quack physicians rather than diminish their numbers. Finally, the statute chartering the New York Medical Society contained a reserve clause which read, "It shall be in the power of the legislature to alter, modify, or repeal this act whenever they shall deem it necessary or expedient."[49] This was the first use of a reserve clause in New York statutes, and it highlighted the growing desire to retain some explicit public control over the incorporation of public service organizations.[50]

Unlike previous general incorporation statutes, the general incorporation statute for county medical societies continued to generate political controversy after it was enacted. The state continued to regulate the medical profession, usually following the recommendations of the New York Medical Society. The Society worked closely with the Regents of the University toward the twin goals of mass literacy and some degree of academic training for medical doctors. The Medical Society's report of 1809 said, in a circular letter, "the medical profession can only be respectable in a well informed community, as the ignorant and illiterate are the only dupes of empyricism. The county medical societies will see the usefulness of exerting their influence to promote education, and of uniting their efforts with the Regents of the University for such purposes."[51] This partnership attempted to gradually improve the standards of medical training. The Regents tried to limit the number of medical schools to those with viable endowments, and some formal medical training was made advantageous for licensing by exempting the graduates of chartered medical schools from examination by boards of censors. On occasion, however, the legislature followed a contrary policy because of political or geographical pressures, as it did in 1807, when apothecaries and herbal doctors were exempted from examination, or later when it preempted the Regents' incorporating power for colleges and established a medical college at the relatively remote location of Geneva, New York.

In 1818, Governor DeWitt Clinton recommended that candidates for a medical diploma be required to attend one of the state's medical schools during the course of their training. The legislature responded by requiring four years' apprenticeship instead of three, and that one of these years could be spent at either a literary college pursuing a general course of study, or at one of the state's medical schools attending a course of lectures. The legislature also revived an old regulation that required a doctor to be at least twenty-one years old and to have completed his studies after his sixteenth year. Doctors trained in out-of-state medical schools were required to present a diploma to the local county medical society before they could begin practice, and all doctors in the state were required to be members of the local county medical society.[52]

The revised statutes of 1828 increased the powers of the county medical societies by omitting the provision that a degree conferred by a state medical college was the equivalent of a license to practice medicine. All medical school graduates had to be examined by a county medical society before they were licensed to practice. Under the broad wording of these regulations, the county medical societies resumed licensing herbal doctors and other sectarian physicians. They strongly objected and in 1830 herbal doctors were again exempted from state regulation.[53]

The annual meetings of the state Medical Society from 1829 to 1833 objected to the exemption and petitioned to end it. The legislature did not act until 1834, when herbal doctors were again brought under licensing by county medical societies, but in the following year they were again exempted.[54] Following this victory, the herbal doctors, or Thompsonite physicians, began a long fight to repeal the law that barred unlicensed doctors from using the courts to collect fees and to repeal the 1830 statute that heavily fined persons convicted of practicing medicine without a license. The New York Medical Society bitterly fought the attempt by Thompsonite physicians to repeal the legal disabilities for sectarian medical practitioners; however, the Thompsonites had considerable popular support from the anti-monopoly Workingman's Party and its successor, the Equal Rights or Locofoco Democrats. These rebel Democrats described the exclusive supervisory powers of the New York Medical Society as a monopoly that was odious to the people. A significant number of the leaders of these two political factions were medical doctors, and it was the Locofocos who acted as the cutting edge of the movement to democratize business opportunities in New York.[55]

In 1839, the Society succeeded in bringing the licensing of pharmacists in New York City under the control of the local medical society or alternatively, requiring all pharmacists in the city to be graduates of a pharmacy college. Five years later, in 1844, the Thompsonite physicians succeeded in ending the licensing of all medical doctors. The repealing statute, however, prescribed a very stiff fine for any person charging fees for medical services who was convicted of malpractice, gross ignorance, or immoral conduct. The statute ended the Medical Society's exclusive supervisory authority over regular medical doctors and prompted a number of prominent Society officers to call a national medical convention. It was held in 1846 at New York University where plans were laid to organize the American Medical Association, which was done two years later.[56]

Until the repeal of the medical licensing law, the New York Medical Society had acted as a statewide medical regulatory commission, which had attempted to enforce a basic level of medical competence and improve medical training. It was also a source of technical information for the legislature. In return, the state had allowed it to meet in public buildings in Albany while the legislature was in session, printed its transactions, and passed much of the legislation it thought necessary for the public welfare. It had the same relationship to the state regarding medical policies as the Regents of the University had regarding educational policies.

In 1853, a general incorporation statute was passed for medical colleges. This statute followed the Regent's recommendation of having the legislature set a policy for all future incorporations of colleges. This statute followed the Regents' recommendation of public hospitals with one hundred or more beds to train physicians and grant medical degrees, when approved by the local medical society. The newly incorporated New York Academy of Medicine supported this plan because it would liberalize the "business of instruction and republicanize our medical schools."[57]

The rural structure of American society was one of the principal reasons for the failure of medical licensure in New York and in other states where it was attempted. The attempt to set a high standard of training was based on European experience where the political structure was highly centralized and the social structure was partially urbanized. There were always enough trained physicians in American cities, but in rural areas there was a continuing shortage. Apprenticeship training was the only effective means of meeting rural needs and most doctors were trained this way. Furthermore, during the 1830s and 1840s, improvements in medical science had not convincingly demonstrated, to a large portion of the population, the overwhelming advantages of regular medicine over the various sectarian practices; nor had the medical schools trained enough new doctors for the rapidly growing population. Until regular medicine established its superiority through research and clinical training, and until the nation was rich enough to heavily endow medical schools, pay the salaries of full-time instructors, and subsidize qualified students, sectarian doctors continued to account for about 10 percent of the nation's physicians. By 1855, medical regulation by state societies had failed, but the attempt did not end. Regulation passed quietly into the hands of a growing number of medical colleges located in the large cities, and it was within this framework of formal training that medical standards were gradually raised and the profession self-regulated.[58]

Licensing of dentists was not a public issue in New York. Dentistry did not emerge as a distinct branch of medicine in the United States until about 1830, at about the time medical licensing by state societies was beginning to break down. Some attempts were made to secure dental licensing before 1838, but most practitioners rejected this policy because it was thought that licensing would legitimize quacks about as frequently as trained men. The need for standards remained, however, and in 1840 in New York City, the American Society of Dental Surgeons was organized. It attempted to set standards of competency by defining curriculums at dental colleges. This failed because the standards were too high to train enough dentists to meet the health needs of rural areas and small towns. A large portion of dentists continued to be trained by apprenticeship.[59]

AGRICULTURAL SOCIETIES

The New York Agricultural Society was incorporated in 1793. Its sponsors were the political, social, and commercial leaders of the state; and all members of the legislature were honorary members. It was organized to help discover and disseminate improved agricultural techniques to practical farmers and to promote household spinning and weaving. The state printed its bulletins and annual reports, as it did for the New York Medical Society and the Regents of the University; however, practical farmers were not interested and its charter was allowed to expire.

After the Embargo was passed in 1808, the state directed its efforts to encouraging sheep raising in order to grow enough wool for the state to become self-sufficient in textile production. Each township was allowed to license taverns and dogs and the revenue was to be used to buy a pedigreed merino ram to improve local bloodlines. Furthermore, the state provided small cash bounties during the next ten years to encourage household weaving of higher quality textiles. In 1819, the enouragement of wool growing and household weaving was replaced by a scheme that was aimed at improving agricultural techniques.[60] An 1819 statute appropriated $10,000 a year for two years, to be distributed as prizes for agricultural produce and household products of superior quality, but the state funds had to be matched by funds raised by each county agricultural society.[61] Appropriation for cash bounties continued until 1825, by which time the purpose of the law had been accomplished—to encourage the organization of county agricultural societies that would sponsor annual fairs. The county agricultural societies did not require incorporation because they owned no real property. Their main function was to organize a county fair while title to the fairgrounds vested in the county government.

Elkanah Watson was the driving force behind this statute, but it was strongly backed by Governor DeWitt Clinton. Watson had organized the first county agricultural fair in western Massachusetts in 1811 and began promoting similar fairs in New York while collaborating with Clinton in promoting the Erie Canal. County fairs were an instantaneous success.

A general incorporation statute for agricultural and horticultural societies was not enacted until 1853. The idea of incorporating horticultural societies was probably borrowed from Massachusetts where a similar statute was passed six weeks earlier. The New York statute authorized one society per county or township, but several townships could combine to form a regional society. Nearly identical statutes were passed in 1853 and 1855 without repealing the earlier one.[62]

CLASSES OF ORGANIZATIONS NEVER GRANTED GENERAL INCORPORATION

Unlike the medical profession, no statutes were ever passed that set standards for legal training or legal competence; nevertheless, lawyers were regulated. When the legislature first attempted to regulate medical practice (1797), the New York Supreme Court adopted rules that set the standard for legal training. Lawyers who wished to practice before the Supreme Court had to serve a seven-year clerkship, but up to four years of classical studies could be accepted as part of this preparation if it were taken after the age of fourteen. The apprenticeship period was reduced to four years in 1803, plus four years of practice.[63] By setting these standards, the New York Supreme Court became the regulatory commission of the state's legal profession; thus, there was no need to pass a general incorporation statute for county bar associations.

Fire fighting companies were another type of organization that were never granted the privilege of general incorporation in New York, although general organizational statutes were passed for them in 1815, 1832, and 1847.[64] Fire companies, however, frequently received special charters of incorporation, but they were always placed under the jurisdiction of a unit of local government. Firemen were recognized as valuable public servants; they were always granted some degree of exemption from militia, jury, and highway duty.

In 1815, the directors of incorporated textile companies were authorized to organize fire companies on the grounds of their factories. This statute recognized the fire hazards connected with the accumulation of lint around stoves and the distance that most rural, water-powered textile mills were from the nearest municipal fire company. In 1832, a general organizational statute was passed for rural township fire companies, but there was no authorization to levy a tax to purchase fire-fighting equipment. In 1847, a similar statute was passed for village fire companies, but a company could not be organized until the electorate authorized a tax to purchase firefighting equipment.

The problem of partitioning jointly owned land arose very early in the colony, mainly because of the practice of granting large blocks of land to a few persons with each owner's share being described in very broad language. There was frequent litigation among the heirs. The first statute aimed at solving these problems was passed in 1708, but it expired in 1721. Another statute was passed in 1762, and re-enacted by the state legislature in 1785, but unlike Massachusetts, commonly owned lands were not incorporated to help clarify their legal title. The usual way of solving these problems was for the court to appoint temporary commissioners under the provisions of a 1785 statute, which made these commissioners agents of the court.[65]

Occasionally, other public bodies such as assessment, drainage, and highway maintenance districts were organized, but none of these units were incorporated. Only when a public body owned real property, such as a school house or mortgages by loan commissions, was there a need for incorporation. If an organization did not own real estate, it was unlikely to be incorporated unless it performed a regulatory function. An attempt was made to apply this rule to militia companies, which owned or had use of stores of arms and equipment, but did not own an armory. Incorporation was rejected as contrary to the state's militia law, because it jeopardized the principle of centralized command.[66]

NOTES

1. Charles Z. Lincoln, *The Constitutional History of New York*, Vol. 1, 540–546.

2. John W. Pratt, *Religion, Politics and Diversity: The Church-State Theme in New York*, 90–93, 100. *New York Laws*, Ch. 18, 1784, 71, Vol. 1, Greenleaf. New Jersey passed a general incorporation statute for religious congregations in 1786, John W. Cadman, *The Corporation in New Jersey, 1791–1875*, 5–6. Pennsylvania passed a similar statute for literary charitable, and religious corporations in 1791.

3. William G. McLoughlin, "The Role of Religion in the Revolution: Liberty of Conscience and Cultural Cohesion in the New Nation," Stephen G. Kurtz, James H. Hutson, eds., *Essays on the American Revolution*, 209–211, 220–221, 234–248, 253. Timothy L. Smith, "Congregation, State, and Denomination: The Forming of the American Religious Structure," *William and Mary Quarterly*, Vol. 25, 1968, 164, 175–176. In 1815, Justice Story of the United States Supreme Court strongly approved of these laws. In reference to Virginia's law incorporating religious congregations, he said that this was the best way to protect their benevolent purposes. *Terrett* v. *Taylor*, 1815, 9 Cranch 49.

4. *New York Laws*, Ch. 61, 1788, 132, Vol. 2, Greenleaf; Ch. 25, 1795, 188, Vol. 3, Greenleaf.

5. Irvin G. Wyllie, "The Search for an American Law of Charity, 1776–1844," *Mississippi Valley Historical Review*, Vol. 46, 1959, 207. James Kent, *Commentaries on American Law* (1827), Vol. 2, 195, 227-228.

Senate Journal 1784, 44–49. *New York Laws*, Ch. 87, 1798, 475; Ch. 122, 1850, 195.

6.   *Williams* v. *Williams*, 1853, 8 New York 537–538. See also James Kent, *Commentaries on American Law* (1827), Vol. 2, 227–232. Carl F. Zollman, *American Law of Charities*, 17–19, 28–33. Irvin G. Wyllie, "The Search for an American Law of Charity, 1776–1844," *Mississippi Valley Historical Review*, Vol. 46, 1959, 206–217. *Philadelphia Baptist Association* v. *Hart's Executors*, 1819, 4 Wheaton 499.

7.   Patrick J. Dignan, *A History of the Legal Incorporation of Catholic Church Property in the United States, 1784–1932*, 11–12, 25, 52–66, 73–74, 92, 122–123, 169, 193–196, 205–208. *New York Laws*, Ch. 218, 1854, 494; Ch. 230, 1855, 338.

8.   Beverly McAnear, "College Founding in the American Colonies, 1745–1775," *Mississippi Valley Historical Review*, Vol. 42, 1955, 24–28, 42–44. Milton M. Klein, *The Politics of Diversity*, 104–107. Guy F. Wells, *Parish Education in Colonial Virginia*, 33–37.

9.   John W. Pratt, *Religion, Politics and Diversity: The Church-State Theme in New York*, 164. Timothy L. Smith, "Protestant Schooling and American Nationality," *Journal of American History*, Vol. 53, 1967, 687. Kenneth A. Lockridge, Literacy in Colonial New England, 38–29, 55–69, 83, 99–100. Lawrence A. Cremin, *American Education: The Colonial Experience, 1607–1783*, 36–41. The curriculum used in the common schools or gospel schools of New York had a large religious content, especially Bible reading.

10.   Frederick Rudolph, ed., *Essays on Education in the Early Republic*. See especially Benjamin Rush's "Plan for the Establishment of Public Schools" (1786), and Noah Webster's "On the Education of Youth in America" (1790). Bernard Bailyn, *Education in the Forming of American Society*, 18–29, 78–82. Ernest E. Bayles, Bruce L. Hood, *Growth of American Educational Thought and Practice*, 11–19.

11.   *Messages from the Governors of New York*, Vol. 1, 200, Jan. 21, 1784, George Clinton. *Laws of the State of New York, 1777–1784* (1886), Vol. 1, Ch. 51, 1784, 686.

12.   Elsie G. Hobson, *Educational Legislation and Administration in the State of New York, 1777–1850*, 21–22. Sidney Sherwood, *The University of the State of New York*, 65, 81–82.

13.   Joseph S. Davis, *Essays in the Earlier History of American Corporations*, Vol. 1, 102.

14.   *Compiled Laws, 1813*, Vol. 2, 262, Sec. 9. Frank C. Abbot, *Government Policy and Higher Education*, 7, 25–28. James Kent said that the visitorial power was an ancient right given to those who created or who

were benefactors to charitable institutions, in order to watch over their welfare. James Kent, *Commentaries on American Law* (1827), Vol. 2, 242.

15.   *New York Laws*, Ch. 67, 1786, Sec. 11, 282, Vol. 1, Greenleaf. Ch. 199, 1813, 319. See Ch. 22, Sec. 8, 1782 for an earlier local statute that was its prototype. The sale of one lot of land per township to aid public education in the 1786 New York statute was the model for a similar provision of the Northwest Ordinance of 1787, passed by the United States Congress.

16.   Richard J. Gabel, *Public Funds for Church and Private Schools*, 203–214. *New York Laws*, Ch. 75, 1795, 248, Vol. 3, Greenleaf. See also, *The Perpetual Laws of the Commonwealth of Massachusetts* (1801), Vol. 2, Ch. 19, 1789, 39. Connecticut also established a school fund in 1795, using capital obtained from the sale of western lands.

17.   Carl. F. Kaestle, "Common Schools Before the Common School Revival: New York Schooling in the 1790's," *History of Education Quarterly*, Vol. 12, 1972, 480–486. Carl F. Kaestle, *The Evolution of an Urban School System: New York City, 1750–1850*, 64–88.

18.   John A. Muscalus, *The Use of Banking Enterprises in the Financing of Public Education, 1796–1866*, 30–34. William O. Bourne, *History of the Public School Society of New York*, 4–5. *New York Laws*, Ch. 66, 1805, 248; Ch. 193, Sec. 4, 1808, 364. *Assembly Journal 1811*, 153, 260. The idea of taxing banks to aid education was probably borrowed from New Jersey, which passed a tax on bank capital in 1810.

19.   *New York Laws*, Ch. 422, 1812, 490. This statute was drawn up by a five-man commission appointed to survey public education statutes of other states: Ch. 246, 1811, Sec. 54; Ch. 52, 1813.

20.   The office was abolished in 1821 when an unfit person was appointed during a patronage fight between Governor DeWitt Clinton and the Regency. Jabez D. Hammond, *The History of Political Parties in the State of New York*, Vol. 1, 570. The Secretary of State administered the common school system from 1821 to 1854 when these duties were vested in the newly created office of Superintendent of Public Instruction.

21.   John F. Dillon, *Treatise on the Law of Municipal Corporations*, 32. James Kent, *Commentaries on American Law* (1827), Vol. 2, 167. *Assembly Journal 1814*, 77. *New York Laws*, Ch. 192, 1814, 229; Ch. 252, Sec. 7, 1815, 260. School districts were a form of municipal or quasi-public corporation possessing very limited powers. They were not benevolent public service corporations in the sense of privately endowed academies.

22.   *Messages from the Governors of New York*, Vol. 2, 1048, Nov. 7, 1820, DeWitt Clinton. *Legislative Documents 1821*, Assembly No. 33. *New York Laws*, Ch. 61, 1821, 54.

23.   *Messages from the Governors of New York*, Vol. 3, 212, Jan. 1, 1828, DeWitt Clinton. Burke A. Hinsdale, *Horace Mann and the Common*

School Revival in the United States, 59–60. Ernest E. Bayles, Bruce L. Hood, *Growth of American Educational Thought and Practice,* 65–68.

24.   Elsie G. Hobson, *Educational Legislation and Administration in the State of New York, 1777–1850,* 39. *Legislative Documents 1825,* Senate No. 132. *Senate Journal 1825,* 123–124. The members of the Literature Committee were not opposed to the Regents continuing to incorporate educational institutions but used this anomalous holdover to attack the Regency's bank incorporation policy.

25.   *New York Laws,* Ch. 544, 1851, 1002. New York's first proprietary high school had been incorporated in 1827 and the number of these schools slowly grew as the number of cities increased.

26.   *Senate Documents 1853,* No. 22.

27.   *New York Laws,* Ch. 184, 1853, 354; Ch. 433, 1853, 828. *Assembly Documents 1843,* No. 14, 4–5.

28.   In 1843, the Secretary of State refused to distribute the report of the Museum of Natural History, which had been printed at state expense, because the statute authorizing the printing had not been passed by a two-thirds vote. He said the authorization was unconstitutional because the Constitution required all public expenditures to receive a two-thirds majority. John S. Jenkins, *History of Political Parties in the State of New York,* 454–455.

29.   George F. Miller, *The Academy System of the State of New York,* 27–46, 71–72. Elsie G. Hobson, *Educational Legislation and Administration in the State of New York, 1777–1850,* 42.

30.   Jesse H. Shera, *Foundations of the Public Library,* 59–70. Joseph S. Davis, *Essays in the Earlier History of American Corporations,* Vol. 1, 100–101; Vol. 2, 17. E. V. Lamberton, "Colonial Libraries of Pennsylvania," *Pennsylvania Magazine of History and Biography,* Vol. 42, 1918, 193–198. *New York Laws,* Ch. 43, 1796, 320, Vol. 3, Greenleaf. New Jersey followed New York's lead in 1799 and amended its general incorporation statute for seminaries to allow the incorporation of libraries.

31.   *New York Laws,* Ch. 80, 1835, 65.

32.   *Messages from the Governors of New York,* Vol. 3, 651, Jan. 2, 1838, William L. Marcy. *New York Laws,* Ch. 237, 1838, 220; Ch. 177, 1839, 150.

33.   *New York Laws,* Ch. 395, 1853, 788.

34.   Simeon E. Baldwin, "American Business Corporations before 1789," *American Historical Review,* Vol. 8, 1903, 457, 462. It was modeled on a similar corporation to aid the dependents of deceased Presbyterian clergymen that was chartered by Pennsylvania in 1759.

35.   *New York Laws,* Ch. 190, 1811, 338; Ch. 114, 1817, 102. *Legislative Documents 1820,* Senate No. 73.

36. *New York Laws*, Ch. 62, 1788, 133; Ch. 64, 1788, 151; Ch. 65, 1788, 174, Vol. 2, Greenleaf; Ch. 180, Sec. 7, 1801, 559.

37. *Jackson* v.*Corey*, 1811, 8 Johns 385.

38. *Jackson* v. *Hartwell*, 1811, 8 Johns 422.

39. *Denton* v. *Jackson*, 1817, 2 Johns Chancery 325.

40. *Overseers of Pittstown* v. *Overseers of Plattsburgh*, 1820, 18 Johns 407.

41. *Todd* v. *Birdsall*, 1823, 1 Cowen 260; *Grant* v. *Fancher*, 1826, 5 Cowen 309.

42. James Kent, *Commentaries on American Law* (1827), Vol. 2, 225, 245. *Revised Statutes 1828*, Vol. 1, Ch. 11, Title 1, 337; Ch. 12, Title 1, 364.

43. William Livingston, William Smith, Jr., eds., *Laws of New York, 1671-1751* (1752), Ch. 666, Sec. 11, 1737. This statute was extended in 1743 (Ch. 745); 1744 (Ch. 768); 1750 (Ch. 897). Theodore Thayer, "The Land-Bank System in the American Colonies," *Journal of Economic History*, Vol. 13, 1953, 145-153. Bray Hammond, *Banks and Politics in America from the Revolution to the Civil War*, 10-12. Don C. Sowers, *The Financial History of New York State from 1789 to 1912*, 259.

44. Forest McDonald, *We the People, The Economic Origins of the Constitution*, 292-296. Beatrice G. Reubens, "State Financing of Private Enterprises in Early New York," Columbia University Dissertation, 140-146, 228-231. *New York Laws*, Ch. 40, 1786, 240, Vol. 1, Greenleaf; Ch. 25, 1792, 400, Vol. 2, Greenleaf; Ch. 215, 1808, 300.

45. *New York Laws*, Ch. 36, 1792, 425; Vol. 2, Greenleaf. The colonial government, however, had previously regulated medical practice in 1760. *Compiled Laws*, 1813, Vol. 2, 219, footnote.

46. This statute was probably copied from New Jersey statutes of 1783 and 1786, which made any two judges of the State Supreme Court a licensing commission to appoint competent persons to examine practicing doctors and surgeons, and issue licenses. *New Jersey Laws*, Nov. 26, 1783; Nov. 2, 1786.

47. *New York Laws*, Ch. 45, 1797, 417; Vol. 3, Greenleaf. See Joseph F. Kett, *The Formation of the American Medical Profession*, 181-182 for a table of New York medical legislation to 1853.

48. Richard H. Shryock, *Medical Licensing in America, 1650-1965*, 24. Joseph S. Davis, *Essays in the Earlier History of American Corporations*, Vol. 2, 304. *Mass. Laws*, Ch. 43, 1803, 109; Ch. 138, 1806, 437. In 1787, the Connecticut legislature refused to charter the Connecticut Medical Society because it would be a dangerous monopoly. County medical societies overcame this objection.

49.   *New York Laws*, Ch. 104, 1807, 246; Ch. 63, 1812, 94. *Transactions of the Medical Society of the State of New York, 1807–1831*, 32.

50.   There is a close relationship in time and purpose between this first reserve clause and a veto opinion that James Kent wrote for the Council of Revision on the day this statute was passed. His veto opinion dealt with the scope of state regulation over turnpike corporations, another variety of public service corporation.

51.   *Transactions of the Medical Society of the State of New York, 1807–1831*, 27. *New York Laws*, Ch. 181, 1809, 565.

52.   *Messages from the Governors of New York*, Vol. 2, 905, Jan. 27, 1818, DeWitt Clinton. *New York Laws*, Ch. 206, 1818, 192.

53.   James H. Young, *The Toadstool Millionaires*, 52–57, 63. *Revised Statutes, 1828* Vol. 1, Ch. 14, Title 7, 453–454. The New York Medical Society had petitioned for this power since 1822: *Legislature Documents 1822*, Assembly No. 90; 91; *1823*, Assembly No. 73; *1825*, Assembly No. 107.

54.   *New York Laws*, Ch. 126, 1830, 141; Ch. 68, 1834, 72; Ch. 305, 1835, 354. *Assembly Documents 1833*, No. 198.

55.   Walter Hugins, *Jacksonian Democracy and the Working Class*, 167–171, 219–220.

56.   Joseph F. Kett, *The Formation of the American Medical Profession*, 171. *Transactions of the Medical Society of the State of New York, 1840–1843*, 230–231, 245–250, 490–512. *New York Laws*, Ch. 275, 1844, 406.

57.   Philip Van Ingen, *The New York Academy of Medicine*, 54.

58.   Joseph F. Kett, *The Formation of the American Medical Profession*, 171–173, 176–180. Richard H. Shryock, *Medical Licensing in America, 1650–1965*, 28–29, 34–39. Philip Van Ingen, *The New York Academy of Medicine*, 54–60. *New York Convention Manual, 1867*, Part 2, Statistics, 218–221. *Senate Documents 1853*, No. 22. *New York Laws*, Ch. 184, 1853, 354.

59.   Robert W. McCluggage, *A History of the American Dental Association*, 20–21, 32–37, 49–52, 89.

60.   Nathan Miller, *The Enterprise of a Free People*, 15–17. David M. Ellis, *Land Lords and Farmers in the Hudson-Mohawk Region, 1790–1850*, 143–149. *New York Laws*, Ch. 186, 1808, 359, Ch. 187, 1808, 361.

61.   *New York Laws*, Ch. 107, 1819, 125.

62.   Ulysses P. Hedrich, *A History of Agriculture in the State of New York*, 123–130. Donald B. Marti, "Early Agricultural Societies in New York, The Foundations of Improvement," *New York History*, Vol. 48, 1967, 314–315, 318–321. *New York Laws*, Ch. 339, 1853, 716; Ch. 425, 1855, 777.

63. Anton-Hermann Chroust, *The Rise of the Legal Profession in America*, Vol. 2, 36–37, 250–252. *Reports of Cases of Practice Determined in the Supreme Court of Judicature of the State of New York*, Caines and Coleman's Cases, 1808, 7–18.

64. *New York Laws*, Ch. 202, 1815, 204; Ch. 222, 1832, 401; Ch. 151, 1847, 146. Virginia passed a general incorporation statute for fire companies in 1788 and Kentucky in 1798, Joseph G. Blandi, *Maryland Business Corporations, 1783–1852*, 10.

65. *New York Laws*, Ch. 39, 1785, 165; Vol. 1, Greenleaf. On occasion, the New York legislature did erect the heirs of commonly held land into a corporation to facilitate dividing it; Ch. 202, 1808. Colonial Massachusetts first used this device in 1713 and this law was re-enacted by the state legislature in 1784; *The Acts and Resolves, Public and Private of the Province of Massachusetts Bay*, (1869), Vol. 1, Ch. 19, 1713, 704.

66. *Assembly Documents 1839*, No. 409. Assessment districts were authorized in 1823; Ch. 262, Sec. 10, 1823.

2

Internal Improvement Corporations

TURNPIKES

One of the first statutes passed after peace was restored regularized the procedure for laying out and maintaining public highways. The statute applied to only a few counties along the Hudson River. It authorized town meetings to choose from three to five highway commissioners, who were to divide the township into highway districts and see that each district chose an Overseer of Highways. The Township Highway Commission was granted powers of eminent domain, and a procedure was laid down to establish a fair price for rights-of-way.

In 1797, this statute was extended to most counties in the state, and a County Highway Commission was erected in each county, consisting of three persons appointed by the Governor for three-year terms. Its duty was to coordinate activities of the several township highway commissions and to superintend the local use of state highway funds.[1] Neither the county superintendents of highways nor the township highway commissioners were given corporate status (in contrast to the trustees for school districts and loan officers) because neither of these commissions owned any real property. Almost all road-building and maintenance equipment was owned by local farmers and contracted for on a seasonal basis.

Beside the public highway system, there was constructed, after 1800, an extensive system of turnpike toll roads. The first turnpike corporation in New York was chartered in 1797, and thereafter, they were the most frequently incorporated business in New York in the first fifty years of the nineteenth century. Between 1797 and 1847, about 500 charters were passed, plus many more charter amendments.

The great era of turnpike construction was between 1800 and 1819. Turnpikes were used primarily to extend the trading radius of established villages, although a trunkline system was built across upper New York from the Massachusetts border to Lake Erie. As early as 1800, Governor John Jay admonished the legislature that it was spending too much time passing private and local statutes, leaving too little time for proper consideration of public measures. Governor Jay probably had the example of the Manhattan Company in mind when he said this, but it could just as well have applied to turnpike companies.[2]

Governor George Clinton said the same thing two years later, and suggested that a "summary mode ought . . . to be prescribed to exact a compliance from those companies with the intentions of government." He said the same thing the following year, but dropped any hint that a general incorporation statute should be passed. He said, "The difficulties which occur in devising amendments to acts of this kind, without invading corporate rights . . . should lead . . . to great care and circumspection in framing future ones."[3]

This led the legislature to insert in most of the turnpike charters passed in 1802 a provision that the turnpikes had to be inspected by one or more state-appointed turnpike commissioners who had no interest in any turnpike corporation, to verify that ten miles of road was in usable condition before the corporation began collecting tolls. These commissions were modeled on the office of the County Highway Commission, except that they were a temporary body. Two years later, the Governor and Council were authorized to appoint a three- to five-man commission for each county, but it could only investigate complaints. An amendment passed in 1806, however, authorized county commissioners to issue written orders to open toll gates when a turnpike was found out of repair.[4]

Chancellor James Kent, writing for the Council of Revision, objected to the summary authority vested in turnpike commissioners because "the order of the commissioners is to be peremptory in the first instance, and requires instantaneous obedience. The bill, therefore, vests in these commissioners an arbitrary power over the interest and property of individuals which is unknown to the Constitution . . ." because there was no provision for a judicial hearing or right of appeal. This opinion strongly implied that there was some sort of a contractual relationship between the state and incorporated turnpike franchises, and in addition, it hinted that there was a violation of "due process of law," because there was no provision for review of a nonjudicial order. Kent's opinion was a short summary of the arguments contained in a memorial submitted to the legislature by the Great Western Turnpike Company, which opposed state regulation. The corporation viewed its charter as "a solemn contract between the government and the stockholders."[5] The legislature ignored Chancellor Kent's argument and passed the statute over the Council's veto.

Improvements in overland transportation were the greatest need of the time. The people expected their representatives to facilitate these improvements. Turnpikes were popular investments, not necessarily because they were expected to be profitable, but because they improved access to markets, raised local land values, and lowered the costs of goods that had to be teamed in. Shares were of low par value and were widely held. Turnpike promoters were treated indulgently by state legislators. Joseph A. Durrenburger did not find a single instance in New York, Pennsylvania, or Maryland, where a legislature refused to grant an extension of a nonuser clause when a company found it difficult to raise sufficient capital.[6]

In 1806, Governor Morgan Lewis again admonished the legislature for spending too much time passing private statutes, especially turnpikes. He said this could be avoided "by establishing general principles on which all such companies shall in the future be incorporated."[7] The legislature passed a concurrent resolution, directing the Attorney General to draw up a bill fixing the terms by which turnpike charters would be granted. A general regulatory statute was the device chosen. It required each charter to be passed separately because turnpikes were franchises and because investors wanted assurance that the road would actually be built somewhere near their residences. It was passed in 1807.[8]

The general regulatory statute required a public notice of intent to incorporate, specified the width of the roadway, who was exempted from tolls, penalties for avoiding tolls, number of directors, the number of corporation officers and how they were to be chosen, how shares were to be subscribed, procedure for forfeiting shares if calls for capital were not met, a nonuser clause, and a system of regressive voting that encouraged the widespread holding of shares. All turnpike companies were delegated the power of eminent domain, with the procedure for appraising and taking land being the major portion of the statute. Public highways could be used if compensation was paid to the local township in the same manner as for private land, but the final route of the turnpike had to be approved by two of the three special commissioners appointed by the state. Tolls could not be collected until ten miles of road were completed and had been inspected by these commissioners. These last features (the right of eminent domain and the power to collect a public toll) made turnpikes into franchise corporations because they could not operate unless these powers were granted to them by the state.

The legislature retained the power of judging each charter application on its own merits. Each act was a short form, which specified capitalization, number of shares and the value of each, route, rate of tolls, and temporary directors until permanent ones could be properly elected. The statute received perfunctory legislative approval because the public benefits conferred by turnpikes far outweighed the private profits they were expected to earn and this made them essentially noncontroversial.

The statute did not have a reserve clause, but it provided that "the legislature may dissolve the said corporation when the income arising from said tolls shall have paid and compensated the said corporation for all monies they have expended in purchasing and making said road, together with an interest thereon of ten percent per annum, besides the expense of repairing and taking care of said road." Thereafter, the turnpike would become a public highway. No turnpike corporation was taken over by the state, and after the completion of the Erie Canal of 1825, toll road construction rapidly declined until the late 1840s when plank roads were built in enormous numbers. A general incorporation statute for plank roads and turnpikes was passed in 1847 that contained most of the provisions of the 1807 statute.

CANAL CORPORATIONS

The state's first monetary aid to regional internal improvements was given in 1791 when the Commissioners of the Land Office were authorized to survey the potential road and canal routes from the upper Hudson Valley to the west, and a year later two companies were incorporated to build canals from near Albany northward to Lake Champlain and westward to Lake Ontario. Thereafter, private canal corporations were frequently chartered (until the advent of the depression in 1838), but after the state began construction of the Erie Canal, most of the corporate canals were short, feeder lines.

No general incorporation statute for canals was ever passed because the state wanted to prevent any competition that might affect the credit rating of the state's canal bonds. With the advent of railroads, the legislature went to great lengths to prevent railroads from competing with the publicly owned canals, even to the extent of subsidizing the construction of the New York and Erie Railroad along a route not competitive with any canal.

BRIDGE CORPORATIONS

The first toll bridge corporation was chartered in 1797, and thereafter they were a very frequent source of legislation until a general incorporation statute was passed in 1848. The greatest number of toll bridge charters were passed from 1800 to 1820. After 1835, such charters were far less frequent and state appropriations to build free bridges were far more numerous.

AQUEDUCT CORPORATIONS

The first aqueduct company was chartered in 1799, although in 1790 the City of Hudson was authorized to regulate an unincorporated association that was supplying water to subscribers in the city. Aqueduct corporations were chartered in fair numbers between 1800 and 1810, and less frequently thereafter; however, they were never allowed creation by a general incorporation statute as they were by Massachusetts in 1799.[9]

STEAMBOAT CORPORATIONS

Steamboat corporations were a relatively late type of incorporated enterprise, although the New York legislature had encouraged the developers of a practical steamboat. The first steamboat corporation was not chartered until 1813, and thereafter, these corporations were frequently incorporated and regulated in the interests of passenger safety.

In 1808, the New York legislature granted a thirty-year monopoly to the Livingston interests to operate steamboats on New York waters. This monopoly was the source of the litigation resolved by *Gibbons* v. *Ogden* in 1824. In the following year, the federal decision was adhered to in New York in *North River Steamboat Co.* v. *John R. Livingston*; however, the state decision recognized the continued operation of the monopoly on the state's inland waters, such as the Finger Lakes and the canals.[10] From 1825 to 1838, the legislature incorporated steamboat companies to operate on these waters, but these companies were explicitly confined to named lakes and stockholders were not given limited liability. In most respects, this put the licensees of the Livingston monopoly, whether corporate or individual, on the same competitive basis. No charters for inland steamboat corporations were passed from 1838 until 1854, because after the expiration of the monopoly, the steamboat business became a competitive free-for-all in which limited liability would have been deemed an unfair competitive advantage. Incorporation of steamboat corporations was resumed in 1854 because by then they were in full competition with railroads and they needed all the advantages they could get. On the other hand, from 1814 to 1838, the stockholders in ocean steamship corporations were readily granted limited liability because such enterprises required a larger capitalization and the competition was international.

FERRY FRANCHISES AND CORPORATIONS

Ferry operations were a frequent object of legislation from 1785 to 1855. A general licensing statute was passed in 1797 that gave the judges of the county courts the power to grant licenses. Some ferry businesses were granted charters, but more frequently they were unincorporated franchises, or alternatively, were prohibited from operating within competing distances of toll bridges. A general incorporation statute for ferries was passed in 1853, but such corporations could not impair the vested rights of existing franchises unless the local government or the local county judge approved of the competition. From 1853 through 1855, eleven corporations were formed under this statute.[11]

STAGE FRANCHISES AND CORPORATIONS

The state granted the first stagecoach franchise, to use public highways, in 1785 and continued the practice until 1817. A general incorporation statute for stagecoach companies was never passed, although one for urban omnibus companies was passed in 1854 that was designed to meet the needs of New York City. Omnibus corporations had to be licensed by the Common Council and they could change or extend their routes only if the city council and two-thirds of the stockholders approved. The Common Council was forbidden to terminate a franchise, once granted, unless two-thirds of the Council approved and unless the city compensated the company for the loss of their business. Stockholders in this relatively new type of enterprise were fully liable for all the debts of the company, so that they had minimal advantages over individually owned omnibus enterprises already in operation.[12]

DAM FRANCHISES

As early as 1735, Massachusetts passed a de facto general incorporation statute for neighborhood grist mills that allowed dams to be built to power waterwheels without the millowners first owning the land that would be flooded after a dam was built. In effect, mill-dam laws delegated the power of eminent domain to millowners and thus conferred on them the status of a public utility. In 1796, the colonial statutes were updated, but the state continued to authorize millowners to flood land without owners' permission provided an annual rent was paid for the use of the land.

Massachusetts courts later extended the eminent domain privilege to the owners of textile mills because of the obvious benefits such operations contributed to the state's general welfare.

The first New York legislation that allowed construction of a dam was a private act passed in 1800 and, thereafter, dams were a frequent source of legislation because, at an early date, the state had defined streams as public highways. The statutes that authorized dam construction were like the franchise statutes the state granted stage lines operating on public highways, but the New York legislature never granted millowners (corporations or partnerships) the power of eminent domain to create mill ponds. Millowners had to own the land they flooded. However, New York courts, in 1805, approved of millowners controlling the flow the water, to the point of stopping it, in order to maximize production, because the most productive use of water was in the public interest.[13]

DOCK AND WHARF FRANCHISES

Massachusetts had chartered wharf associations during the colonial period and passed a de facto general incorporation statute for them in 1784 (*Mass. Laws*, ch. 39, 1784). New York did not charter a dock corporation until 1825 (then it was a dry dock), but thereafter, dock charters were frequently passed. Like turnpikes, incorporated public docks were franchises that allowed local entrepreneurs to build a local internal improvement.

SUMMARY

The early commentators on American law observed that the development of corporation law in the United States was almost wholly indigenous, especially in matters of corporation creation and contracts. It appears they were correct. Blackstone had not clearly distinguished between municipal corporations, benevolent public service corporations, and business corporations, and the other classes of English corporations he discussed did not exist in the legal and social structure of the United States; therefore, organizations like independent religious congregations, loan commissioners, and townships needed statute definition to be corporations.

Few English corporate decisions are cited in early American cases unless they dealt with municipal corporations, court procedure, or jurisdiction. Parliament passed very few individual charters of incorporation for business enterprises and no general incorporation for business corporations until 1844. Large businesses in England, after the Bubble Act (1720), were carried on by joint-stock associations, which were unincorporated companies but legally were only expanded partnerships; therefore, both the case and statute laws of England dealt almost entirely with partnerships and single proprietorships, although these businesses might be called companies.[14]

The laws that encouraged the creation of local units of religious and secular education defined the policies that led the legislature to pass laws that encouraged the development of business corporations: both types of organizations strongly contributed to the public welfare. During the first forty years of national existence, all American Protestant denominations chartered new congregations in very large numbers, and some types of benevolent organizations were also chartered in very large numbers. As a result, entrepreneurs who sought to make new products or replace household manufactured products by similar products made in factories, understood how incorporation helped to protect real property and helped to secure the patronage of the state for their undertakings. All communities were also familiar with the benefits that both of these types of corporations contributed to public welfare.

They performed functions that the state or local governments were unable or unwilling to do, and whether they built a church building, schoolhouse, or textile mill, the improvements they made were highly visible. For several reasons, the corporation became a common entrepreneurial form of organization in the United States before it did in Europe. Americans were familiar with its operation because it was used as a means of securing state patronage to perform new types of public services, and it offered efficient protection of real property; and later it was equally efficient at limiting stockholder liability.[15]

The transfer of the public service function from benevolent to business goals was easy to make in the late eighteenth and early nineteenth centuries because both forms of organizations performed their services on the local level where their contributions to local prosperity were clearly recognized. A turnpike or textile mill was a public improvement that was as useful and as visible as a church building or schoolhouse. The earliest legal distinction was not between benevolent and business corporations but between public (municipal) and private corporations (all other classes of corporations).[16] Private corporations included all varieties of voluntary organizations composed of private individuals who associated for some limited purpose. These corporations were private in the sense that their officers held no public office by virtue of their corporate title. This definition made it of secondary importance whether a private corporation performed a benevolent service or one for profit so long as its function was recognized as a valuable contribution to local public welfare; therefore, the organization of these corporations was encouraged by general laws.

Furthermore, the benevolent corporations were all voluntary, and most were governed by the bodily participation of their members. As long as franchise businesses performed local services, they had much the same organization except that voting was by shares owned instead of by bodily participation. In most local franchise corporations, shares were widely owned. Incorporation lent the prestige of the state and the sanction of the law to privately managed projects, which clergymen, teachers, and entrepreneurs strongly desired. It was also a device that allowed the state to define the civil powers of corporations to the public's advantage.

Religion, literacy, and commerce need not be closely related, but it seems they were in the northern United States (at least in New York and New England). One of the implicit selling points in promoting public education in Calvinistic Christian communities, and getting the local community to tax itself to pay for it, was the necessity of reading the Bible. This made the organization of a system of public education in Protestant Christian communities relatively easy, especially in communities that had a large proportion of New England settlers. In the first half of the nineteenth century, nearly the entire native-born population of New York, even in pioneering communities, had attended common schools to the level of functional literacy.[17]

Furthermore, in the early national period, the religious motivations for achieving mass literacy were re-enforced by the civil desire to have all republican citizens able to read the constitutions and laws of the state and nation. This relationship between mass literacy, religion, and republican government strongly contributed to training local entrepreneurs because the use of the corporation device to organize associations that promoted mass literacy was a local training ground where many men learned how to organize associations that could be used to earn private profits. The general incorporation statutes for benevolent organizations were an extremely useful legal encouragement that could easily be modified to provide equality of opportunity for profit-making ventures on a larger scale than could be undertaken by single proprietors or partnerships.

The experience of the English Calvinists in the northern colonies in trying to institutionalize their political and religious values and the necessity, during the early national period, of organizing new congregations and new schools on newly settled land in a secular state, called into existence laws (from a friendly government) that encouraged men to pool their labor and capital resources in order to undertake larger scale public welfare projects. The social demands of organizing local benevolent and charitable corporations created a large reservoir of persons experienced in organizing voluntary self-help ventures that could be used to exploit local commercial opportunities. Joseph A. Schumpeter's definition of the entrepreneurial function fits this situation. "We have seen that the function of entrepreneurs is to reform or revolutionize the pattern of production by exploiting an invention or more generally, an untried technological possibility for producing a new commodity or an old one in a new way. . . . To undertake such new things is difficult and constitutes a distinct economic function. . . . To act with confidence beyond the range of the familiar beacons and to overcome that resistence requires aptitudes that are present in only a small fraction of the population and that define the entrepreneurial function. This function does not essentially consist in either inventing anything or otherwise creating the conditions which the enterprise exploits. It consists in getting things done."[18]

The entrepreneurial function is essentially one of organizing. The local pools of organizing skills in existence by the end of the eighteenth century were a major ingredient in the rapid industrialization of the United States. In Europe, as in the United States, the more famous entrepreneurs of the industrial revolution made their reputations as organizers of business corporations, not as inventors or merchants.[19] According to Thomas C. Cochran, "This rapid adoption of the corporation for a wide variety of enterprises in the United States within the course of a single generation must be regarded as one of the most important developments of the Business Revolution."[20] Even though the earliest factories were largely experimental and used machinery that did not require high capitalization, and the available markets were usually small, it was advantageous to be incorporated because incorporation in New York offered the protection of limited liability for investors in speculative enterprises. Even though these businesses could have been organized as single proprietorships or partnerships, incorporation was eagerly sought and readily granted.

The earliest business charters fell into three categories: internal improvement companies (turnpikes, toll bridges, canals, water supply); monied corporations (banks, insurance); and manufacturing companies (textiles, iron and steel, glass, earthenware). In the beginning, almost all business corporations had some degree of franchise relationship to the state, or performed services or made products that New York wished to encourage as a means of making the state and nation economically self-sufficient. Before 1800, about 66 percent of the business charters in the United States were for turnpikes, while banks and insurance corporations accounted for another 20 percent, and manufacturing companies for less than 4 percent.[21]

There was, however, a class of public corporation that was less frequently incorporated. This class performed a regulatory function over a professional activity that affected the welfare of the whole state. Two examples of this class of corporation are the New York Medical Society and the Regents of the University. These organizations were incorporated to facilitate the collecting of information and to advise the legislature on the proper policies that would make these services safe and responsive to public need. In effect, they served as permanent regulatory commissions that continuously supervised these areas of public concern at a time when the only existing statewide regulatory agency, the court system, was ineffective in supervising either medical practice or secondary education. Because they were vital to the public welfare, the legislature enacted the first reserve clause to protect the public interest. Reserve clauses allowed the legislature to amend or repeal any charter at any time and for any reason. It was first used in the organizing statute of the New York Medical Society in 1806; its second application was the Regents of the University in 1813.

NOTES

1. *New York Laws*, Ch. 52, 1784, 105; Vol. 1, Greenleaf; Ch. 43, 1797, 466; Vol. 3, Greenleaf.

2. *Messages from the Governors of New York*, Vol. 1, 450, Jan. 28, 1800, John Jay.

3. *Messages from the Governors of New York*, Vol. 1, 511, Jan. 25, 1802, George Clinton.

4. *New York Laws*, Ch. 81, 1804, 296; Ch. 160, 1806, 558.

5. Alfred B. Street, ed., *The Council of Revision of the State of New York*, 338. *Legislative Documents 1806*, March 19, 1806.

6. Joseph A. Durrenburger, *Turnpikes: A Study of the Toll Road Movement in the Middle Atlantic States and Maryland*, 82, 103–104.

7. *Messages from the Governors of New York*, Vol. 1, 574, Jan. 28, 1806, Morgan Lewis.

8. *New York Laws*, Ch. 38, 1807, 102. The Massachusetts legislature passed a general regulatory statute for turnpikes in 1805: *The Laws of the Commonwealth of Massachusetts, 1780–1807* (1807), Vol. 3, Ch. 125, 1805, 285.

9. *The Laws of the Commonwealth of Massachusetts, 1780–1807* (1807), Vol. 2, Ch. 59, 1799, 843.

10. *New York Laws*, Ch. 225, 1808, 333. *North River Steamboat Co. v. John R. Livingston*, 1825, 3 Cowen 713, 755.

11. *New York Convention Manual, 1867*, Part 2, Statistics, 38. *New York Laws*, Ch. 65, 1797, 447, Vol. 3, Greenleaf; Ch. 142, 1853, 213.

12. *New York Laws*, Ch. 142, 1854, 325.

13. Harry N. Scheiber, "Property Law, Expropriation, and Resource Allocation by Government: The United States, 1789–1910," *Journal of Economic History*, Vol. 33, 1973, 237–240. Morton J. Horwitz, "The Transformation in the Conception of Property in American Law, 1780–1860," *University of Chicago Law Review*, Vol. 40, 1973, 251–256. *The Acts and Resolves, Public and Private, of the Province of Massa-*

chusetts Bay (1874), Vol. 2, Ch. 5, 1735, 758. *The Law of the Common-wealth of Massachusetts, 1780–1807* (1807), Vol. 1, Ch. 49, 1796, 729.

14.   H. A. Shannon, "The Coming of General Limited Liability," *Economic History*, Vol. 2, 1931, 270–275, 279–281. Edwin M. Dodd, *American Business Corporations until 1860*, 93–99. James W. Hurst, *Law and the Conditions of Freedom in Nineteenth Century United States*, 17–18.

15.   Oscar Handlin, Mary F. Handlin, "Origins of the American Business Corporation," *Journal of Economic History*, Vol. 5, 1945, 5.

16.   Joseph K. Angell, Samuel Ames, *A Treatise on the Law of Private Corporations Aggregate* (1832), 7-9, 16-20, 35. Henry W. Rogers, "Municipal Corporations, 1701-1901," *Two Centuries Growth of American Law, 1701-1901*, 269. William Blackstone, *Commentaries on the Laws of England* (1778), William G. Hammond, ed. (1890), Vol. 1, 844–845. *Terrett v. Taylor*, 1815, 9 Cranch 52.

17.   Whitney R. Cross, *The Burned-Over District*, 89–98. Kenneth A. Lockridge, *Literacy in Colonial New England*, 66–69, 83, 97–100.

18.   Joseph A. Schumpeter, *Capitalism, Socialism and Democracy*, 132.

19.   Charles Wilson, "The Entrepreneur in the Industrial Revolution in Britain," *Europe and the Industrial Revolution*, Sima Liberman, ed., 381. George R. Taylor, ed., *The Early Development of the American Cotton Textile Industry*: Nathan Appleton, "Introduction of the Power Loom and Origin of Lowell"; Samuel Batchelder, "Introduction and Early Progress of the Cotton Manufacture in the United States," xxvi–xxxi.

20.   Thomas C. Cochran, "The Business Revolution," *American Historical Review*, Vol. 79, 1974, 1459.

21.   Joseph S. Davis, *Essays in the Earlier History of American Corporations*, Vol. 2, 24–25.

3

Early Business Corporations

THE GROWTH OF NEW YORK'S BANKING SYSTEM TO 1815

Merchants organized the first state banks because they wanted to use the credit the banks created. The states also had a direct interest in promoting banks because they would help revive domestic and foreign commerce and they could print a specie-based paper currency that could provide an adequate circulating medium in a peacetime economy where specie was perpetually in short supply. Banks could also make loans to state governments, and were often required to do so. All of these functions were valuable public services. Merchants had pre-Revolutionary experience with long- and short-term credit from English export houses, and the banking business was not entirely unfamiliar; therefore, all of the early banks were relatively large-scale enterprises. This situation was sharply different from constructing the first canals or starting the first manufacturing ventures under the factory system, where there was only a small reservoir of technical and management skills.

The first bank chartered by the New York legislature was the Bank of North America, in June 1782, but this action reincorporated a bank chartered by the Congress of the United States. It never went into operation in New York. The first state bank was the Bank of New York, which began operation in 1784, at the time trade resumed with England, but the bank was not chartered until 1791. From their beginnings in North America, banks were consistently profitable, and several states insisted on investing in them in return for granting charters of incorporation.[1] After 1795, charters for all classes of businesses were granted with increasing frequency, but bank charters were the most desired.

By 1805, bank promoters in all states were reluctant to accept the state as a competitor for investment opportunities, but because banks were highly profitable, several state governments insisted on the right to subscribe to shares of stock in new banks in exchange for incorporation. This occurred in New York. Banking in New York became the perfect business with which to perpetuate the political alliance between the Federalist party and businessmen, particularly urban businessmen. During the 1790s, only Federalist-dominated banks were chartered in New York in order to bring the commercial interests of the city to the support of Federalist political policies. Federalist economic policy had a brilliant beginning by chartering the Bank of the United States and the earliest state banks, but the party's leaders could not continue to dominate the engine of commerce they set in motion.

Under Aaron Burr's leadership, the Republicans resorted to a political ruse to get a Republican bank chartered by a Federalist-controlled legislature. In 1799, the Manhattan Company was chartered for the laudable purpose of supplying New York City with pure water, and in a single clause embedded in its charter it was authorized to assume banking powers. The full significance of this clause was not recognized by either the legislature or Governor John Jay, although the Chief Justice, sitting on the Council of Revision, wrote an objection. He was ignored. The Manhattan Company then used its considerable influence to help elect a Republican-controlled legislature and governor in 1800, which rendered certain the election of Thomas Jefferson in an otherwise very close presidential contest. This event secured the Vice-Presidential nomination for Aaron Burr and made him a powerful figure in the 1800 balloting by the electoral college because he represented northern Republican commercial interests.[2]

When the Republicans gained control of the New York legislature, they refused to charter any more Federalist-controlled banks, so Federalist entrepreneurs became private bankers and began circulating notes based on deposits and personally owned specie. This practice threatened a deluge of unreliable banknotes, and the Republicans in 1804 passed a statute limiting the banking business to corporations.[3] This restraining statute was copied from a Massachusetts statute of 1799, passed by a Federalist legislature. It converted all subsequent banking legislation into corporate legislation and made the banking business into a political, as well as an economic, franchise. The twin objects of the restraining statute were to preserve the profits of the banking to Jeffersonian entrepreneurs and provide the state with a reliable paper currency.

Concomitant with the passage of the first restraining statutes by the states, the national government began to exert some centralized control over the credit practices of the state banks through the agency of the Bank of the United States. The loans of one bank when deposited in another become an asset on which more loans could be made. Banking soon became very complex because the transfer of credit was the first corporate interstate commerce on any scale, and because banking and currency were inseparably intertwined. This interdependence welded all banks into one system, so that the credit practices of one state bank affected the credit practices, stability, and integrity of the whole system within that state. Unless there was some centralized control over individual state banks, the whole system was subject to being thrown out of gear, with only the strongest surviving a period of financial stringency.[4]

As the United States passed into the nineteenth century, the nation was served by five classes of currency, kept reliable by the good management of the Bank of the United States. These classes were: specie coined by the national government, banknotes issued by the Bank of the United States, banknotes issued by the state-chartered banks, and banknotes circulated by private bankers where not prohibited, plus private paper (bills of exchange, warehouse receipts, promissory notes). In the third and fourth classes of currency, there were as many varieties of notes and degrees of integrity as there were agents of issue. Restraining statutes were an attempt to provide some degree of integrity for a state's currency by limiting the issue of banknotes to incorporated banks.

Credit was the type of money banks provided. It was one of two kinds: deposit credit and banknote credit. Deposit credit is the type we know today in which a person's bank account is credited with a sum of money that is gradually expended by checks. Banknote credit was created by giving the borrower a bundle of banknotes representing the amount of the loan, except that the agent of redemption for these notes was the bank of issue. Usually, the only place where these notes had to be redeemed was at the head office of the bank. There, and only there, could they be exchanged for gold and silver on demand, and for this purpose a reserve of specie was kept in the bank's vault. In most country banks, the specie reserve amounted to 5 percent or less of the value of its notes in circulation, but the reserve was as high as 30 percent for the city commercial banks. Banknotes were the usual form of currency and credit in the nation, and they strongly tended to prevent a wide circulation of specie.

The Bank of the United States, by having the largest depositor in the economy, the federal government, as its customer, became the general creditor of all state banks. By its day-to-day practice of discounting, the Bank of the United States automatically exercised a centralized restraint on the credit practices of all state banks. The banknotes of state banks could be discounted slightly or heavily, or not accepted as payments for excise taxes, land, custom duties, fines, or for bills of exchange drawn on its branches; or the banknotes of state banks could be collected and presented for redemption in specie at the state bank's home office. The Bank of the United States could use one or all of these restraints on the volume of banknotes circulated by state banks because it was usually the creditor of the state banks. The Bank was not directly concerned with how local credit resources were allocated by a bank's directors, but by its policies, it strongly contributed to the reliability of the local banknotes. In effect, the Bank was an incorporated regulatory commission supervising the nation's credit policy. The supervision ended with the bank's extinction in 1811.

The Bank's dissolution was an open invitation to banknote inflation. All states took advantage of it. From 1810 to 1812, New York chartered ten new banks, but this was a conservative number compared to those chartered by other states. In 1813, the Pennsylvania legislature tried to charter twenty-five in a batch, but the bill was vetoed. In the following year, forty-one banks were simultaneously chartered by a statute passed over the governor's veto. Governor

Daniel D. Tompkins of New York was not saying anything new in 1812 when he warned the legislature about the increase in the number of incorporated institutions. In particular, he warned against banks. Petitions for bank charters had deluged the legislature, and if all were passed, the banking capital of the state would more than double. The Governor listed many reasons why no new banks should be chartered; the chief reasons, however, were that they circulated paper money in increasing quantities, thus aiding speculation and inflation, and they discouraged manufacturing and agriculture by collecting specie in vaults where it was easier to export. The Governor's criticism strongly implied that bank loans would normally be made to farmers and manufacturers and the ability to make these loans was one of the principal reasons for the banks' incorporation.

The end of the Bank of the United States could not have come at a worse time—on the eve of a war that demanded an immense amount of credit. The vacuum was filled with notes issued by state banks, on which there was little restraint. The result was runaway inflation leading to a general suspension of specie payments in 1814, except in New England. Suspension meant that banks could issue notes without the responsibility of redeeming them in specie on demand. Inflation had a disastrous effect on financing the war. The federal government floated about 80 million dollars in bonds, but received only 34 million in cash. The national government was bankrupt and the state banking systems were shaken to their foundations. On the return of peace in 1815, the need for a new central bank was obvious, President Madison's earlier constitutional scruples notwithstanding.[5]

The constitutional authority for states to charter corporations, other than banks, was never questioned. It was part of their sovereignty not alienated to the national government. However, the states had wholly surrendered their power to issue bills of credit. Was it logical or constitutional for the states to grant the power of creating paper money to their corporate creatures when they themselves did not possess this power? "When the constitution was fresh, the question probably occurred to no one, for the people were familiar with bills of credit and with banknotes as quite distinct things. . . . To identify the two as one . . . would . . . have seemed metaphysical. But twenty or more years later, as banks increased in number and their credit in the form of circulating notes came to provide a volume of currency which before could not have been imagined, the fact that the notes were money became obvious, and its unexpected implications began to emerge."[6] The constitutionality of banknotes issued by state-chartered banks was not tested in the United States Supreme Court until 1837, in *Briscoe* v. *Bank of Kentucky*, when they were found constitutional.

In the controversy over re-chartering the national bank, "John C. Calhoun . . . argued in February 1816, that the federal convention of 1787 had intended to give Congress exclusive control of the monetary system; that subsequently there had sprung up great numbers of state banks; that as a result there had been 'an extraordinary revolution in the currency of the country'; that 'by a sort of undercurrent the power of Congress to regulate the money of the country had caved in'; that the state banks had usurped it, 'for gold and silver are not the only money,' since whatever is 'the medium of purchase and sale' was the money of the country."[7] At least 90 percent of the current money was state banknotes.

The second Bank of the United States was chartered in 1816 to bring order to the large volume of paper currency that had been put into circulation by the vastly enlarged number of banks chartered by the states after the demise of the first Bank of the United States. It began operations in January 1817. By a joint resolution passed in April 1816, Congress directed the Treasury not to accept the banknotes of any state bank after February 20, 1817, that was not redeeming its notes in specie. In the meantime, in New York from 1814 to 1818, the suspension of specie payments presented a great opportunity for speculative profits if a general incorporation statute for banks were passed.

When the first Bank of the United States ceased operation, there was a persistent demand for more bank charters, and all varieties of speculators tried to lobby bank charters through the legislature. State Senator Martin Van Buren gained firsthand experience in 1814 with the political possibilities of banking legislation when the legislature was pressed with twenty-two new applications plus granting banking powers to the Commission Company and the New York Coal Company. A general incorporation bill was passed by the Federalist-controlled Assembly and Van Buren introduced a bill in the Republican-controlled Senate to repeal the restraining statute (of 1804). Both bills failed to pass because of the political deadlock, but both bills found strong support among speculators and entrepreneurs eager for the profits of banking but even more eager to use the credit that many banks could supply.[8]

After the war, New York politics were chaotic. The Federalists were discredited because they had done little toward supporting the war, and the dominant Republicans were deeply divided. Republican leadership polarized around two persons: State Senator Martin Van Buren, the very effective legislative leader, and DeWitt Clinton, a strong supporter of internal improvements and former presidential candidate. Based on his experience of 1814, Van Buren's faction set about forming an alliance with the state's banking interest. Banks were the key business because they could supply credit, and the new breed of entrepreneurs called into existence by the war demanded credit to exploit the wealth of the interior and the business opportunities of the city. New York's economic history is particularly important after 1815, because, according to Bray Hammond:

> The New York City business community . . . was already foremost in the country in energy, originality, and aggressiveness. Its political ties within the state were powerful and were becoming so in Washington. It still had much to win from its rivals, especially Philadelphia, but it was on its way. Moreover, what happened in New York displays the forces and interests that were at work throughout the economy. The resources of America that for three centuries had lain in desuetude for lack of industrial techniques were now acquiring values that filled men with excitement. To exploit them money was needed, and to provide money there must be banks. So banks there were everywhere.[9]

The immediate question the Republican Party had to face was whether to restrict banking to individually chartered corporations, as in the past, or enact a general incorporation statute that opened the banking business to all persons who could mobilize sufficient capital. The Albany Regency, the policy-making committee of the Republican party, worked out a politically advantageous arrangement between 1815 and 1819. Banks would be allocated on a highly political basis. The allocation of bank charters was one of several means that the Regency used to weld an alliance of factions into a disciplined party. It was during this same period that Martin Van Buren emerged as the leader of the Regency.

INSURANCE CORPORATIONS

New York's first insurance corporations were chartered by the legislature in 1798: two were stock and one was mutual. The stock companies modeled their charters on the Insurance Company of North America, which was granted a Pennsylvania charter in 1794. The mutual company's charter was modeled on the articles of association of the London Amicable Society, which had served as the model for two mutual corporations organized in Philadelphia.

By 1807, there was effective interstate competition in underwriting marine insurance.[10] In that year, the New York legislature passed a statute excluding out-of-state insurance corporations from selling policies in New York. James Kent, in a veto message for the Council of Revision, raised a very strong constitutional objection to the shortsighted policy of excluding out-of-state or foreign corporations. He said the statute was "inconsistent with the second section of the fourth article of the Constitution of the United States which declared that 'the citizens of each state shall be entitled to all privileges and immunities of citizens of the several states. . . . ' If the bill had prohibited all insurance by private individuals or companies, by means of agents . . . then there would have been an equality between the citizens of this and the other states and the present objection would not have applied."[11] The veto was sustained.

Although insurance corporations were monied corporations, like banks, they aroused comparatively little political controversy because they were not connected with the currency. From the beginning, however, they were forbidden to own large amounts of real estate. By 1807, when the Embargo was enacted, corporate marine insurance was firmly established in the United States. After the War of 1812, when American commerce was recovering from almost complete prostration, a rate war developed among American insurance corporations, with the result that, while agricultural exports boomed and the shipbuilding industry rapidly expanded, marine insurance companies found it difficult to stay in business. Many became bankrupt or switched to underwriting fire risks, especially in the rapidly growing cities. To facilitate marine companies going out of business, the 1817 legislature passed a statute allowing the dissolution of insurance companies in New York City, provided they presented a balance sheet showing the company's assets exceeded its debts.[12]

In 1824, the agents for all out-of-state fire insurance corporations were required to post a $1,000 bond with the Comptroller, and to aid New York insurance companies, a 10 percent tax was imposed on the policies sold by out-of-state companies. The conflagration that swept New York City on December 16–17, 1835 bankrupted most of the city's fire insurance corporations because they had concentrated their risks there. Only three of the city's twenty-six insurance corporations survived. The role that out-of-state insurance corporations played in spreading risks was belatedly recognized and the 10 percent tax was reduced to 2 percent. As a result of these bankruptcies, the public distrusted stock insurance corporations and most fire insurance businesses chartered in the next eighteen years were mutual companies.[13]

THE GROWTH OF NEW YORK MANUFACTURING ENTERPRISES

Immediately upon the return of prosperity following the adoption of the Federal Constitution, the New York legislature began aiding entrepreneurs engaged in manufacturing; and it continued to be responsive to the needs of new manufacturers as settlement moved westward from Albany and costs increased for transporting goods into the interior from older factories located near tidewater. The 1790 legislature authorized loan of £ 200 at 5 percent interest for three years to enable an individual to import European labor and complete his factory for making earthenware, and three years later a loan was made for £ 3,000 (at 5 percent interest for eight years) to encourage the manufacture of cotton, linen, and glass. Another loan for £ 6,000 was made in 1795 to a manufacturer of scythes, nails, and tobacco products. The Hamilton Manufacturing Society, which made glass, was exempted from taxes for five years in 1796, and its employees were excused from jury duty, working on the highways, and from the militia except in cases of invasion or insurrection. In the following year, it was granted a charter of incorporation.[14]

A systematic program of encouraging manufacturing entrepreneurs began in 1805 when the legislature set up the School Fund and appropriated 500,000 acres of vacant land to it. The capital realized from land sales was to be loaned at the discretion of the Comptroller for as long as three years on the security of mortgages. The School Fund was a very useful source of long-term working capital for many manufacturers when such capital was in exceedingly short supply.[15]

The passage of the Embargo in 1807 and subsequently the Non-Intercourse Act resulted in an acute shortage of consumer goods, especially textiles. The state met this emergency with several programs. The 1808 legislature authorized the state to borrow $450,000, which was then lent to residents of northern and western counties in amounts between $50 and $500. While it was not stated why these small loans were made it can be supposed they encouraged textile manufacturing by extending credit to farmers to purchase household looms or breeding sheep. To dispense this money, the Governor and Council appointed two loan officers in each county. Upon their taking an oath, their office became a corporation. Like the earlier loan statutes, incorporation facilitated dealing with problems of mortgage foreclosure and the sale of real property.

Two additional statutes encouraged the household manufacture of woolen cloth. County judges were authorized to select the best quality cloth submitted to them for examination and award a cash prize from the state treasury; and the Society of Useful Arts was authorized to judge the best pieces of cloth made in the state and award prizes from state funds. The legislature also encouraged the importation of at lease one thoroughbred Merino ram into every county by offering a $50 reward to the person who kept one for breeding purposes where one was lacking.[16]

The speculative opportunity of the Embargo was eagerly grasped by New York entrepreneurs, just as it was by those in New England. The usual means of entering the thread manufacturing business was to convert an existing mill (grist, saw, or forge) to spinning, if the expensive machinery could be obtained. New capital was generally needed to make the conversion. Existing mills were usually organized as partnerships or unincorporated associations (joint-stock companies) in which the associates were bound together by a private agreement. All members were personally liable for the debts of the company, which made them little more than expanded partnerships. Actually, they were something more. The agreements usually specified most of the powers of corporations except the two key ones, perpetual existence and a single legal entity. These could only be granted by the state.[17]

When existing mills supplied only a local market, the owners usually knew the credit ratings of most of their customers; therefore, incorporation was not crucially important. Incorporation became desirable when new and expensive machinery had to be purchased and the raw material (cotton) had to be imported, and the finished product (thread) had to be sold on an anonymous market because the mill would produce far more thread than the local community could weave into cloth. Incorporation would make the business into a single legal entity, facilitate the ownership of property and the sharing of profits among a larger number of persons, help mobilize capital, and give easy access to the courts. It was hoped that it would also grant limited liability to shareholders. Incorporation was a valuable legal incentive that encouraged people to take advantage of the speculative opportunities created by the Embargo.

Governor Tompkins' messages of 1808 and 1810 admonished the legislature to prepare for war, but he also mentioned the need to encourage manufacturing because economic self-sufficiency was a major ingredient in waging a successful war.[18] The demand for manufacturing charters, particularly for textiles, accelerated during these years and entrepreneurs were encouraged to come to the legislature to seek incorporation. In 1810, seven charters were granted for companies making textiles, five for producers of glassware, one for paper making, one for iron implements, one for slate mining, and one for evaporation of salt from brine, and in the next year, fourteen more manufacturing or mining enterprises were incorporated. This was an extraordinary number of manufacturing incorporations compared with the few previously passed. The legislature learned much about the needs of manufacturing companies and the lack of political opposition to them. A major reason for the lack of opposition to textile mills was that they made only thread, which was the raw material for household weaving. There was no conflict of interests between weavers and spinners. Cheap and abundant thread was to the weaver's advantage at a time when the price of textiles was rising. It was not until after 1815 that cloth was woven on water-powered looms in the United States.

In the years immediately before 1811, the charters for textile manufactories were of fourteen or fifteen years' duration and their average capitalization was about $100,000. The promoters frequently advertised that they were using domestic raw materials, implying that their product had never before been made in the United States and that it was in the public interest to be economically independent of foreign nations. More often than not, there was a limited liability clause, but if one was absent, common law prevailed. Under common law, a chartered corporation possessed limited liability unless otherwise specified. Each share was generally given one vote, and there was almost always a provision for proxy voting because this privilege had to be expressly granted in New York or it did not exist.[19] Occasionally, a manufacturing corporation was allowed to own shares in another corporation, but unless this privilege was explicitly granted, it was illegal. A reserve clause was never added.

The legislature of 1811 urged its members to return to the next session clad in woolens of American manufacture, but at the same time it restricted loans to manufacturers from the School Fund because factory buildings had a low resale value in the event of foreclosure. Loans to manufactories had to be secured with improved agricultural land, which found a ready market.

A general incorporation bill was introduced on the model of the general incorporation statute for religious congregations: "A Bill to Encourage the Manufacture of Woolen Cloth, also Cotton, Hemp, and Flax and for other Purposes." Textile manufacturing appeared to be a new form of public service corporation that was as noncontroversial as turnpikes, and since these manufactories did not collect a public toll, they could be safely created by a general incorporation procedure. One of the strongest memorials for their self-incorporation was the Treasury Department's 1810 census of manufacturing in the United States, which was completely reprinted in the *Senate Journal*. New York still had many accessible water-power sites, and the statute encouraged their rapid exploitation. When the bill was printed, its title was shortened to "An Act Relative to Incorporations for Manufacturing Purposes."[20] It passed easily. It was essentially an emergency measure to encourage investments in enterprises that would produce thread for household weaving at a time when the European textile supply was cut off. Under these circumstances, textile manufacturers performed a vital public service.

THE GENERAL INCORPORATION STATUTE FOR MANUFACTURING CORPORATIONS

The general incorporation statute of 1811 was to be in effect for five years. It allowed five or more persons to self-incorporate for manufacturing woolen, cotton, and linen textiles, and for making glass, bar iron, steel, anchors, nail rods, hoop iron, and ironmongery from ore, sheet lead, shot, and white and red lead. In the previous three years, manufactories of all these items had secured individual acts of incorporation. The statute involved no innovations. It was an aggregate of generalized provisions from the charters passed during the preceding three years. In contrast to turnpikes, manufactories usually had a small number of shares of high value, which meant that the investors were local and few in number. In many respects, these early enterprises were expanded partnerships that produced for the needs of the immediate region and used local raw materials (except cotton). They usually had a small number of employees, from ten to fifty.[21]

In order to incorporate, promoters had to acknowledge their intentions before a local judicial officer and file a copy of the articles of incorporation with the Secretary of State. Corporations had a life of twenty years and their maximum capitalization was $100,000. There could be no more than nine trustees (directors) and they were granted broad powers to manage the business. The term *trustee* was borrowed from the 1784 general incorporation statute for religious congregations, a connection that is also found in Massachusetts.

Two complementary corporations were also chartered: the New York Manufacturing Company in 1812, to produce iron and brass wire for carding wool and cotton, and the Commission Company in 1813.[22] The New York Manufacturing Company was also granted banking powers because of "the difficulty in inducing persons to invest their money in untried enterprises." In this instance, the profitability of banking was directly linked to the economic policy of encouraging textile manufacturing. The Commisson Company was capitalized at the huge sum of $600,000. Its purpose was to make loans to American manufacturers and to facilitate the sale of their products, on commission, to the residents of New York City during the wartime shortages caused by the cessation of imports. It was an emergency public service corporation whose stockholders were granted limited liability as a means of attracting capital, but it also contained the first explicit reserve clause applied to a business corporation. It allowed the legislature to alter or repeal its charter at any time after five years. The reserve clause was designed to protect retail and wholesale merchants from unfair corporate competition if the venture proved successful because the Commission Company was competing with businesses that were totally organized as full liability enterprises. At the same time, the legislature authorized and directed the Comptroller to make a large number of long-term loans from the School Fund to manufacturing operations distributed throughout the state. After the war was over, a second Commission Company sought incorporation, in 1815, but it was rejected.[23]

After the end of the war (1815), the provisions of the general manufacturing state were broadened to cover makers of clay and earthenware products, and in the following year, coverage was extended to makers of pins, ale, porter, and beer, and extracting lead from ores; but the law itself was renewed for only a year, to May 1817. An amendment passed in April 1817 brought makers of Morocco leather in Green and Delaware counties under its provisions, but the law was not extended. Ten months after it had expired, it was revived for five years when Governor DeWitt Clinton pointedly told the legislature that national dignity depended on self-sufficiency in textile manufacturing. Oneida County was added to the counties where Morocco leather manufacturers could incorporate (1819) and in 1821 the same legislature that authorized calling the 1821 Constitutional Convention enacted the statute without time limit and extended its coverage to makers of coarse salt in the western part of the state.[24]

The 1811 statute was of major commercial importance. From 1811 to 1848, there were 362 incorporations under its provisions. During the same period, the legislature passed only 150 special charters for manufacturing purposes. The 1811 act lifted a significant burden from the legislature during the tense times preceding and during the War of 1812. From 1811 through 1815, 210 incorporations were registered under its provisions out of the total of 362 corporations that used it during the law's lifetime. Of the 362 charters granted by general incorporation, 226 were for making textiles, 62 for metal products, and 15 for glassware. In its early years, the statute was of major importance to upstate manufacturers located on dispersed water-power sites. Only six of the first 129 enterprises incorporated under its provisions were located in New York City, but after 1820 when efficient steam engines became available, it was extensively used by New York City entrepreneurs engaged in metalworking trades.[25]

After the end of the War of 1812, many of the newly incorporated textile manufactories went bankrupt. English textile manufacturers tried desperately to recapture their American market. Lord Brougham clearly perceived the situation when he advised British textile exporters that "it is worthwhile to incur a loss upon the first exportation in order, by the glut, to stifle in the cradle those infant manufacturers in the United States, which the war has forced into existence."[26] Against these dumping tactics, the New York legislature granted what relief it could. The machinery, raw materials, and inventories of textile manufacturers were exempted from distress sale in 1815, but this provided insufficient relief. In February 1816, Governor Tompkins recommended that the textile industry be granted the state's "patronage and protection" because the United States could not be a truly independent nation when it was dependent on another for its clothing. In November he recommended that the state augment the partial protection of the newly passed national tarriff (1816) because the investors in textile manufactories "had, from the purest motives of patriotism, and when the best interests of the country required it, adventured their property."[27]

It was not until 1817, however, after a series of eight articles in the *Commericial Advertiser* supporting subsidies for New York manufacturers, that the legislature exempted from state and local taxation the machinery, inventory, and buildings of all manufacturers of thread and cloth.[28] The measure was passed near the bottom of the depression being experienced by domestic textile producers and when its benefits were combined with the protective tariff of 1816, it helped the stronger textile manufacturers to weather the distress. Furthermore, the wording of the statute was broad enough to include the looms and inventory of all hand weavers, which greatly increased its political appeal. The only litigation concerning the statute arose out of the interpretation of its liability clause. This was almost inevitable because of the large number of bankruptcies after 1815.

LIABILITY UNDER THE 1811 GENERAL INCORPORATION STATUTE FOR MANUFACTURING CORPORATIONS

The case of *Slee* v. *Bloom* was filed in the Court of Chancery April 1819, and decided in 1821.[29] It was taken to Chancery to untangle a morass of conflicting liability claims. Chancery had jurisdiction in civil suits where there was a multiplicity of parties and where there appeared to be no question of interpreting a statute.

The case grew out of the bankruptcy of the Dutchess Cotton Manufactory that was organized in December 1814 at Poughkeepsie under the provisions of the 1811 general incorporation statute. It spun cotton thread. Late in 1815, business conditions became strained, and heavy calls were made upon the stockholders for capital. Most stockholders ignored the calls, and in October 1816, it was decided to discontinue the business. The accumulated debts, although substantial, were owed mostly to one man who had sold his mill to the corporation for part stock and part cash. The cash had never been paid. In 1817, the original mill owner, Samuel Slee, sued to collect the unpaid cash from the other stockholders who had ignored the calls for capital on the shares to which they had subscribed. In his suit, Slee maintained that the corporation was dissolved because it had no assets and had not elected officers for two years. If the corporation was dissolved, then the liability provision of the 1811 statute would apply. The statute said that, "for all debts which shall be due and owing by the company at the time of its dissolution, the persons then composing such company shall be individually responsible to the extent of their respective shares of stock in said company and no further."[30]

Chancellor Kent was of the opinion that the corporation was still in existence because it had not been judicially dissolved. The only way a corporation could be dissolved was through the courts of law, using *scire facias* or *quo warranto* proceedings. The dissolution of corporations was within the jurisdiction of the common law courts, not of Chancery.[31] Even if the corporation was not dissolved, Kent added, Slee could not call upon the individual stockholders for his claims against them because the corporation's board of directors had settled for less and he had assented to this settlement when he was a member of the board. The decision was immediately appealed to the Court for the Correction of Errors, the highest court in the state.

The two points involved in this appeal concerned the time a corporation was dissolved and the extent of stockholder liability under the 1811 statute. Chief Justice Ambrose Spencer held that the corporation was dissolved because it was without assets, and because a judicial remedy was needed to reach the corporation's stockholders to pay the corporation's creditors. When this happened, the court presumed a virtual surrender of the corporation's charter. This overruled Kent, and the case went back to Chancery for compliance. The Chancellor was "to enter a decree declaring all the respondents . . . liable, individually, to the extent of their respective shares of stock in the said company."[32] This opinion appeared to be an affirmation of the common law doctrine that liability extended only to the par value of the stock, because only a small part of the par value of each share had actually been paid-in at the time of the corporation's dissolution. The corporation's debts would have been satisfied if only part of the share's par value was paid-in; therefore, the real meaning of the liability clause remained ambiguous. Modern limited liability was not the only interpretation of the statute; it could also mean double liability.

Justice Spencer's preface to the decision leaves the impression that he meant modern limited liability. He said:

> The object and intention of the legislature in authorizing the associa-
> tion of individuals for manufacturing purposes was . . . to facilitate
> the formation of partnerships without the risks ordinarily attending
> them, and to encourage internal manufactures. There is nothing of an
> exclusive nature in the statute; but the benefits from associating and
> becoming incorporated . . . are offered to all who will conform to its
> requisitions. There are no franchises or privileges which are not
> common to the whole community. In this respect incorporations
> under the statute differ from corporations to whom some exclusive. . .
> privileges are granted. The only advantages of an incorporation under
> the statute over partnerships . . . consist in a capacity to manage the
> affairs of the institution by a few . . . agents, and by an exoneration
> from any responsibility beyond the amount of the individual sub-
> scriptions.[33]

The statement is worth an extended quote because Spencer was a member of the 1821 Constitutional Convention, which attempted to limit the number of new corporations by the two-thirds clause, yet tacitly exempt from its provisions all classes of corporations that could be organized under pre-existing general incorporation statutes.

The remanded case was put in the hands of a Master in Chancery to make another attempt to resolve the conflicting liability claims. In the course of this work, the Chancellor faced the two new prob-lems of whether or not the corporation's property supplied by Slee, in exchange for stock, was overvalued, and whether or not the judgment of the Court of Errors was binding on the individual stockholders, as it most certainly was on the corporation's direc-tors. The Chancellor said the directors of the company were not agents of the individuals composing it; and, although the company was bound by their acts, the individuals were not. The decision was again appealed to the Court of Errors, and *Slee* v. *Bloom* came before Judge Spencer a second time, in November 1822.

To the second of these questions, Chief Justice Spencer could "perceive no escape from the conclusion that the respondents are individually liable to the same extent that the company itself was liable. . . . The trustees could not bind the individual members beyond the funds of the company, with this qualification, that they could bind the individual stockholders in the event of the dissolution of the corporation, to the extent of their respective shares, and no further."[34] It was still not entirely clear whether Spencer meant limited liability in the modern sense, or double liability; but he did not have to face this issue because the stockholders would only have to pay in about half of the $100 par value of the shares to discharge their liability.

Spencer then disposed of the charge of fraud in valuing Slee's mill.

> The subscription to the stock took place after the agreement by the trustees to purchase; and if the stockholders, with their eyes open, and the means of information at hand, were content to become members of the corporation, without due consideration or examination, they must ascribe their losses to their own want of prudence and caution. But we do not hear a lisp of complaint until the events of peace had materially changed the aspect of affairs and rendered the stock less valable . . . .and indeed there is no trace of any complaint as to the fairness of the transaction of sale until the concerns of the establishment were overwhelmed with ruin. . . . Had political events terminated differently, it appears, from all the evidence, that the speculation would have been a profitable one.[35]

In other words, the company's debt to Slee was not fraudulent, and the judgment of the Court of Errors was binding on the stockholders in their individual capacities to the extent of the debt owed him; but in this case, the debt averaged less than the par value of each share. The exact definition of stockholders' liability was yet to be determined.

In 1812 the Cambridge Farmers Woolen Manufactory was incorporated under the general incorporation statute. In the course of its operation, its stock was fully paid-in and the company accumulated additional debts. In January 1818, it was bankrupt. The shareholders sought to preserve the corporation from dissolution because they claimed that no suit to recover debts could be maintained against a corporation without assets until such a corporation was dissolved. They said the corporaton was not dissolved and pointed to the election of a board of directors in 1818 as evidence. A suit was commenced in July 1819. In *Penniman* v. *Briggs*, the Court of Chancery judged the corporation dissolved and ordered the debts of the corporation to be prorated among the stockholders.[36]

The case was appealed in *Briggs* v. *Penniman*, and came before the Court of Errors in December 1826. Justice Woodworth interpreted the liability clause of the 1811 statute to mean that "every stockholder in a company of this description incurs the risk of not only losing the amount of stock subscribed, but is also liable for an equal sum, provided the debts and owing at the time of dissolution are of such magnitude as to require it." Senator John C. Spencer[37] elaborated, saying, "Surely the legislature did not mean to declare that the stockholders should be liable . . . at common law. Something more was intended; and it is to my mind very clearly expressed that the extent of the stock held by them should be the measure of their individual liability to creditors."[38] This is unmistakable double liability: stockholders of manufacturing corporations organized under the 1811 statute were liable for paying corporate debts to the full face value of the shares they owned plus a sum equal to this amount.

PRIVATEERING ASSOCIATIONS

News of the fall of Napoleon reached New York City in June 1814 and was received with mixed reactions. The High Federalists rejoiced at his fall, but more sober minds knew that an attack on New York City from the sea could be expected. In August, British troops landed in Maryland and burned many public buildings in Washington, D.C. In the meantime, defense preparations were frantically rushed to repel both land and sea assaults. The battles of Plattsburg and Lake Champlain were fought on September 11, 1814, and, although the British regulars were repulsed, the closeness of the contest threw the state into a panic. The legislature passed a general incorporation statute for privateering associations in October.[39] Prior to 1813, New York City had spawned 120 such vessels, but after 1813 the blockade was nearly ship-tight.

The statute had a preamble which said: "Whereas a barbarous warfare on our coast and frontiers by pillage and conflagration is carried on by the enemy, and a determination is avowed to lay waste our cities and habitations. . . . " Preambles had gone out of style around 1800, but it was felt that this extraordinary class of legislation needed some extraordinary justification. There were no previous special charters for privateers. Privateering associations had to be licensed by the United States government and operate under the United States statutes governing privateers, and their charters automatically expired one year after the end of the war. James Kent, as a member of the Council of Revision, objected, but his colleagues did not accept it and it was passed. Kent believed the statute tended to "impair the public morals" and, besides, it was a national and not a state issue.[40]

OTHER INCORPORATED BUSINESS ENTERPRISES

New classes of business ventures and the application of steam power to older skills found it easy to secure incorporation in New York. When whaling developed into a large-scale business in the 1830s, promoters in New York, unlike those in Massachusetts, readily obtained charters of incorporation. There were no existing New York whalers and incorporation was a way of attracting a new industry to the state. On the other hand, the legislature never incorporated a shipbuilder or canal boat transportation company because such businesses were traditionally full-liability enterprises and highly competitive; and for the same reason, the capitalization of salt makers and Morocco leather manufacturers under the 1811 statute was less than was allowed for other businesses.

SUMMARY

The familiarity with corporate organization combined with a state government that willingly gave legal and economic encouragement to potential entrepreneurs had an accelerating effect on New York's economic growth. It created a very favorable climate for corporate business activity not only in frontier areas of potential commercial development but also in cities where larger scale enterprises were organized. The result was that New York's geographic advantages were exploited at an early date and on a large scale.

Before 1820, most incorporated businesses could be classed as public service franchises because they required a grant of one or more special powers from the state in order to perform a service closely linked to public welfare. The franchise relationship is obvious with internal improvement corporations because they needed state authority to acquire a right-of-way and charge a public toll, but incorporated banks were also a type of franchise because they supplied the paper currency and a large part of the credit in the area they served. Manufacturers of glassware and textiles also had some aspects of public service corporations because they made articles that had formerly been imported or provided a market for locally grown wool as well as producing yarn for local household weavers. Limited liability was a means of attracting capital into these new, relatively large scale or technically sophisticated enterprises, which could not readily be undertaken by single proprietors or partnerships possessing full liability.

These new businesses lacked entrenched opposition from full-liability businesses and were organized as corporations from their inception. The political controversy over corporations was not between single proprietorships and partnerships being driven out of business by corporations, but whether or not it was desirable or sound public policy to open the privileges of incorporation to all entrepreneurs in those classes of businesses where the corporation was the usual form of organization. Until banking instability emerged after 1811, there appeared to be no strong objection to general incorporation statutes and limited liability for all businesses that did not take land by eminent domain proceedings and did not compete with full-liability enterprises.

Some classes of corporate businesses began as public service corporations but with changing circumstances lost this status. Manufacturing corporations best illustrate this transition. The incorporation of manufactories was part of a policy of encouraging entrepreneurs to make New York self-sufficient in the production of some basic manufactured goods. During the Embargo, when the supply of English textiles was cut off, textile manufacturers occupied a position in the community similar to turnpikes and academies. The general incorporation statute for manufacturing corporations of 1811 was an emergency statute designed to promote the production of textiles during the cessation of imports. It was highly successful. With the resumption of imports in 1815 and a firmly established textile industry, these corporations ceased being vital to public welfare and became pure business corporations exploiting an anonymous market.

The emergency nature of the 1811 statute is indicated by the incorporation of two complementary enterprises, the New York Manufacturing Company in 1812 and the Commission Company in 1813. Both companies supported the textile industry, one by manufacturing carding wire and the other by facilitating the distribution of finished products. Both operations involved high risks; therefore, they were granted extraordinary powers to attract capital: banking in the case of the New York Manufacturing Company and limited liability in the case of the Commission Company. The privateering general incorporation statute of 1814 was a similar emergency statute.

At the war's end, there were strong doubts about the political expediency of keeping the 1811 manufacturing statute in force, as well as doubts about its utility because of its infrequent use after 1816. Its ambiguous political position is clearly indicated by the legislature's vacillation about renewing it before it was permanently enacted in 1821. The same doubts about its political expediency were evident in New Jersey where an identical statute was passed in 1816 but repealed in 1819 before it expired. The 1811 statute remained in force in New York because entrepreneurs found it convenient to seek incorporation without having to relate their business to a narrow definition of public service, and the state found it convenient because manufacturing corporations were politically noncontroversial. They did not require the use of eminent domain; they did not collect a public toll; they were not involved with the currency; and they facilitated the rapid application of costly steam power technology to older skills, such as running textile machinery.

The first New York bank was chartered to perform three public functions: to extend short-term credit to merchants, to circulate the state's paper money, and to loan money to the state. Because it issued paper money with the state's approval, it was a franchise business. Newer businessmen outside the Federalist political and commercial circle wanted full access to the advantages of credit but, because of a hostile Federalist legislature, the only way a

Republican bank was chartered was by means of the Manhattan Company subterfuge. As long as a few banks supplied the state with paper money, the franchise nature of banking was obvious, but with a multiplicity of banks, the franchise relation was obscured.

After 1800, banking was a highly profitable business that attracted many entrepreneurs. Those who failed to obtain a bank charter became private bankers. Under common law, all individuals could loan money and circulate evidences of debt as a form of currency. In order to control the growing volume of unreliable paper money circulated by private bankers, and protect the chartered banks from competition, the New York legislature, in 1804, limited the banking business to corporations and then proceeded to charter an increasing number of banks without any provision to regulate their banknote credit practices. New York was saved any serious embarrassment by the policy of the Bank of the United States regulating the credit practices of all state banks. The Bank kept the paper money of the state banks somewhere near par by its discounting practices and this unseen regulation almost totally concealed the franchise nature of banking.

NOTES

1. Bray Hammond, *Banks and Politics in America from the Revolution to the Civil War*, 48–59, 71, 144, 192–193. Bray Hammond, "Long and Short Term Credit in Early American Banking," *Quarterly Journal of Economics*, Vol. 69, 1934, 80, 83. Joseph S. Davis, *Essays in the Earlier History of American Corporations*, Vol. 2, 44–46. Henry W. Domett, *A History of the Bank of New York, 1784–1884*, 6–10, 18–19, 28–35. John W. Cadman, *The Corporation in New Jersey, 1791–1875*, 61–65. Don C. Sowers, *The Financial History of New York State from 1789 to 1912*, 48–50, 260–261. Edwin M. Dodd, *American Business Corporations until 1860*, 203–208. Joseph G. Blandi, *Maryland Business Corporations, 1783–1852*, 18. Benjamin J. Klebaner, "State-Chartered American Commercial Banks, 1781–1801," *Business History Review*, Vol. 53, 1979, 529–534.

2. Howard L. McBain, *DeWitt Clinton and the Origin of the Spoils System in New York*, 70–71. Bray Hammond, *Banks and Politics in America from the Revolution to the Civil War*, 160–161. Alfred B. Street, ed., *The Council of Revision of the State of New York*, 423. *New York Laws*, Ch. 23, 1797, 50.

3.   Bray Hammond, *Banks and Politics in America from the Revolution to the Civil War*, 149–159. *New York Laws*, Ch. 117, 1804, 476.

4.   Bray Hammond, *Banks and Politics in America from the Revolution to the Civil War*, 197–199.

5.   *Messages from the Governors of New York*, Vol. 2, 697, Jan. 28, 1812, Daniel D. Tompkins. Bray Hammond, *Banks and Politics in America from the Revolution to the Civil War*, 218, 227–232.

6.   Bray Hammond, *Banks and Politics in America from the Revolution to the Civil War*, 564.

7.   Bray Hammond, *Banks and Politics in America from the Revolution to the Civil War*, 565.

8.   Jabez D. Hammond, *The History of Political Parties in the State of New York*, Vol. 1, 371–375. *New York Laws* (37th Session, 1814), 285–286 (Appendix). *Assembly Journal 1814*, 412.

9.   Bray Hammond, *Banks and Politics in America from the Revolution to the Civil War*, 164.

10.   Joseph S. Davis, *Essays in the Earlier History of American Corporations*, Vol. 2, 234–242. Both John W. Cadman, *The Corporation in New Jersey, 1791–1875*, 71, and Joseph G. Blandi, *Maryland Business Corporations, 1783–1852*, 89–90, say that insurance was the first large-scale interstate corporate business, but neither of them defines the transfer of credit through banks, particularly the branches of the Bank of the United States, as interstate business.

11.   Alfred B. Street, ed., *The Council of Revision of the State of New York*, 345–347.

12.   Lester W. Zartman, ed., *Yale Readings in Insurance*, 18, 314. Marquis James, *Biography of a Business, 1792–1942: The Insurance Company of North America*, 112–114. *New York Laws*, Ch. 146, 1817, 150.

13.   *New York Laws*, Ch. 277, 1824, 340; Ch. 30, 1837, 21 (New Jersey passed identical retaliatory legislation in 1826). *Documents of the Convention of the State of New York, 1846*, No. 111, 12–15. Lester W. Zartman, ed., *Yale Readings in Insurance*, 24–25. Joseph K. Angell, *A Treatise on the Law of Fire and Life Insurance* (1854), 38–45. Nathan Miller, *The Enterprise of a Free People*, 173–180.

14.   *New York Laws*, Ch. 56, 1790, 392, Vol. 2 Greenleaf; Ch. 47, 1793, 70; Ch. 45, 1795, 213; Ch. 54, 1796, 331; Ch. 68, 1797, 451, Vol. 3 Greenleaf.

15.   Nathan Miller, *The Enterprise of a Free People*, 12–14. Only the larger loans to manufacturers required statute authorization: *New York Laws*, Ch. 148, 1808, 324; Ch. 185, 1813, 288. See *Legislative Documents 1824*, Senate No. 32, for a list of the loans made by the Comptroller to en-

courage manufacturing. The great majority were made between 1812 and 1816 for amounts between $500 and $2,500.

16.   Don C. Sowers, *The Financial History of New York State from 1789 to 1912*, 259-261. Carter Goodrich, ed., *The Government and the Economy: 1783-1861*, 196-199. *New York Laws*, Ch. 216, 1808, 392; Ch. 186, 1808, 359; Ch. 187, 1808, 360.

17.   Joseph S. Davis, *Essays in the Earlier History of American Corporations*, Vol. 2, 258-262. Caroline F. Ware, *The Early New England Cotton Manufacture*, 37, 43-57. Wolfgang P. Strassman, *Risk and Technological Innovation*, 80-82.

18.   *Messages from the Governors of New York*, Vol. 1, 622, Jan. 26, 1808; Jan. 30, 1810, Daniel D. Tompkins.

19.   Joseph K. Angell, Samuel Ames, *A Treatise on the Law of Private Corporations Aggregate* (1832), 67. *Phillips* v. *Wickham*, 1829, 1 Paige Chancery 598. The Connecticut Court ruled in 1812 that proxy voting could be provided by by-laws, *State* v. *Tudor*, 1812, 5 Day 329, and Massachusetts followed Connecticut's lead: Edwin M. Dodd, *American Business Corporations Until 1860*, 227. New Jersey, on the other hand, followed New York's policy: John W. Cadman, *The Corporation in New Jersey, 1791-1875*, 305.

20.   *New York Laws*, Ch. 67, 1811, 111. *Senate Journal 1811*, 117, 162-164, 400. *Documents of the Convention of the State of New York, 1846*, No. 40, 2-3.

21.   Ronald E. Seavoy, "Laws to Encourage Manufacturing: New York Policy and the 1811 General Incorporation Statute," *Business History Review*, Vol. 46, 1972, 86-95. Robert K. Lamb, "The Entrepreneur and the Community," William Miller, ed., *Men in Business*, 97-103, 116. Lamb emphasizes that new manufacturing enterprises often began as a closely held family business, and that the more successful of them usually had a member who had extensive experience in the use of credit, so that from the beginning factory manufacturing was associated with the organization of banks. He also points out that these enterprises depended for their success on the social acceptance of their corporate activity. This is one of the major themes of the present book—that the corporate organization of local religious congregations provided a favorable social climate for the growth of corporate business activity.

22.   *New York Laws*, Ch. 175, 1812, 354; Ch. 150, 1813, 239. The statute that incorporated the Commission Company was entitled, "An Act for the Encouragement of American Manufactures." *Mass. Laws, 1780-1807*, Vol. 1 (1807), Ch. 51, 1786, 282. *Mass. Laws*, Ch. 65, 1809, 464. *Mass. Archives 1812*, No. 7289: "An Act Concerning Cotton and Woolen Factories."

23.   Joseph Dorfman, "Chancellor Kent and the Developing American Economy," *Columbia Law Review*, Vol. 61, 1961, 1308-1309.

24.   *New York Laws*, Ch. 47, 1815, 44; Ch. 58, 1816, 58; Ch. 233, 1817, 265; Ch. 67, 1818, 53; Ch. 102, 1819, 119; Ch. 14, 1821, 9; Ch. 231, 1821, Sec. 19. *Messages from the Governors of New York*, Vol. 1, 899, Jan. 27, 1818, DeWitt Clinton. New Jersey attempted to aid the depressed textile industry by passing a general incorporation statute for manufacturing enterprises, but it was repealed in 1819, before it expired. John W. Cadman, *The Corporation in New Jersey, 1791-1875*, 20-25.

25.   William C. Kessler, "A Statistical Study of the New York General Incorporation Act of 1811," *Journal of Political Economy*, Vol. 48, 1940, 877-882. The use of New York's 1811 statute compares very favorably with the number of special manufacturing charters passed in Massachusetts from 1800 to 1817. The Massachusetts legislature incorporated 318 business corporations, plus 86 in Maine. In New England (Conn., Maine, Mass., N.H., R.I., Vt.) from 1800 to 1817, there were 280 manufacturing and mining charters passed, all by special acts. William C. Kessler, "Incorporation in New England: A Statistical Study, 1800-1875," *Journal of Economic History*, Vol. 8, 1948, Tables 1 and 2. Maryland showed a similar spurt in manufacturing activity during the same years. Joseph G. Blandi, *Maryland Business Corporations, 1783-1852*, 93-96. Beatrice G. Reubens, "State Financing of Private Enterprises in Early New York," Columbia University Dissertation, 201, 216. Carroll W. Pursell, *Early Stationary Steam Engines in America*, 50-53, 72. See Allan Pred, "Manufacturing in the American Mercantile City, 1800-1840," *Annals of the Association of American Geographers*, Vol. 56, 1966, 307-312, 315-325, for the types of manufacturing enterprises that were located in New York City.

26.   Arthur H. Cole, *The American Wool Manufacture*, Vol. 1, 146: from *Niles Register*, Vol. 11, 284.

27.   *Messages from the Governors of New York*, Vol. 2, 855, Feb. 2, 1816; 875-876, Nov. 5, 1816, Daniel D. Tompkins.

28.   Dixon R. Fox, *The Decline of Aristocracy in the Politics of New York, 1801-1840*, 324. *New York Laws*, Ch. 64, 1817, 54.

29.   *Slee* v. *Bloom*, 1821, 5 Johns Chancery 366. Stanley E. Howard, "Stockholders' Liability under the New York Act of March 22, 1811," *Journal of Political Economy*, Vol. 46, 1938, 501-513.

30.   *Dutchess Cotton Manufactory* v. *Davis*, 1817, 14 Johns 238. The wording of the liability provision was taken from the 1809 charter of the Albany Manufacturing Society, which in turn was taken from the 1798 charter of the United Insurance Company of the City of New York.

31.   Joseph K. Angell, Samuel Ames, *A Treatise on the Law of Private Corporations Aggregate* (1832), 511. James Kent, *Commentaries on*

American Law, Vol. 2 (1827), 252–253. New York had an exception to this rule. The Court of Chancery could dissolve incorporated insurance companies under the provisions of Ch. 146, 1817 and Ch. 148, 1821.

32. *Slee* v. *Bloom*, 1822, 19 Johns 484.

33. *Slee* v. *Bloom*, 1822, 19 Johns 474.

34. *Slee* v. *Bloom*, 1822, 20 Johns 684.

35. *Slee* v. *Bloom*, 1822, 20 Johns 688.

36. *Penniman* v. *Briggs*, 1824, 1 Hopkins 300.

37. Chief Justice Ambrose Spencer retired in January 1823 and in March 1824 was appointed Mayor of Albany. He served until December 1826. Senator John C. Spencer was his son who served in the State Senate from 1825 to 1828, and was one of the revisers of the state laws published in 1828. Stanley E. Howard, "Stockholders' Liability under the New York Act of March 22, 1811," *Journal of Political Economy*, Vol. 46, 1938, 512.

38. *Briggs* v. *Penniman*, 1826, 8 Cowen 392, 395.

39. Alexander C. Flick, ed., *History of the State of New York*, Vol. 5, 241–246. *New York Laws*, Ch. 12, 1814, 11.

40. Alfred B. Street, ed., *The Council of Revision of the State of New York*, 440. Kent served on the Council of Revision frm 1798 to 1823, first as a Justice of the Supreme Court, then as Chief Justice; and from 1814, as Chancellor. The Council consisted of the Governor, Chancellor, and justices of the Supreme Court. It reviewed acts of the legislature and exercised the veto power. The veto could be overruled by two-thirds of the legislature. It was abolished by the 1821 Constitution and the veto power vested solely in the Governor. Between 1804 and 1822, Chancellor Kent was the Council's spokesman, writing all but one of its opinions.

4

Bank Policy During the Formative Years of the Regency, 1815-1829

THE MARRIAGE OF BANKS AND POLITICS UNDER THE REGENCY

After the War of 1812, the Federalist party was discredited because it had sponsored the Hartford Convention and had done little toward supporting the war. By default, the Jeffersonian Republicans became the dominant political party, and by 1820, the only party in New York. It was an awkward party composed of a congeries of antagonistic factions loyal to various politicians, to one section of the state, or to a powerful interest group. It lacked discipline and cohesion. The organizing efforts of Martin Van Buren, between 1815 and 1819, produced the first modern political party in the United States.

A modern political party has approximately these characteristics: (1) voting discipline on major issues; (2) voting discipline in support of nominations made by the executive, caucus, convention, or primary; (3) partisan dispensing of patronage; (4) an alliance with one or more major economic interest groups; and (5) image building through the public media such as newspapers, radio, and television. By 1819, Van Buren's expert political management had made his faction, the Bucktails, the ascendent majority within the Republican party. The leadership of the reorganized party was collective and was centered in the legislature because DeWitt Clinton occupied the governor's chair. By 1821, the Albany Regency emerged as the executive council of the New York Republican party.

One of Van Buren's major incentives to create a new party organization was to check the political ambitions of DeWitt Clinton and advance his own political fortunes. Clinton's political future was at a low ebb at the beginning of 1815 because he had been the presidential candidate opposed to James Madison (in the election of November 1812) after war had been declared in June. Clinton had been critical of United States involvement in the war and even more critical of its early, inept conduct. When peace was restored in December 1814, politicians who had been critical of the war were under a cloud, and in order to recoup his popularity, Clinton strongly favored the immediate construction of the Erie Canal. In order to get the needed legislation enacted, he addressed rallies throughout the state and made alliances with several Federalist-oriented factions in the legislature.

When Governor Tompkins of New York was elected Vice-President of the United States in 1816, the Republicans had to nominate a successor. One of the obvious candidates was Clinton, but Van Buren opposed him because Clinton was a lone wolf and unmanageable; however, Clinton was nominated, and in the election he received Van Buren's full support. Clinton exhibited superior intellectual attainments and vigorously advocated projects and policies that encouraged the rapid commercial and industrial growth of New York. Sometimes, however, his contemptuous conduct toward his associates combined to defeat his best intentions. Clinton was a politician of the old style, who dispensed rewards for personal loyalty. Van Buren usually supported Clinton's economic programs but was strongly opposed to his criteria for political preferment.[1]

After the Erie Canal proved such an enormous financial success, both Van Buren and Clinton adopted identical policies opposing federal aid for internal improvement projects elsewhere in the nation, although at the time the Erie Canal was being promoted, both men had vigorously solicited federal aid. Projects in other states might require federal taxation at New York's expense and could hurt New York's position as the preferred entry into the west; however, after the success of the Erie Canal was assured, Van Buren and Clinton differed on the number of internal improvement projects the state could finance. Clinton favored as many projects as the credit of the state could support. Van Buren was more cautious.

Van Buren began reorganizing the party in 1815 when he was appointed Attorney General (he remained a state senator). This office gave him sufficient political leverage so that by 1819 he and his associates had achieved discipline over a substantial part of the party's legislators. The means of achieving discipline was the caucus and the means of enforcing its decisions was patronage. In the caucus, a majority vote determined the party's policies, who would be nominated for elective offices, and who would be appointed to the principal administrative positions. All persons who participated in making these decisions were expected to adhere to them in public, regardless of their personal preferences, doubts about the expediency of the course decided upon, or their personal distaste for a person nominated for a certain office.

Marcy summed up the rule of party regularity in 1825, after the system had been perfected. "An opposition to a candidate which is abstractly right may be politically wrong. We had better support a man that we believe to be unsound than to oppose him, if by so doing we insure success to others equally unsound and at the same time, hazard the election of political friends who are worthy of our confidence and whose success is necessary to the triumph of our cause."[2] A bitter personal rivalry developed between the Clintonians and the Bucktails because Clinton's supporters served the personal ambitions of their leader and Clinton did not hesitate to advance himself by repudiating policies and nominations made in the caucus.[3]

The open break between Van Buren and Governor Clinton occurred at the beginning of the legislative session of 1819 when Clinton ignored the Republican party's caucus nomination for Speaker of the Assembly and, with Federalist help, elected his personal choice. The *Albany Argus* newspaper changed its editorial policy and supported Van Buren's majority of the party, who then made war on Clinton. This placed the *Argus* irrevocably in Van Buren's camp and under his editorial guidance, which added an essential ingredient to the reorganized Republican party. The *Argus* was used to disseminate the party's policies to its adherents, which made the achievement of discipline easier because every member knew what was expected of him. In return, the *Argus* was guaranteed a continuation of the state printing contract. In 1820, Van Buren arranged for half-interest in it to be purchased by his brother-in-law and the rest by friends.

The greatest political prize, however, was control of the Council of Appointment, and when Van Buren's faction gained control of it, only regular party men were appointed. Comptroller William L. Marcy described how systematic patronage worked: "I must, I need not say to any man of discernment, how pernicious would be the example of selecting for the presiding officer of the popular branch of the legislature a person brought forward and elected by the railers and scoffers of regular nominations and all party discipline."[4] The second great prize was the Canal Board. It preferred to hire only regular Republicans and award its construction and maintenance contracts to friendly entrepreneurs. In order to further isolate Governor Clinton, Van Buren seems to have influenced Clinton's enemies in New York City to drop their opposition to canal construction, so that a judicious use of patronage could detach some of Clinton's upstate supporters from his personal influence.

The last major ingredient in Van Buren's scheme of political management was banking. Van Buren got his first experience with banking five years after he began legal practice in his home county. In 1808, he went to Albany to lobby for passage of a charter for the Hudson Bank, and when it was passed, he became its legal counsel and a director. In 1812, as a candidate for the state Senate, he witnessed the major political battle over granting a state charter to the New York branch of the defunct Bank of the United States. Even though it was a sound commercial bank, the dominant Republicans tried to block its incorporation because its directors were Federalists, but widespread bribery secured a charter in spite of the Republican Governor proroguing the legislature in an effort to defeat it. The Governor used this maneuver because he lacked the veto power. In the future, visible corruption could be avoided if commissioners were appointed by the legislature, to distribute bank stock upon its initial offering (which had first been done in 1811).

From 1811 to 1818, the legislature chartered twenty-three banks. Most of them were incorporated immediately after the dissolution of the first Bank of the United States when there were frequent changes in control of the legislature because of widespread discontent created by the Embargo and the War of 1812. Bank charters were used to reward political supporters or acquire factional support, and they were often granted to inexperienced or irresponsible persons. During these years, banking proved especially profitable because the Bank of the United States no longer existed to restrain the expansion of credit, and the suspension of specie payments from 1814 to 1817 (with only partial resumption until 1820) allowed New York banks to issue their notes without having to redeem them.

During the lapse of specie payments, when Van Buren's faction was trying to achieve party discipline, it was also groping for a business alliance that would counteract Clinton's strong support among those groups who expected to benefit by the completion of the Erie Canal. Banking lent itself to political management, but the management had to be systematized. Until the right formula was found, the banks were protected. In 1815, the Senate blocked the passage of a tax on bank capital after the Assembly had passed it, and this was repeated in 1818 and 1819. In 1816, the Bank of Niagara in Buffalo sought a charter that would have allowed it to issue banknotes without requiring their redemption in specie. The Council of Revision strongly objected to this deficiency, but Van Buren appears to have defended it; however, the rest of the Senate would not approve it. Shortly afterwards, a resolution was offered in the Senate requiring the Comptroller to investigate the several banks that had stopped specie payments, and find out the amount of specie in their valuts. The Senate did not act on it.[5]

Another factor that aggravated the postwar currency disruption was the suspension of the small bill statute in 1815 and 1816. A statute had been passed in 1807 to encourage the circulation of the state's limited supply of specie by prohibiting the circulation of banknotes under five dollars. The 1815 and 1816 statutes suspending the 1807 statute were designed to secure an adequate circulating medium in an economy that chronic wartime inflation had denuded of specie and small coins. Its suspension allowed banks to issue a flood of small notes called tickets, with values of 6¢, 12¢, 50¢, and 75¢. They were seldom redeemed because day-to-day business depended on them. The law was a very attractive speculative opportunity, and many organizations entered the banking business. The result was to increase the unreliability of the currency, which generated enormous political pressure to decrease the volume of banknotes and limit the number of banks that could issue them.[6]

Jacob Barker took advantage of this speculative situation in April 1815 by organizing the Exchange Bank. It was a private bank in which he was the sole owner. Barker was a recent business associate of Van Buren's and a leading Tammany Hall politician. Public opinion forced Attorney General Van Buren to file a suit to halt its operations on the grounds that it violated the 1804 restraining statute. Barker argued that the 1804 statute forbade only associations and corporations from the banking business, not individuals. He claimed that individuals could continue to participate in banking under the authority of common law. The state Supreme Court sustained Barker.[7]

The newly chartered Utica Insurance Company also entered the banking business. Attorney General Van Buren sought an injunction from Chancellor James Kent to halt its operations on the grounds that the legislature never intended to grant it banking powers. Kent declined to issue an injunction. He said that the 1804 restraining statute had transformed the banking business into a corporate franchise and the Utica Insurance Company's banking business was not a public nuisance. The legality of its entering the banking business was a point of law and not of equity.[8] Van Buren immediately took the case to a court of law. Counsel for the Utica Insurance Company argued that under the restraining statute, banking was not a franchise but a business in which all corporations could engage unless there was a specific prohibition in their charter. Such prohibitions had been placed in over fifty charters following the Manhattan Company affair, but one was not inserted in the charter of the Utica Insurance Company. The Utica Insurance Company was not incorporated for the sole purpose of underwriting insurance, "but for all other purposes not unlawful or expressly prohibited." This argument was directly based on English common law, which held that chartered business corporations could undertake any lawful business not specifically forbidden.[9]

In reply, Van Buren quoted Chancellor Kent's recent opinion in the *Attorney General* v. *Utica Insurance Company* where he described the political nature of banks under the 1804 restraining statute: "Banking has now become a franchise derived from a grant of the legislature and subsisting in those only who can produce a grant." Van Buren admitted that the restraining statute did not use the word *corporation*, but it did use the word *person*. He then quoted a legislative opinion in 1804, when the New York City Chamber of Commerce asked the legislature to explain the purpose of the restraining statute. The legislature said it applied only to persons, associations, or companies engaged in banking and would not restrict any other business activity. In the context of the time, the statute was designed to restrain all individuals and organizations from entering the banking business unless specifically authorized by the state.

Justice Smith Thompson of the state Supreme Court wrote the court's opinion in which he made two very important points: where a statute's wording was ambiguous the court would follow the intent of the legislature, and the word *person*, as used in the restraining statute included corporations. This appears to be a reversal of the court's opinion fifteen months earlier when he had delivered the opinion in *Bristol* v. *Barker*, in which he had said "individuals" had the right to enter the banking business in spite of the same restraining law. In any case, he was relieved of the embarrassment of changing his mind for political motives by the passage of the restraining statute of 1818. The 1818 statute prohibited individuals and unincorporated associations from keeping offices of deposit as well as from circulating and discounting paper currency. It did nothing, however, to limit the number of banks or restrain their tendency toward inflation, and no policy the state afterwards pursued was a serious check on these tendencies. Only Jacob Barker was exempted from its provisions, and then for only three years.

Barker had to use all of the political influence he could get in order to secure this exemption. Prior to the opening of the 1818 legislative session, he retained Van Buren's law partner, Benjamin F. Butler, as his lobbyist. His major objective was to secure a charter for the Exchange Bank (located in New York City), which would allow it to open branches. He hopefully confided that he foresaw little objection because it was only fair that, if the legislature should prohibit all unincorporated banking, his operating bank should be granted a charter.[10] When the session opened, it was immediately apparent that a restraining law would be enacted, especially since Governor Clinton's annual message said that the currency situation required immediate correction.

Clinton further admonished the legislature not to incorporate any more banks in remote places where there was no commercial need for them. These country banks were founded on fictitious capital and their main purpose was to force banknotes into circulation. This caused inflation and an unstable currency and might, in the near future, jeopardize the whole banking system. The Assembly's Banking Committee followed Clinton's lead and charged that the banking "influence too frequently, nay, often, already begins to assume a species of dictation altogether alarming and unless some judicious remedy is provided by the legislative wisdom we shall soon witness attempts to control all selections to office in our counties, nay the elections to this very legislature. Senators and members of the Assembly will be indebted to banks for their seats in this capital and thus the wise ends of our civil institutions will be prostrated in the dust by corporations of our own creation." The Assembly then passed a resolution calling for an investigation of how banks obtain charters and whether any undue means was used to force their notes into circulation. The Senate under Van Buren's influence did not concur with the resolution.[11]

The aroused opposition of the Assembly meant that it would be impossible to obtain a charter for the Exchange Bank because its notes were circulating far below par. When he was apprised of this, Barker switched tactics and suggested that the legislature allow the Washington and Warren Bank, a chartered bank he controlled, to open an office of discount and deposit in New York City. This request was in the nature of a bargaining point to be conceded in order to secure exemption for the Exchange Bank from the restraining law. When he got his exemption, he was very thankful.

In this whole episode, Barker contrasted the interests of the country banks to the interests of the city banks and he identified the Exchange Bank and the Washington and Warren Bank as country banks. The main asset of the country banks was their charter, which allowed them to circulate banknotes. They were supposed to be redeemable on demand for specie at the bank's home office, but the Washington and Warren Bank had to borrow specie in order to have any specie reserve at all. Its remote location (fifty miles north

of Albany at Sandy Hill, now Hudson Falls) was counted on to prevent its notes from ever being redeemed. As a reward for his lobby-
ing success, Butler was made president of the Washington and
Warren Bank where, from March 1819 to June 1820 he had the job
of trying to maintain the appearances of solvency. It was a job tinged
with fraud because in May 1818 its debt structure made it
bankrupt, and in June 1819, the bank had only $200 in gold in its
vaults. By June 1820, the value of Washington and Warren notes
had fallen to 37.5¢, and Butler returned to Albany where he resumed
his legal partnership with Van Buren.[12]

In 1816, one-third of the state's funds were directed by law to be
deposited in the Mechanics and Farmers Bank of Albany. The
deposits consisted of the notes of country banks that were used to
pay state taxes, purchase state lands, pay fines, and later pay canal
tolls. If the Regency had desired, these deposits could have been used
to restrain the volume of banknotes issued by the country banks.
The Mechanics and Farmers Bank could have acted as the central
bank for upstate New York and created a reliable currency within a
short time, as was done by the Suffolk Bank of Boston. The Regency never pursued this policy.

The Suffolk Bank became the central bank of New England after
the Panic of 1819, and its operation created a reliable currency for
New England that lasted until the outbreak of the Civil War. The
Suffolk Bank restrained the excessive circulation of banknotes by
country banks by forcing them to keep specie deposits with it.
When the notes of the country banks were spent in the Boston area,
they were redeemed out of the country banks' deposits. If a country
bank expanded its banknote circulation in great excess of its
deposits with the Suffolk Bank, the Suffolk Bank began to collect
the excessive notes and take them to the bank's home office and demand their redemption. The laws of both Massachusetts and New
York required the redemption of a bank's notes only at its home office. The threat to redeem an excessive circulation was a constant
restraint on the excessive issue of banknotes (inflation) by the country banks, and helped create and preserve a reliable paper currency
in New England. The system evolved between 1818 and 1822.[13]

The purpose of the Suffolk system was to conserve the specie
reserves of the Boston banks. The port of Boston was a major
center of imports and Boston merchants had to pay tariff duties in

specie, as required by the national government. The quickest and cheapest way for Boston merchants to obtain specie was to redeem the notes of the Boston banks. They circulated at par, while the notes of the country banks were discounted. The discounted notes of the country banks were not presented for specie redemption because merchant-importers would not get their full face value in specie as they would when they redeemed the notes of Boston banks. The constant redemption of the notes of Boston banks depleted their specie reserves and compelled them to lessen the volume of their loans, which reduced their profits. The notes of country banks circulated at a discount because they were distant from their offices of redemption. By requiring the country banks to keep specie deposits with it, in order to redeem their notes on demand, the Suffolk Bank kept the notes of the country banks at par with the notes of Boston banks. When this occurred, after 1822, the notes of country banks could be presented for redemption for specie in Boston and used to pay the tariff, thus ending the disadvantageous specie drain on the Boston banks in relation to the country banks.

The Regency had to make a fundamental decision: was there greater advantage in restricting banking to a limited number of corporations whose charters could be apportioned to political advantage, or was it better to open the banking business to all entrepreneurs who had the capital, and claim the rewards for producing a more reliable but less inflated banking system? Van Buren's experience told him that individually incorporated country banks could be more easily managed. It could be done in two ways: during the process of chartering, the promoters of a new bank and most of its initial stockholders had to be Republican; and almost as important, they had to be Republicans who would support a disciplined party. Secondly, the Republican party would continue to support highly inflationary policies, which the country banks wanted. The Republican party leaders who looked to Van Buren for guidance opted for a politically managed bank policy. The necessity for systematic management was highlighted in 1818 when the Catskill Aqueduct Company succeeded in getting a charter with banking privileges by a subterfuge similar to the Manhattan Company affair.

When Attorney General Van Buren borrowed Chancellor Kent's idea that bank charters were franchises (in 1818), in order to win his case against the Utica Insurance Company, he must have realized in explicit terms that the restraining statutes were the key to a managed bank policy. A managed bank policy was possible if a disciplined legislative majority, particularly in the Senate, could pass or defeat a bank charter on its political merits. The votes to achieve the desired results could be secured by allowing Republican legislators the first opportunity to subscribe to the initial offering of stock. Furthermore, a managed bank policy could be launched on a popular base because the 1818 restraining law had been passed at the insistence of the Governor and the legislature.

Another major step toward a politically managed bank policy was taken in 1820 with the decision to sell the state's investment portfolio of bank stock. It was worth over $950,000. The disposal of these shares (which cut the state's revenue from bank dividends from $318,000 in 1820 to $24,000 in 1821) satisfied for a time the desire of Republican politicians and businessmen for opportunities to invest in banks and the businessmen's desire to exclude the state from a business that yielded substantial private profits. "Bank stock was better calculated to be in the hands of individuals than in the possession of government."[14] Actually, the first step in the political management of the banking business had been taken in 1814 when the state stopped subscribing to shares in newly chartered banks or requiring the promoters of new banks to give a bonus to the state for their charters.

After 1819, the collective leadership of the reorganized Republican party forged an alliance with the chartered banks. The legal foundations of this alliance were the restraining statutes of 1804 and 1818 and the decision in *The People* v. *Utica Insurance Company*, augmented in 1821 by the two-thirds clause of the new constitution. Banks were a major source of strength because they bound men to the party through interest and because they could exercise considerable political influence in rural areas. They were one of the principal means that enabled Van Buren's faction to remain the ascendent majority within the Republican party.

When the leadership council of the reorganized Republican party solidified into the Albany Regency, about 1820–1821, it did not adopt the policy of linking banking privileges to the financing of internal improvement or public service projects such as was done with the Manhattan Company in 1799, the Manufacturers Bank in 1812, or the Catskill Aqueduct Company in 1818. Other states frequently used hybrid banks to finance internal improvement projects, while southern states often floated bonds to secure capital for Planters Banks to supply agricultural credit. On other occasions, many states passed bank charters on the condition that some shares were contributed to the state's School Fund or the bank purchased shares in a turnpike, canal, or railroad corporation. After 1818, banking profits were put into the hands of Republican politicians and businessmen, and only on three occasions (1824 and 1825), when the Regency lost control of the legislature, were hybrid corporations again chartered.

Bank charters had too much political value in New York to be squandered on hybrid corporations. The Regency judiciously limited the number of banks, which made each one into a regional credit monopoly—and enhanced its political influence. Furthermore, bank shareholders were always granted some form of limited liability, even after the panic-depression of 1819 when this became a burning public issue.[15]

THE POLITICAL IMPACT OF INFLATIONARY BANKING

The years following the end of the War of 1812 had been prosperous, except for manufacturing. Bad European harvests and the pent-up demand for food and staples provided a ready market for American agricultural surpluses, and the unrestrained credit expansion of New York banks fueled this prosperity to a highly inflationary level. The Panic of 1819 put New York's over-extended banking system under severe strain. The drastic fall in agricultural prices meant that credit extended during the inflationary years had to be repaid during stringent times. The second Bank of the United States, after it became operative in 1817, rode the speculative tide instead of restraining the credit practices of state banks. The Bank's excessive long-term loans (on agricultural commodities and land) jeopardized its profitability at the same time the United States Supreme Court affirmed its constitutionality in sweeping terms. In the process of regaining its liquidity, it had to press state banks to pay their short-term credits at the bottom of the depression. State banks were forced to squeeze their creditors much against their inclination, at a time when it was extremely painful. Most banks, and particularly the Bank of the United States, found themselves strongly distrusted by a large portion of the population.

During the 1819 legislative session, the Assembly's Banking Committee reiterated Governor Clinton's warning of the year before: the danger of banks no. needed by the commercial community, whose only purpose was to print and circulate banknotes.[16] However, the Senate did nothing to force the country banks to increase their real capitalization or limit their circulation. The depressi. .1 that followed the panic caused a large number of bank insolvencies. When a bank became insolvent, the stockholders lost either part or all of their investment, and the noteholders of an insolvent bank generally got nothing. This was a major political grievance. The public felt that these franchise corporations, chartered by the state to provide an adequate circulation of paper money to meet the state's commercial needs, should protect noteholders to the full value of the banknote before granting limited liability to stockholders. The circulation of depreciated or worthless banknotes, or notes that could not be redeemed for specie was not a public service.

In 1811, the public was willing to accept the corporate form of business organization for those businesses that did not compete with full-liability enterprises. State banks were not yet fully associated with exclusive economic or political privileges; however, after the disastrous currency disruptions in 1814 and 1819, the public did associate exclusive privilege with banking corporations. Agrarians who had a relatively fixed income and lacked economic mobility were badly hurt by the wartime and postwar inflationary spiral. Inflation raised the price of the basic manufactured articles they bought and the price of land they wanted to buy, while at the same time it put them in the position of having to accept highly depreciated banknotes, on a take-it-or-leave-it basis, if they wanted to exchange their agricultural surpluses for manufactured necessities.

In 1820 and 1821, further attempts were made to exert some state control over the currency circulated by the state banks. It was proposed that all banks keep regular banking hours (which would facilitate redemption); that the State Treasurer receive only notes from specie-paying banks; and that such notes be promptly redeemable at par in all towns between Utica and Poughkeepsie, and in New York City. If a bank failed to redeem, the Treasurer would have the authority to ask the Attorney General to investigate it.[17] The bill failed to pass in both years because it would have restrained the credit practices of the country banks allied to the reorganized party. Nor did the legislature act on the other alternative to secure a stable currency—full liability for bank stockholders. The initiative for these reforms came from the Assembly where Governor Clinton retained considerable influence. The main roadblock was the Senate where the leadership of the reorganized party was concentrated. By 1820, the legislature had failed to provide a means of guaranteeing a reliable paper currency and the credit-restraining policies of the second Bank of the United States were just beginning to be felt.

Two currency disruptions in five years, a severe inflation followed by a panic-depression forced ten of the state's forty-three banks into insolvency by 1825, mostly in the years 1819 and 1820.[18] Banks were a politically explosive issue and there was a strong demand to limit their numbers and thereby limit the volume of banknotes in circulation. Many persons felt that a currency consisting wholly of specie would better serve the public because specie had a fixed and permanent value. This was the attitude many delegates carried in New York's Constitutional Convention of 1821.

THE CONSTITUTION OF 1821

Banking was not the major issue of the convention. The most important issue was whether or not to end all suffrage requirements for white males over twenty-one. Other important issues were whether the Council of Revision and Council of Appointment should be abolished and how to recast the state's judicial system.[19]

The question before the convention concerning banks was not their elimination but how to control them. All grievances about banks were discussed at the convention, even if they did not find their way into the record but, unfortunately, they were not discussed under circumstances that allowed intelligent criticism. The result was the two-thirds clause, requiring all charters of incorporation to be passed by at least a two-thirds majority of all elected members of the legislature. It was designed to limit the number of banks the legislature could create, in order that a thorough investigation could be made into the need for each new bank, and into the characters of the men who petitioned for the charter. Article 1, Section 9 of the Constitution said:

> The assent of two-thirds of the members elected to each branch of the legislature shall be requisite to every bill appropriating the public moneys or property for local or private purposes, or creating, continuing, altering, or renewing any body politic or corporate.

Jacob Radcliff, a Supreme Court justice from 1798 to 1804, questioned its inclusive wording. He said the inclusive wording was impolitic, but Rufus King, the chairman of the Incorporations Committee and Regency ally, said that if anyone had questioned the policy of limiting the number of corporations twenty-five years ago, it would have been considered political heresy. All corporations were privileged organizations. They were exceptions to the common law; the process of creating them should be closely guarded; and their numbers ought to be diminished as far as was consistent with preserving vested rights.[20]

Radcliff persisted, saying that he believed this also, but only as it applied to banks and monied corporations, and not to village, bridge, or turnpike corporations. Another delegate said that two-thirds would never be lacking to incorporate a village or turnpike corporation, and King added that general laws already provided for the incorporation of religious societies and turnpike companies. Furthermore, the common law abhorred monopolies (which he equated with chartered banks), and great mischief was caused in proceeding against them. Another delegate went to the heart of the issue: he wanted to have the value of paper currency as stable as specie. He proposed to accomplish this by making bank stockholders personally liable for the redemption of all banknotes. Regency leadership rejected this proposal in favor of the inclusive wording of the two-thirds clause, which was routinely passed without division.[21] Thus, in the name of reform, the convention adopted the Regency's bank policy. The two-thirds clause constitutionalized party discipline as it had been used to allocate bank charters because a disciplined majority was essential to secure a two-thirds approval for these controversial corporations.

The Constitution of 1821 retained Article 36 from the 1777 Constitution, which confirmed all crown charters and land grants made before 1775, but expanded it in Article 7, Section 14, to limit the impairment of any corporate charter granted by the state or its agents since that date. In effect, the Constitution recognized charters as contracts and corporations as artificial persons. This reflected not only the recent *Dartmouth College Case* (1819), but also New York's own legal development. These two concepts produced no political controversies in the future, although the charter-contract concept was soon negated by adoption of the reserve clause. In fact, these concepts helped define a legal status for corporations that was advantageous to business corporations.

The convention also constitutionalized the Regency's appointment policy. Van Buren was chairman of the Committee on Appointments and, over strong opposition, succeeded in getting the delegates to grant the legislature (particularly the Senate) a large measure of control over future appointments. The major state offices such as Secretary of State and Comptroller were filled by nominations coming from the legislature. If both houses jointly nominated the same man, he was automatically appointed, but if they disagreed, the appointment was made by a combined vote of both houses. The same policy was applied to most local offices where the county boards of supervisors or city councils filled the major offices. The state's judicial offices, however, were appointed by the Governor with the approval of the Senate, but the Court for the Correction of Errors, composed of all Senators, remained the court of last resort. The four-year term for Senators was unchanged, and membership of the Senate was set at 32 so that it had a great political advantage over the 128 annually elected members of the Assembly. When Van Buren went to Washington, D.C. in December as United States Senator, a complete apparatus had been established for building and maintaining the reorganized party.[22]

In succeeding years, the banking-currency controversy centered around the Regency's enforcement of the 1804 and 1818 restraining statutes and the two-thirds clause when applied to banks. Regency leaders were happy with the two-thirds clause, and existing banks had no objection because it increased their profit potential by making the chartering of competing banks more difficult. However, the political management of the two-thirds clause in relation to banks raised the broader question of the proper political and economic relationship of all business corporations to the state. This problem became a source of great confusion and great controversy before it was satisfactorily settled by the Constitutional Convention of 1846.

LIMITED PARTNERSHIPS

In 1822, at its first session under the new Constitution, the legislature enacted a limited partnership statute, which was intended as a substitute for many uses of the business corporation. Coming at this time, it reflected the anti-corporation sentiment of the Convention. The statute authorized two classes of partners: general partners who managed the business and limited partners who contributed capital but who had no part in the management of the enterprise. Limited partners were liable only to the extent of their initial investment, while the general partners were personally liable, as in the case of co-partners. The capital furnished by the limited partners could not be withdrawn during the duration of the partnership in the guise of dividends, and in the event of the partnership's bankruptcy, the limited partner's capital could not be considered among the claims of creditors.

The statute was lifted bodily from the contemporary French commercial code, which in turn was based on the 1673 French ordinance *la Société en Commendité*. It was the first limited partnership statute in the United States. In the next twenty years, however, similar statutes were passed in most states, usually as a measure intended to curb the increase of business corporations. In New Jersey, which was typical, the limited partnership was infrequently used and then for petty enterprises of a short duration. It was usually used to organize a family enterprise that involved high risks, an application somewhat similar to a syndicate. One of the reasons for its limited use was the increasing availability of corporation charters with limited liability.[23]

CORPORATION TAXATION UNDER THE 1823 TAX STATUTE

By 1822, according to Governor Clinton, those New York textile corporations that had survived the depression were operating at a profit. This statement was a boast about industrial prosperity, not an invitation to tax them. In the following year, however, a comprehensive tax law was passed which applied to all business corporations. The all-inclusive wording of the statute duplicated the all-inclusive wording of the two-thirds clause of the Constitution, a policy that admirably expressed the inchoate anti-bank and anti-corporation sentiment of the Convention.

The first corporation tax bill had been introduced in 1822, based on simple and lucrative bank capitalization taxes operating in Massachusetts and New Jersey.[24] The presidents of ten banks and eighteen insurance companies in New York City petitioned against its passage. One of the most effective arguments insisted that it would tax business confidence because it would, in effect, tax credit, and credit was the basis of the state's continuing prosperity. When the tax was defeated, a concurrent resolution was passed asking the Comptroller to draw up a report on corporation taxes levied by other states.[25] This report served as the basis for the corporation sections in the tax law of 1823.

The tax aimed to collect the existing personal property tax on corporation shares at the corporation's head office. Shares of stock had always been taxable as personal property but had seldom been declared for assessment. The statute defined all corporations as legal persons, following the dictum laid down in two earlier corporation cases.[26] This was necessary to end all legal doubts about collecting a personal property tax at the corporation's head office, instead of from individual stockholders. The tax was collected by withholding the personal property tax from a shareholder's dividend. The withheld money was paid to the nearest local government and then forwarded to the county treasurer who forwarded it to the State Treasurer. The State Treasurer deducted the state's share of the personal property tax and sent any remaining money to the county treasurer where the shareholder lived—not necessarily to the same county where the tax was collected. There it was sent to the township or municipality where the shareholder lived. In New York, unlike other states, the revenue from the corporation tax was shared by the state with local governments until 1826, when the state dropped its personal property tax. Thereafter, the corporation tax was a local tax, which was of substantial benefit to New York City and other growing cities.

The statute did not aim to tax corporations as such; it aimed to tax shareholders, and especially those classes of corporations where shares were held in large blocks—mainly commercial banks and insurance corporations. The highly capitalized commercial banks and insurance corporations were located principally in New York City and ownership was concentrated there. The statute required the secretaries or cashiers of all business corporations to submit an annual statement to the local assessors where the enterprise was located, plus a list of shareholders with the number of shares each owned and their residences. Taxes on shares owned by nonresidents of New York remained with the state. Corporations strongly resisted supplying this information.

The corporation tax was computed by the following formula. The corporation's assets were divided into the two categories of real estate and paid-in capital. The amount of real estate was subtracted from the amount of paid-in capital because the corporation had already paid local real estate taxes. The rest of the capital represented liquid or personal property assets. Only these assets were taxed. The formula bore heavily on banks and insurance corporations, which seldom owned more than their office buildings and had a high percentage of their capital invested in loans or securities. The formula was borrowed from a Massachusetts Supreme Court opinion of 1813.[27] It avoided double taxation in those classes of corporations like turnpikes and toll bridges where all or nearly all of the company's capital was invested in real estate, which had already been taxed. If a corporation wished to avoid this confusion, it could pay a flat 10 percent on its dividends, profits, or income. This wording made no distinction between operating profits, net profits, and dividends and caused a vast amount of confusion that delayed the tax's collection until 1825.

In levying the tax, the state assumed that all corporations were profitable and that the tax would be paid out of dividends. Insofar as it assumed that all corporations were profitable, this was an income tax; but insofar as this was not true, it was a tax on corporation capital. The tax placed a tremendous burden on the assessors and collectors in rural areas, who were sometimes poorly rewarded for their efforts, because it frequently happened that most of the stockholders lived elsewhere. In these areas, the tax was frequently ignored.

One of the first acts of the 1824 legislature transferred enforcement from the State Treasurer into the capable hands of Comptroller William L. Marcy. The statute's workability did not improve and in the next year, the corporation tax was completely revised, following Marcy's suggestions. The revision allowed turnpike, bridge, canal, and manufacturing corporations to pay 5 percent of their net profits in lieu of all other taxes (including state and local real estate taxes), provided their net profits did not exceed 5 percent on their invested capital. A distinction was made between gross income and net profits, which allowed marginally profitable corporations to escape most taxation. Marcy said that the provisions that permitted manufacturing and other classes of business corporations to commute all their real estate taxes for a 5 percent levy on their net profits allowed them to pay anywhere from 5 to 50 percent of the taxes they would normally have paid.[28] This tax exemption was an incentive for manufacturing enterprises to incorporate under the 1811 statute. Thus, the state's tax policies encouraged incorporation for businesses that had been granted incorporation from their inception.

The 1825 law appeared to end the 1817 tax exemption that textile manufacturers enjoyed on their machinery, inventories, and buildings. Almost immediately, the occasion arose to test the statute's meaning. When an attempt was made to tax a textile manufacturer, a group of mill owners petitioned the legislature to confirm their exemption. An advisory opinion from the Attorney General confirmed the exemption of 1817 but added that the legislature was the final judge in the matter. The Assembly concurred with the Attorney General but added that it had not been the intent of the legislature to exempt textile manufacturers when the statute was passed. The Senate refused to confirm the tax exemption.[29] The issue went into immediate litigation and came before the New York Supreme Court in 1825, which held that the 1817 tax exemption had been virtually repealed by the 1823 statute. From 1823 to 1826, the corporation tax yielded a considerable public revenue: banks paid $223,000 and insurance corporations contributed $174,000, but there was no way of knowing how much of this tax money represented local real estate taxes paid on corporate-owned land and how much was withheld personal property taxes on capital shares.[30]

The revised statutes of 1828 attempted to simplify the collection of corporate taxes. They declared that "all monied or stock corporations deriving an income or profit from their capital or otherwise shall be liable to taxation on their capital." This changed the tax from a withheld personal property tax into a capitalization tax. Such a tax was easier to collect. The revisers added marine insurance corporations to businesses that could commute all their taxes by paying 5 percent on the paid-in capital, and the provision was abandoned that the secretary of each company had to submit a list of stockholders to the Comptroller.[31]

The second major case of litigation under the corporation tax law dealt with railroads, a new class of business enterprise. Railroad directors wanted an authoritative opinion on their tax obligations. The Chancellor explained,

> When it went into effect . . . no railway charter had been granted. It is not surprising, therefore, that no special provision in relation to such companies should be found in the tax laws. . . . I think it is evident that such companies, whose stock or the principal part thereof, is vested in the lands necessary for their roads . . . are taxable on that portion of their capital, as real estate, in the several towns or wards in which such real estate is situated. . . . Such companies, of course, are not taxable upon their capital as personal estate, except upon so much thereof, if any, as remains after deducting all of their real estate at cost, including the railway itself.[32]

This ruling virtually exempted railroads from the capitalization tax since railroads had a large part of their assets and their bonded debt tied up in rights-of-way, buildings, and rolling stock. The same formula was applied to insurance corporations in 1832, when the Senate asked Attorney General Greene C. Bronson for an opinion on the statute as it applied to insurance companies. He said they could deduct such amounts of their capital as were invested in shares of stock that had already paid a capitalization tax or local property tax; however, in 1832, very little insurance capital was invested in railroad or manufacturing stocks.[33]

This formula could not apply to banks because they were forbidden to invest in shares of other corporations. Most of a bank's capital was loaned for short terms or retained as liquid assets. This formula left a relatively large amount of capital that could be taxed, which was the intent of the statute. However, did a bank's capital include undivided profits, which it employed in the same way as its legal capitalization? This question was answered in the negative in 1834: only a bank's legal paid-in capital was subject to taxation.[34] In 1836, the question was raised as to whether or not the legislature intended to tax gross profits on invested capital regardless of whether or not it yielded a net profit. Chief Justice Samuel Nelson said that the revised statutes were quite clear. The tax on corporations was a capitalization tax. "In all the discussion of the assessment law, we are not aware that the principle was ever advanced or defended that the taxation of capital should depend upon the question whether it had been profitably employed or not." This interpretation was subsequently confirmed and applied to free banking associations in 1841.[35]

CORPORATION BANKRUPTCY

Personal insolvency laws were passed in colonial New York in 1755 and 1761 and were among the earliest acts of the state legislature (1784 and 1788). They were designed to allow old debts to be liquidated in the hopes that this would facilitate the revival of commerce. The financial distress caused by the Embargo led to the passage of two additional laws in 1811. The first one benefited individuals, allowing relief without the assent of any creditors and the discharge of all debts and contracts made before and after its passage. It was repealed a year later. The second bankruptcy statute comprehended the dissolution of corporations, mainly marine insurance corporations.[36]

It was the 1811 individual insolvency statute that was litigated in *Sturgis* v. *Crowninshield* in 1819, when the United States Supreme Court ruled unconstitutional that portion of the New York statute that applied to contracts made prior to the passage of the statute. This overruled the New York Supreme Court.[37] State bankruptcy or insolvency statutes could offer relief only to contracts made after the passage of the statute; otherwise, they were in conflict with "impairing the obligation of contract" clause in the United States Constitution. The Court also held that state bankruptcy and insolvency laws (the distinction between them was impossible) were not in conflict with the bankruptcy clause of the United States Constitution as long as the national government did not act. When Congress chose to act, the state laws would be suspended insofar as they covered the same issues.

In the same way that the 1823 corporation tax fell mainly on banks, the corporation insolvency statute of 1825 was specifically aimed at banks. The immediate reason for its passage was an attempt by three supposedly defunct banks to resume business after they had suspended specie payments during the Panic of 1819, but more generally, the statute penalized bank officers and shareholders because of the excessive number of bank failures after 1819.[38] Every bank insolvency was deemed fraudulent unless otherwise determined, and bank officers and directors found guilty of using fraudulent practices were penalized with full liability and the stockholders of these banks were subject to double liability. Fraud, however, was very difficult to prove.

The three suspending banks were immediately prosecuted under the provisions of the new law. Two of them, the Bank of Washington and Warren, and the Bank of Niagara, had been organized during the formative years of the Regency, and they had been granted indulgent charters that allowed them to suspend their business operations if they could not redeem their notes in specie. In other words, they could become temporarily insolvent; but if they suspended a second time, the Attorney General was authorized (but not compelled) to prosecute them. In order for the Washington and Warren Bank to reopen, Jacob Barker, who still controlled it, had bought $150,000 worth of its notes that had been unredeemable for over five years at discounts of between 50 and 75 percent. The attorney who defended its right to resume business was its ex-president Benjamin F. Butler. The third bank was the Bank of Hudson, where Van Buren had been a director.

The court found that the resumption of business by two of the banks in 1824 was legal under the provisions of their charters. "It seemed the legislature anticipated the insolvency of this bank and provided that while insolvent and unable to pay, it should cease doing business as a bank until it should be able to redeem its paper."[39] In the case of the Hudson Bank, the court held that it was in fact bankrupt because its assets had been put into receivership. When this happened, the rule of *Slee* v. *Bloom* applied: a corporation automatically surrenders its charter when it ceases to perform the function for which it was created.[40]

CORPORATION POLICY AND THE CONSTITUTION OF 1821

The business corporation, in its modern form, is a convenient organization to maximize the profits of its stockholders. It is a public service organization only because it provides employment and pays taxes. Business corporations in this sense emerged from franchise corporations about 1815–1820, in the same way that franchise corporations emerged from benevolent public service corporations in the 1790s. The emergence of the modern business corporation was closely associated with a rapid increase in business opportunities that followed the application of new technologies to industrial production, the radical lowering of long distance overland transportation costs by canals and steamboats, and the expanded use of bank-provided capital and credit. These developments vastly increased the volume of domestic and foreign trade. The confluence of these events produced a marked shift in the public's attitude toward private debts.

In New York, the public was less interested in protecting the creditors of corporations than in opening the new opportunities for business profits to all investors and entrepreneurs who wanted to use the corporation to mobilize capital or supply credit. This attitude became public policy when the New York legislature adopted all the Revised Statutes of 1828: full limited liability was granted to all corporation stockholders provided their shares were fully paid-in.[41] The great exception was banks.

Banks became the focal point of the corporation controversy because they supplied almost all of the state's currency and a large part of its business credit. When a loan was made, the usual procedure was to give the debtor a bundle of banknotes issued by the local banks instead of having his account credited with the amount of the loan. He spent these banknotes directly instead of issuing personal checks on his bank deposit. This banking-credit-currency relationship required steady regulation in order to avoid an inflationary disaster like the one that befell the nation from 1814 to 1819.

The Bank of the United States performed this unseen regulation from 1791 to 1811 and from 1823 to 1834 and gave the nation a sound currency and credit structure. Regulation was achieved by receiving banknotes from state banks as deposits in the several branches of the Bank, for payment of lands sold from the public domain, excise taxes, or for bills of exchange. When these banknotes were deposited, the Bank forced the state banks to redeem them in specie if their issue of banknotes was excessive, but the local citizenry did not always have the choice of forcing redemption, expecially if the banknotes came from a distant bank. They often had to accept an unsound banknote or not do business. In New York, much of the doub ul currency was circulated by country banks having a close political connection to the state. This made banking a highly political issue. In the four years following the 1821 Convention, the legislature passed ten new bank charters, which increased the number of state banks by over a third. There was great pressure to charter even more. This pressure was aggravated by the defeat the Regency suffered in the election of 1824.

The Regency lost control of the Democratic-Republican party in 1824 for several reasons. There was a squabble over the method of selecting presidential electors. Van Buren favored appointing them by the legislature, which would give them to William H. Crawford, while supporters of Andrew Jackson and John Quincy Adams favored some form of popular election, either at large or by districts. The Regency-controlled Senate defeated a bill that would have allowed their popular election and the public was aroused. The public also favored the election of local justices of the peace instead of having them appointed, and the Regency was slow in sponsoring the needed constitutional amendment. Furthermore, DeWitt Clinton was summarily removed from the Canal Board on the eve of the Canal's completion, and this caused an immense public stir. This tender political situation was further inflamed by the reopening of three supposedly defunct banks. The Democratic-Republican party lost its legislative majority in the election of 1824 and Clinton was re-elected governor after receiving the nomination from a convention of the Peoples party. Thereafter, all political parties in New York used the convention device to make nominations for state offices, but the legislative caucus of the Democratic-Republicans, when they regained control of the legislature, continued to dispense a large amount of patronage and allocate investment opportunites in banks.

Although anti-Regency factions controlled the legislature in 1824 and 1825, they never effectively organized it. In this political vacuum, the sponsors of the Chemical Bank secured a charter by massive bribery, and several Lombard (loan) companies secured charters and immediately issued bonds designed to circulate as money.[42] The Chemical Bank scandal led entrepreneurs to demand that the banking business be opened to all persons who had the necessary capital. They said the restraining laws were being used to exclude legitimate businessmen from organizing needed banks. The agrarians were also disgusted because the two-thirds clause did not prevent the chartering of new banks; it merely raised the ante of political influence and bribery required to secure a charter. The embattled Regency members used all of their efforts to prevent the passage of any long-term banking legislation that might undermine the Regency's banking alliance.

The first attempt was made in 1824. The Senate Banking Committee wanted more commercial credit in the state, and if the incorporated banks could not provide it, then credit associations would. The Committee proposed that the legislature charter non-specie-based associations that would accept commercial paper and issue circulating notes in exchange. These "incorporated associations, possessing no capital, would issue their bills payable to bearer . . . and take therefore the obligations of individuals well secured . . . which paper would ultimately be redeemed and therefore be entitled to the confidence of the public." On the other hand, "the present bank holders [were] a class of citizens who ought not be wantonly assailed."[43]

In 1825, a bill was introduced that would have repealed the restraining statutes and allowed unincorporated banknote brokers to receive deposits and issue circulating notes, provided they deposited security. Such a policy would encourage individuals who possessed capital to establish credit facilities in places that were not large enough to support an incorporated bank but which needed smaller amounts of credit. They believed this would aid rural areas since sufficient capital to incorporate commercial banks was available in the cities. The integrity of the private brokers would be guaranteed by making them personally liable. The limited partnership statute could be amended so it could be used by these brokers, but care had to be taken when repealing the restraining statutes so that no class of corporation except banks could circulate banknotes. A resolution was introduced in the Senate to repeal the restraining statutes, and only the tie-breaking vote of the President of the Senate defeated it. It was recommended again in the following year and again defeated.

Some members of the entrepreneurial interest suggested that a general incorporation statute for banks would be constitutional if it were passed by a two-thirds majority; however, it was obvious that the votes were not available. Instead, a general regulatory statute was drawn up, similar to the one for turnpikes. It suggested that any legitimate request for a bank charter would be granted, as was the practice in Massachusetts. As drafted, the bill would have allowed the Comptroller to investigate the books of all banks created under it.[44] It was not passed, but some of its features were included in the corporation bankruptcy statute of 1825.

On the other hand, the agrarians still feared that the restrained creation of banknote credit would inflate land values and raise the prices of the goods and services they purchased. Above all else, they demanded some method to guarantee the value of the banknotes circulated by the chartered banks. They wanted a paper currency that would be redeemable for specie on demand anywhere in the state. The agrarians would end the scandal over incorporating banks by rigorously exercising the restraints implicit in the two-thirds clause of the Constitution. By not chartering any more banks, the agrarians hoped to restore stable prices. The Regency correctly read popular opinion and, in 1825, when the Assembly passed eighteen bank charters, the Senate concurred in only three; and in 1826, when the Democratic-Republican party regained control of the legislature, the Regency authorized no new bank incorporations until the enactment of the Safety Fund statute in 1829. This policy had the effect of greatly restricting the creation of credit.

Entrepreneurs strongly objected because they believed the most important need of the state, and for their own ambitions, was an abundance of credit. New York's commercial banks were among the most efficient institutions in the nation in mobilizing and magnifying the state's dispersed capital resources and allocating them to the investments with the highest returns. They were in that crucial intermediary position where they saw the business opportunities of the enlarged markets tributary to New York created by the Erie Canal and by the rapid growth of the cotton export trade. The incorporated banks provided vital long-term credit by renewing short-term loans to the owners of local textile factories called into existence by the War of 1812, and similar accommodations were made to other large-scale projects.[45] Entrepreneurs would end the bank scandals of the mid-1820s by incorporating all capitalists who wanted to enter the banking business and thus increase the volume of credit available to aid industrialization or exploit new markets.

It appears that when the legislature, in 1825, requested the Regents to state the authority by which they continued to charter academies (under the new Constitution), it was part of the attack on chartered banks made by agrarians and entrepreneurs. The entrepreneurs wanted to know why the pre-1821 general incorporation statutes continued to operate in spite of the two-thirds clause in the Constitution, yet a general incorporation statute for banks was considered unconstitutional. The agrarians wanted to make the state's incorporation policy logically consistent by requiring all corporation charters to be passed by a two-thirds majority, and by so doing, remove the possibility that there might be exceptions to a literal interpretation of the two-thirds clause. Upon investigation, the whole matter was dropped because it raised two embarrassing constitutional interpretations. The first suggested that any general incorporation statute might be passed by a two-thirds vote of the legislature, and one of the first would probably be for banks. The agrarians opposed this because it would mean an unlimited number of banks; the Regency opposed it because it would destroy the foundations of its bank alliance. The second constitutional interpretation indicated that the two-thirds clause should be literally construed. A literal interpretation would abrogate the 1811 statute for manufacturing corporations and increase the expense of incorporating academies by excluding the Regents. A literal interpretation would also seriously limit the scope of the common school statute. These changes were not politically desirable.

Thus, in the mid-1820s, there was the beginning of a dual attack on the Regency's bank alliance: from the agrarians who wanted to reduce the number of note-issuing banks, and from businessmen who wanted a vastly enlarged supply of credit. It was thought that one goal could be achieved by reducing the number of banks, and the other by increasing their number. These goals were not necessarily irreconcilable. There could be both a reliable currency and an abundance of credit but not from New York's banking system as it was managed from 1821 to 1829. The sometimes reckless creation of credit by the limited number of Regency pet banks was not enough to satisfy businessmen, nor was it put into the hands of the right people. Entrepreneurs wanted to control the bank-chartering process and create much more credit. They would create new banks to aid businessmen and not reward political stalwarts.

In the legislative sessions of 1827 and 1828, the banking issue subsided but did not die while the legislature debated and enacted the first revision of the laws since 1813. The double liability of bank stockholders under the 1825 bankruptcy statute was retained but only after a vigorous attempt was made to impose full liability. The Regency opposed full liability because they claimed it would drive men of integrity out of banking and attract unscrupulous speculators who would sell bank shares to an unsuspecting public, overcirculate banknotes, and then pull out of the business. Community ruin would result. The legislature did, however, insert a reserve clause in the revised statutes, thereby converting all new corporation charters into enabling acts instead of contracts. Business corporation in New York could now be fully regulated at the pleasure of the state, if the majority party chose to act.

The revisers undertook a partial codification of the law, which was especially desirable in matters of corporate powers and regulation since these were the two most confused areas in New York law. The general powers and limitations of all corporations were put in one section and all of the pre-1821 general incorporation statutes were redrawn. The revisers had no doubts about their constitutionality and the legislature agreed, but the legislature had strong doubt about their power to revise them. The two-thirds clause seemed to fossilize them; it seemed to recognize that they were still in force but that they were beyond alteration; consequently, it pursued an inconsistent course. It rejected all of the redrawn general incorporation procedures except the one delegating incorporation powers to the Regents of the University (which was accepted on the basis of the plausible explanation they had presented in 1825), and placed all of the other general incorporation statutes in the third volume as laws not revised but still in force.

In the proposed section on general incorporation procedures, the revisers added one for obituary societies. It was based on an 1826 statute allowing township supervisors to receive land in trust for use as a public burial ground.[46] The revisers favored self-incorporation for obituary societies because they believed that the two-thirds clause did not apply to public service corporations over which there was little controversy, namely, those that received a charter of incorporation whenever they petitioned for it. The revisers saw no reason why the philosophy behind the continued operation of general incorporation laws could not be expanded to meet a public need. At the same time, they adhered to a literal interpretation of the two-thirds clause in relation to banks: that it was meant to limit their numbers.

The Regency-led legislature rejected the innovation of obituary societies because it "was an entirely new provision to our laws, it went the whole length in asserting the right of the legislature to pass general laws for the creation of corporations in the mode which had been practiced previous to the adoption of the present constitution."[47] The Regency saw that such a dual interpretation of the two-thirds clause, literal for banks and broad for other public service corporations, would be a Pandora's box that would reopen the debate over the Regency's banking policy. A general incorporation statute for rural burial grounds was the first general incorporation statute passed by the New York legislature in 1847, after the ratification of the Constitution of 1846.

In the 1820s, if the politics of banking-currency-credit could have been separated from other corporate business enterprises, the two-thirds clause could have been easily interpreted to allow the enactment of general incorporation statutes (passed by a two-thirds majority) for all types of businesses not previously organized by single proprietorships or partnerships. Such a statute was passed in Connecticut in 1837 when the legislature allowed three or more persons to incorporate "for the purpose of engaging in and carrying on any kind of manufacturing or mechanical or mining or quarrying or any other lawful business."[48]

The Regency would not, however, give up its banking alliance. It did, however, set out to improve it. This required that the stigma be removed from banks by setting up a system that would guarantee the value of the banknotes circulated by all of the state's banks. This was the purpose of the Safety Fund statute of 1829.

NOTES

1.   Jabez D. Hammond, *The History of Political Parties in the State of New York*, Vol. 1, 420-424, 436, 449-461. Ronald E. Shaw, *Erie Water West, A History of the Erie Canal, 1792-1854*, 56-64. Marshall Smelser, *The Democratic Republic, 1801-1815*, 245-248.

2.   Marcy to Flagg, Oct. 20, 1825 (endorsed by Edwin Croswell, editor of the *Albany Argus*), in Ivor D. Spencer, "William L. Marcy and the Albany Regency," Brown University Dissertation, 138. In January 1832, Marcy made his more famous statement, "to the victor belong the spoils of the enemy."

3.   Jabez D. Hammond, *The History of Political Parties in the State of New York*, Vol. 1, 479-488; Vol. 2, 114. Michael Wallace, "Changing Concepts of Party in the United States: New York, 1815-1828," *American Historical Review*, Vol. 74, 1968, 456-458, 462-463, 468-469.

4.   Marcy to Flagg, Nov. 26, 1823, Flagg papers, New York Public Library.

5.   William L. MacKenzie, *The Life and Times of Martin Van Buren*,

23-24, 31-37. Beatrice G. Reubens, "State Financing of Private Enterprises in Early New York," Columbia University Dissertation, 60. Davis R. Dewey, *Financial History of the United States*, 144-145. Robert V. Remini, "The Early Political Career of Martin Van Buren, 1782-1828," Columbia University Dissertation, 93, 217, 226-227, 287. *Messages from the Governors of New York*, Vol. 2, 871, April 6, 1816, Daniel D. Tompkins. *Legislative Documents 1815*, Assembly, March 20, 1815. *Senate Journal 1815*, 290; *1816*, 202-203. The proposed bank taxes of 1811 and 1819 were for the benefit of the Common School Fund. The New Jersey legislature first debated a bank tax in 1807 and in 1810 taxed the stock of four named banks at the rate of one-half of one percent annually. Subsequently the tax was applied to all chartered banks. John W. Cadman, *The Corporation in New Jersey, 1791-1875*, 63-68.

6.   Richard H. Timberlake, "Denominational Factors in Nineteenth-Century Currency Experience," *Journal of Economic History*, Vol. 34, 1974, 836-839. John J. Knox, *A History of Banking in the United States*, 49. *New York Laws*, Ch. 173, 1807, 224; Ch. 32, 1815, 35; Ch. 222, 1816, 271.

7.   Bray Hammond, *Banks and Politics in America from the Revolution to the Civil War*, 331, 342. Bristol v. Barker, 1817, 14 Johns 205.

8.   *Attorney General* v. *Utica Insurance Company*, 1817, 2 Johns Chancery 370.

9.   *The People* v. *Utica Insurance Company*, 1818, 15 Johns 366, 375. Justice Ambrose Spencer, a bitter political opponent of Van Buren, wrote a strong dissent; however, the accepted interpretation of charters for business corporations had been made by Chief Justice John Marshall in 1804, when he ruled in *Head* v. *Providence Insurance Company*, that corporation charters must be narrowly interpreted: a corporation possessed only those powers explicitly givern to it or which could be implied by a reasonable construction.

10.   Jacob Barker to Benjamin F. Butler, Jan. 5, 1818; Feb. 7, 1818; Feb. 16, 1818; Feb. 18, 1818. Butler papers, State Library, Albany. *New York Laws*, Ch. 236, 1818, 242.

11.   William L. MacKenzie, *The Life and Times of Martin Van Buren*, 87. *Messages from the Governors of New York*, Vol. 2, 916-917, Jan. 27, 1818, DeWitt Clinton. *Senate Journal 1818*, 163, 166.

12.   William L. MacKenzie, *The Lives and Opinions of Benjamin F. Butler and Jesse Hoyt*, 21-22. William L. MacKenzie, *The Life and Times of Martin Van Buren*, 38-43, 157. *The People* v. *the Bank of Washington and Warren*, 1825, 6 Cowen 212. Barker to Butler, March 2, 1818; Barker to Samuel Young, March 5, 1818 (never delivered); Barker to Butler, April 9, 1818; Butler papers, State Library, Albany.

13.   Bray Hammond, *Banks and Politics in the United States from the Revolution to the Civil War*, 549–556, 562–563. *New York Laws*, Ch. 236, 1816, Sec. 28, 291.

14.   Beatrice G. Reubens, "State Financing of Private Enterprises in Early New York," Columbia University Dissertation, 47–48, 78–79. The quote is from *Assembly Journal 1820*, 616. Don C. Sowers, *The Financial History of New York State from 1789 to 1912*, 49, 325–327.

15.   Davis R. Dewey, *State Banking before the Civil War*, 46–52. Walter B. Smith, *Economic Aspects of the Second Bank of the United States*, 30–31. Bray Hammond, *Banks and Politics in America from the Revolution to the Civil War*, 565–580. Other hybrid banks were the Chemical Bank and Delaware and Hudson Canal Company Bank in 1824; and the Dry Dock Bank in 1825.

16.   Bray Hammond, *Banks and Politics in America from the Revolution to the Civil War*, 242–246, 257–259. *McCulloch v. Maryland*, 1819, 4 Wheaton 316. *Assembly Journal 1819*, 68.

17.   *Legislative Documents 1820*, Assembly, No. 85; 86. *Legislative Documents 1821*, No. 120.

18.   Robert E. Chaddock, *The Safety Fund Banking System in New York, 1829-1866*, 247–250. Victor S. Clark, *History of Manufactures in the United States*, Vol. 1, 378–379: "In 1814 all banks but those in New England suspended specie payments and a flood of paper money inflated prices. Though specie payments were resumed three years later, the depression reached its maximum in 1819. In 1813 the nation's circulation was $70,000,000, two years later it had risen to $100,000,000, and in 1819 it had fallen to $45,000,000—a contraction of fifty-nine percent in three years."

19.   Merrill D. Peterson, ed., *Democracy, Liberty and Property: The State Constitutional Conventions of the 1820's*, 126–128.

20.   King had not changed his opinion since the Constitutional Convention in Philadelphia in 1787 when he argued against granting the power of incorporation to the national government because he associated corporations with mercantile monopolies. He probably took his ideas from Adam Smith's *Wealth of Nations* where Smith had indicated that most British business corporations were franchises or had special privileges that went in the direction of monopoly. Simeon E. Baldwin, "American Business Corporations before 1789," *American Historical Review*, Volume 8, 1903, 464–465. Simeon E. Baldwin, *Modern Political Institutions*, 191–192. King's printed correspondence shows he had almost no interest in his convention duties as Chairman of the Incorporation Committee. Charles R. King, ed., *Life and Correspondence of Rufus King*, Vol. 6, 299–424.

21.   Nathaniel H. Carter, William L. Stone, Marcus T. C. Gould,

reporters, *Report of the Proceedings and Debates of the Convention of 1821*, 446. 645. L. H. Clarke, reporter, *Report of Debates and Proceedings of the Convention*, 225.

22.   Robert V. Remini, "The Albany Regency," *New York History*, Vol. 39, 1958, 341–345. Jabez D. Hammond, *The History of Political Parties in the State of New York*, Vol. 1, 337; Vol. 2, 114–115. Bray Hammond, *Banks and Politics in America from the Revolution to the Civil War*, 178–180, 578–579. Robert V. Remini, "The Early Political Career of Martin Van Buren, 1782–1828." *Columbia University Dissertation*, 308–310. Denis T. Lynch, *An Epoch and a Man: Martin Van Buren and His Times*, 162–163.

23.   James Kent, *Commentaries on American Law* (1828), Vol. 3, 12. Francis J. Troubat, *The Law of Commendatory and Limited Partnerships in the United States*, 47–48. Stanley E. Howard, "The Limited Partnership in New Jersey," *Journal of Business of the University of Chicago*, Vol. 7, 1934, 299–314. *New York Laws*, Ch. 244, 1822, 259.

24.   *Messages from the Governors of New York*, Vol. 2, 1093, Jan. 1, 1822, DeWitt Clinton. *New York Laws*, Ch. 262, Sections 14–16, 1823, 390. The Massachusetts legislature enacted similar legislation in 1812 at the rate of one percent annually: *Mass. Laws*, Ch. 32, 1812, 45. John W. Cadman, *The Incorporation in New Jersey, 1791-1875*, 63-68, 391-392.

25.   *Legislative Documents 1822*, Senate, No. 182; *Assembly Journal 1823*, Appendix C, Comptroller's Report on a General System of Taxation; Appendix D. *Legislative Documents 1823*, Senate No. 88; 92; 93; 202; 203; 214; 216A; 216B.

26.   *Clinton Woolen and Cotton Manufacturing Company* v. *Morse*, 1817 (unreported), cited in, *The People* v. *the Utica Insurance Company*, 1818, 15 Johns 382.

27.   *Salem Iron Factory* v. *Danvers*, 1813, 10 Mass. 517–518.

28.   *Legislative Documents 1827*, Assembly, No. 88. *Assembly Documents 1835*, No. 212. *New York Laws*, Ch. 22, 1824, 16; Ch. 254, 1825, 373.

29.   *Legislative Documents 1824*, Assembly No. 52; 53. *Senate Journal 1825*, 121.

30.   *Columbian Manufacturing Company* v. *Vanderpoel*, 1825, 4 Cowen 556. *Legislative Documents 1825*, Senate No. 19; *1827*, Assembly No. 69; *1828*, Assembly No. 31; *Assembly Journal 1827*, 442.

31.   *Revised Statutes 1828*, Vol. 1, Ch. 13, Title 1, 389–390; Ch. 13, Title 4, 414–418. *Revised Statutes 1828* (1836), Vol. 3, Appendix, 496–501.

32.   *Mohawk and Hudson Railroad Company* v. *Clute*, 1834, 4 Paige Chancery 395.

33.   Edward L. Pierce, *A Treatise on American Railroad Law*, 55. *Senate Documents 1832*, No. 103, 9. *Assembly Documents 1838*, No. 146. *Assembly Documents 1847*, No. 98.

34.   *Bank of Utica* v. *the City of Utica*, 1834, 4 Paige Chancery 399.

35.   *The People* v. *the Supervisors of the City and County of New York*, 1836, 18 Wendell 607-608. *The People* v. *the Assessors of Watertown*, 1841, 1 Hill 617.

36.   *New York Laws*, Ch. 92, 1788, 204; Ch. 123, 1811, 205; Ch. 235, 1811, 434.

37.   *Sturgis* v. *Crowninshield*, 1819, 4 Wheaton 200. *Penniman* v. *Meigs*, 1812, 9 Johns 325.

38.   James Kent, *Commentaries on American Law* (1827), Vol. 2, 252-253. *New York Laws*, Ch. 325, 1825, 448. The Revised Statutes of 1828 made a distinction between bankruptcy proceedings against banks and other corporations: *Revised Statutes 1828*, Vol. 1, Ch. 18, Title 2, 589-594; Vol. 2, Ch. 8, Title 4, 461-472.

39.   William L. MacKenzie, *The Lives and Opinions of Benjamin F. Butler and Jesse Hoyt*, 22. *The People* v. *The Bank of Niagara*, 1826, 6 Cowen 196; *The People* v. *The Bank of Washington and Warren*, 1825, 6 Cowen 211.

40.   *The People* v. *The Bank of Hudson*, 1826, 6 Cowen 217. *Slee* v. *Bloom*, 1821, appears to be the first case of non-insurance corporation being involved in bankruptcy. Justice Nelson, in 1840 (*Bank of Poughkeepsie* v. *Ibbotson*, 1841, 24 Wendell 479) refers to *Briggs* v. *Penniman*, 1826, as setting the accepted Chancery procedure for corporate bankruptcy.

41.   Charles M. Haar, "Legislative Regulation of New York Industrial Corporations, 1800-1850," *New York History*, Vol. 22, 1941, 195-196, 205-206. *Revised Statutes 1828*, Vol. 1, Ch. 18, Title 3, Sec. 5, 600.

On the other hand, in Massachusetts in 1821, the Supreme Court had said regarding the unlimited liability provision of the 1809 general regulatory statute for manufacturing corporations, "The legislature have thought fit, and we think wisely to subject the property of all members of these corporations to a liability for the debts of the company," *Marcy* v. *Clark*, 1821, 17 Mass. 334. Only reluctantly in 1830, after five years of urgings by Governor Levi Lincoln, did the Massachusetts legislature adopt a policy of limited liability for corporation stockholders.

Governor Lincoln said that full liability for stockholders of manufacturing corporations adversely affected the orderly conduct of business and, therefore, had the opposite effect intended. The success of manufacturing corporations was, to a large extent, based on using credit. In order to get credit, owners had to pledge collateral assets, but shares of stock subject to full liability were not readily usable for collateral because they had limited market value. People were unwilling to purchase them or accept them for payment of debts. *Mass. Laws*, Governor's Message, 228–230, Jan. 6, 1830, Levi Lincoln; Ch. 53, 1830, 325. Edwin M. Dodd, "The Evolution of Limited Liability in American Industry: Massachusetts," *Harvard Law Review*, Vol. 61, 1948, 1361–1372.

42.   Jabez D. Hammond, *Life and Times of Silas Wright*, 64–65. Robert E. Chaddock, *The Safety Fund Banking System in New York, 1829–1866*, 247–254. Jabez D. Hammond, *The History of Political Parties in the State of New York*, Vol. 2, 144–175, 196–199. C. H. Rammelkamp, "The Campaign of 1824 in New York," *Annual Report of the American Historical Association*, 1904, 181–183.

43.   *Legislative Documents 1824*, Senate No. 74, 2–3.

44.   Bray Hammond, *Banks and Politics in America from the Revolution to the Civil War*, 572. Davis R. Dewey, *State Banking Before the Civil War*, 145–146. *Legislative Documents 1825*, Senate No. 71, 156. *Senate Journal 1825*, 55, 99–103, 186–188.

45.   Rondo Cameron, *Banking in the Early Stages of Industrialization*, 6–14. Robert G. Albion, *The Rise of New York Port, 1815–1860*, 77–102.

46.   *New York Laws*, Ch. 67, 1826, 47. The 1826 statute was based on a private act of incorporation passed in 1824; Ch. 264, 1824, 325. The original scope of the codification of the state's incorporation laws can be found in the *Revised Statutes 1828* (1836), Vol. 3, Appendix 529.

47.   Hiram E. Sickels, ed., *Opinions of the Attorneys-General of the State of New York*, 62; *Senate Documents 1835*, No. 4.

48.   Edwin M. Dodd, *American Business Corporations until 1860*, 416–418. *Conn. Laws*, Ch. 63, 1837, Sec. 2, 107.

5

The Safety Fund System, 1829-1838

THE SAFETY FUND STATUTE

It was a political necessity in 1829 to pass a bank regulatory statute that could stabilize the value of the state's currency. During the preceding legislative session, the Regency's chief pet, the Mechanics and Farmers Bank, had not gotten a two-thirds majority when it had petitioned for re-incorporation. Nine other banks shared its fate. This balky behavior caused the *Albany Argus* to question the wisdom of the two-thirds clause. "It seems to be an unequal constitutional rule which declares a vote to be in the negative, notwithstanding more than three to one of the members present are in the affirmative. . . . The voters in the negative, we believe, are not so generally from any objections to the immediate renewal of charters, but in consequence of a difference of opinion as to the extent of the restrictions." The Regency did, however, succeed in defeating an attempt to impose full liability on bank stockholders.[1]

Martin Van Buren was elected Governor of New York in 1828 while he was still serving in the United States Senate. He occupied the Governor's chair from January to March 1829, when he resigned to become President Andrew Jackson's Secretary of State. Only if the Regency overcame the grievance against the state's banknote currency could rechartering begin, and it would be highly advantageous to have the rechartering managed by the Regency. This situation would strongly contribute toward giving the Democrative-Republican party a continued lease on office because the charters of most of the state's banks expired within the next three years.

Before offering the Safety Fund plan, Van Buren reviewed the alternatives. He rejected a policy that would have allowed all of the state bank charters to expire and leave the Bank of the United States alone to satisfy the state's credit needs. New York had to have its own banking system. He was of the opinion that there were many merits to a plan for a central state bank with many branches in which the state had an investment like the federal government's interest in the Bank of the United States; but in the final analysis the best plan was to retain the existing banking system. "Experience has shown that banking operations, to be successful and consequently beneficial to the community, must be conducted by private men upon their own account." Private banking, however, required safeguards to remedy the great popular distrust of banks— people got little or nothing for the banknotes they held when a bank failed; as Van Buren said, "The solvency of banks, and consequent stability of their paper is the principal, and almost only point in which the people have much interest." Van Buren also believed that unlimited liability for bank stockholders would contribute to an unstable currency because it would tend to put the banking business into the hands of irresponsible men. Furthermore, "the number of stockholder in comparison with the great body of people is so very small and the stock is so constantly changing hands that the equity of its original distribution becomes a comparatively unimportant matter."[2] The public interpreted this to mean that banking was a business best undertaken by large capitalists because only they could afford to be investors; but the legislators interpreted it to mean that they would have the first opportunity to subscribe to shares in new banks.

Instead of copying the Suffolk System of centralized clearance that continuously regulated the banknote credit practices of participating banks, Van Buren backed a plan for guaranteeing the currency's value through a tax-supported insurance fund—the Safety Fund. Its principle was the same as that of the presently existing Federal Deposit Insurance Corporation. All participating banks paid an annual tax of one-half of one percent on their stock until they contributed 3 percent of their capitalization. This fund would redeem the notes of insolvent banks, but until such an emergency arose, a bank's credit practices were practically unrestrained by the state. This was not a serious problem in the 1820s because the Bank of the United States performed this function through its discounting practices, but if the Bank of the United States were not rechartered, disaster could result if no state machinery was created to take its place.

When the statute was drafted, the inclusive term *debt* was used the increase in the number of corporations because their charters seated consequences that led directly to the Fund's bankruptcy in 1842. If bank examiners discovered an insolvent bank, its assets were immediately audited and if these proved insufficient to pay its debts (outstanding banknotes plus deposits), the Comptroller was authorized to redeem these obligations from the Safety Fund. Stockholders were granted limited liability, instead of double liability as under the 1825 bankruptcy statute or the full liability demanded by the agrarians but directors were still saddled with full liability if fraud was the cause of bankruptcy. The legislature removed this disability in 1830.[3]

The time was right for such a statute. No bank charters had been passed since 1825, and there was a real need for more commercial credit. The statute was proposed by Joshua Forman, a prominent lawyer, a respected promoter of the Erie Canal, and an inventor of an improved method of evaporation to recover salt from the state's salt springs. The statute featured most of the proposals discussed during the bank controversy in 1824 and 1825. It was a general regulatory statute that required each charter application to receive individual consideration. Thus it systematized a banking policy the Regency had already adopted: it preserved the political management of the state's banking system. The alternative was a free banking statute that was strongly supported by substantial numbers of Democratic-Republicans, but a free banking system would be politically unmanageable and in obvious conflict with a literal in-interpretation of the two-thirds clause of the state's constitution.

After the Safety Fund statute was enacted, bills were introduced to recharter twenty-eight operating banks and charter thirty-two new ones. Of these sixty applications, the legislature rechartered sixteen and incorporated eleven new banks. In subsequent years, most operating banks were rechartered and, during the years when President Andrew Jackson was making war upon the Bank of the United States (1833–1836), twenty-eight new banks were incorporated.

The Safety Fund statute was complementary to the two other corporate statutes passed during the 1820s that applied primarily to banks: the corporation taxation statute and the corporation bankruptcy statute. These three statutes brought the banking business under more state supervision than any other class of business. The Safety Fund Statute went one step further by setting up a statewide Bank Commission to inspect the financial integrity of the participating banks, but it had no power to restrain their credit practices. The insurance fund feature, however, did provide enough safeguards on the reliability of the state's banknote currency to calm popular suspicions and allow the legislature to incorporate or reincorporate a total of ninety-three banks between 1829 and 1839.[4] Equally important, the Safety Fund statute was a law that could be politically managed; one that allowed the Regency to interpret capitalists wanting bank charters to mean capitalists of the Jacksonian Democratic persuasion.

The Bank Commission was the first permanent statewide independent regulatory commission in the United States.[5] It was composed of one commissioner appointed by the Governor and two selected by the banks themselves, all of whom were removable at the Governor's pleasure. They could have no direct or indirect interest in any bank. Their duty was to inspect the books of all banks once every four months or oftener if requested by any three banks; and they could examine all the bank's records and take sworn statements from the bank's officers. When a bank was found to be insolvent, they were authorized to apply to the Court of Chancery for an injunction to suspend its operations.

THE POLITICS OF THE SAFETY FUND SYSTEM

The highly capitalized New York City commercial banks resisted joining the Safety Fund because the tax was levied on bank capital and not on banknotes. A tax on banknotes would have forced the country banks to pay a high tax relative to their capitalization, while the city banks, which circulated few notes of their own, would pay little. New York City banks circulated a relatively small volume of notes because they usually credited the accounts of their debtors with the amounts of their loans, which were then expended by checks. The capitalization tax of the Safety Fund forced the city banks to subsidize the integrity of the notes circulated by the country banks. It was, however, a highly tenuous security. The substitution of the word *debt* for *banknote* made the Safety Fund excessively liable because debts also included deposits; and if the Bank of the United States were to cease restraining the credit practices of the country banks, the integrity of their notes would be jeopardized at the first financial stringency because the stronger city banks would charge high discounts when accepting them for deposit.

In order to be effective, all New York banks had to participate. Almost all bank charters had time limits and, as they expired, the banks would be forced to join the Safety Fund if they wanted to continue in business. The Manhattan Company, however, was one of the banks that possessed a perpetual charter. A suit was brought against it in October 1830, which questioned its right to be in the banking business. The state contended that the Manhattan Company was not legally a bank because the restraining act of 1804 restricted banks to corporations specifically chartered for that purpose. The Manhattan Company pointed out that it was specifically exempted from the restraining law by a statute passed at the same time the restraining law was enacted, and thereafter, the state had frequently recognized it as a legitimate bank. The New York Supreme Court sustained the Manhattan Company.[6]

Enactment of the Safety Fund statute just before the beginning of Jackson's war upon the Bank of the United States put New York's banking system in an advantageous position to expand if the Bank failed to be rechartered, but anti-Bank interests had to be mobilized and pro-Bank sentiment neutralized if the Bank was to be destroyed. There were two geographic regions of pro-Bank sentiment in New York, western New York just then emerging into commercial development, and New York City. Both of these regions enjoyed sound banking largely resulting from the effective competition provided by branches of the Bank of the United States.

Western New York supported rechartering the Bank because, in 1831, it had few country banks and the Bank of the United States' branch at Buffalo supplied it with a stable currency and sound credit facilities. In New York City, many officers of the larger commercial banks opposed the Bank War because they were apprehensive about the inflationary pressures that would follow the end of the Bank's credit restraints. The Bank of the United States, by restraining the banknote credit practices of the country banks, preserved conditions for orderly economic growth. On the other hand, New York City commercial banks had much to gain and did not militantly support rechartering the Bank during the Bank War of 1832. They were intensely jealous of the financial primacy of Philadelphia where the headquarters of the Bank was located. The Bank's financial strength depended on the tariff revenues deposited with it. Such deposits generated an enormous amount of credit controlled by the Philadelphia directors of the Bank; but over half of the nation's tariff revenue was collected at the port of New York. If the tariff revenue collected at New York was deposited in New York City banks, it would greatly expand their credit-making capacities, and their profits.

The only way these deposits could be gotten was by destroying the Bank and substituting state banks as depositories. This was accomplished by President Jackson's veto of rechartering the Bank in July 1832, and the process of selecting pet state banks began in September 1833. In January 1834, several New York business leaders proposed that the legislature charter a bank capitalized at ten million dollars, with a quarter of the capital being supplied by the state. Conservative bankers saw this bank as a means of replacing the central banking functions of the Bank of the United States. It could act to curb potential inflation in New York when the Bank's charter expired. In the winter of 1834, Vice-President Van Buren made known his opposition to this proposal and it died.[7]

The heart of the opposition to rechartering the Bank of the United States came from the regions where country banks were most numerous. Most country banks favored the destruction of the Bank because it would allow them to expand the volume of their banknote credit without restraint and raise their interest rates. They would be able to lend at the state's maximum legal interest rate of 7 percent without competition from the Bank's branches in New York City, Utica, and Buffalo. The branches had always attracted the better risks because the maximum interest they could charge was 6 percent. The Regency also strongly favored the Bank's destruction because it would allow the chartering of many more state banks to supply the credit the Bank of the United States had formerly provided. Bank charters were eagerly sought because banking was a highly profitable business, expecially the country banks that specialized in creating banknote credit. In 1833, it was estimated that the average annual profit on banking capital was over 7 percent: 6.14 percent for the city commercial banks and over 9 percent for the country banks.[8]

In 1832, petitions were presented for fifty new banks, and the legislature had to sort them out to see that the potential profits got into the hands of friendly promoters. Party workers were encouraged to subscribe for a few shares at their first offering, when they were sold at par. In 1831 and 1832, when seventeen new banks were chartered and eight existing ones renewed, ten prominent members of the Regency bought over $200,000 worth of stock, and many members of the legislature or their families were conspicuous as repeated subscribers for new bank shares. As soon as a new bank went into operation, many of the initial subscribers sold their shares at an advance.

When the Seventh Ward Bank was chartered in 1833, the commissioners who supervised the distribution of shares directed that one-third should go to their friends and two-thirds to state officeholders. Only forty of the initial 3,710 shares were sold to the public. In the early 1830s, investment in country banks was a way to get rich quickly because they yielded large profits with a minimum of invested capital.[9] A legislator writing to the local Democratic boss at Sacketts Harbor in January 1832 said: "There are more applications for banks this year than ever before. You must make out a complete list of directors, officers, etc., and if obtained, you must know how. It must be a Jackson bank; and the bank junto must be allowed a finger in the pie."[10]

The second greatest opportunity for speculative profits was land. Particularly attractive was land that could be industrially developed; and in the 1830s, the most attractive lands were water power sites in western New York. The easiest site to develop was not Niagara Falls, where the torrent of water was very difficult to control, but at Lockport where the Erie Canal's surplus water could be channeled over the escarpment and used to turn water wheels of turbines. Securing the long-term use of the Canal's surplus water required political connections and, furthermore, much of the credit required to sustain these new manufacturing operations had to come from banks. The Lockport Bank was chartered in 1829. It was a banking opportunity that was sure of initial success, not only because of the local industrial potential, but also because large revenues from canal tolls collected at Lockport needed a local depository.[11]

Many New York entrepreneurs and businessmen tended to support the destruction of the Bank, or were indifferent to its fate, because the looser credit controls that would follow would lead to the creation of more credit. More credit was necessary to exploit the widening variety of business opportunities in the early 1830s, even if it cost 7 percent. Many businessmen looked upon the expiration of the Bank as the first step in putting the creation and management of credit in the hands of the men who used it—local businessmen. It was hoped that the increased credit would be available in the cities where it was needed, instead of being allocated to rural locations where it would increase the supply of unreliable banknotes.

The 1832 veto of the Bank's charter was also popular with large numbers of New York agrarians and tradesmen who opposed the excessive issue of banknotes. The destruction of the Bank of the United States was, in their opinion, the first step toward restoring a stable currency because it killed the "monster" that issued more banknotes than any other bank in the nation. The Bank's destruction was also looked on as a necessary step toward ending the intimate connection between politics and banking, a connection which this group believed was responsible for inflation because the most visible source of inflation was the large volume of discounted banknotes issued by Safety Fund banks. After the destruction of the Bank of the United States, the agrarians wanted to proceed against the Safety Fund banks. The result would be a currency consisting only of gold and silver coins. They got little sympathy from the leadership of New York's Democratic party.

When the national government ceased making deposits in the Bank of the United States late in 1833 and began putting its funds in pet banks, the Bank began tightening credit by reducing the accommodations it had extended to state banks. Governor Marcy responded to the distress cries of New York's banks and recommended passage of a six million dollar loan to aid them. The Whigs accused him of mortgaging the state for the benefit of the Democracy's pets. The loan was authorized in 1834 but not used, because in June of that year, the Bank changed its policy.

The withdrawal of deposits from the Bank of the United States meant there was no longer any effective national restraint on the volume of banknotes state banks could push into circulation. The end of centralized credit controls after 1834 led to the creation of large volumes of new credit in the commercially aggressive states. New York was one of the leaders. Political considerations dictated that the increase in credit be mostly banknotes issued by country banks. Country banks were a convenient way to reward party members. The party caucus could allocate the banks on a geographic basis, and its members could reserve the opportunity to subscribe to a few shares and thus reward themselves for the discipline needed to provide the two-thirds majority.[12]

The Regency not only approved the incorporation of many new country banks, but in 1831, began another policy that strongly reenforced the rapid expansion of banknote credit. It increased the credit-making capacities of the country banks by placing substantial amounts of demand deposits, and later time deposits, among them. These deposits came from the surplus revenue of the Canal Fund, which was distributed on a highly partisan basis. By 1837, fifty-two of the state's ninety banks held Canal Fund deposits, often the largest single capital resource a country bank possessed. Friendly banks paid only 3 ½ percent interest on time deposits, while neutral or unfriendly banks were rejected even if they offered to pay 5 percent. A bank that got a deposit treated it as an asset and made loans on it. There were no restrictions on its use. The Mechanics and Farmers Bank of Albany was the largest and most important beneficiary of this policy, and it rationed the distribution of the Canal Fund's surplus revenue to other Safety Fund banks.[13]

The policy of allowing select country banks to use deposits of state funds as a basis for expanding their banknote credit gave the Regency a commanding voice over the political influence they could exercise against rechartering the Bank of the United States.

The influences they mobilized strongly supported the legislature when it instructed New York's Senators and requested its representatives to vote against rechartering the Bank. Thomas W. Olcott, the cashier of the Mechanics Bank, was the person who brought the country banks into line. "He manages the business of the bank almost exclusively and . . . has more influence on legislative deliberations than any other person I know of."[14] Olcott supplied much of the financial expertise of the Regency, but the Regency's bank policy was made elsewhere, probably in the caucus where the Democratic majority was greedy for the opportunity to invest in bank stocks. This policy had the full support of Governor William L. Marcy and of Marcy's father-in-law, who was president of the Mechanics Bank. Marcy knew the value of building party discipline on the basis of interest. Upon the overthrow of the Bank, the country banks did not want any restraints placed on the creation of banknote credit; therefore, the Regency did not make the Mechanics Bank, its chief bank of deposit, into a state central bank that would restrain their credit practices. The Regency's bank policy was in strong contrast to the policy of the Suffolk Bank of Boston that effectively restrained the banknote credit practices of New England's country banks.

THE POLITICAL USE OF THE TWO-THIRDS CLAUSE

The accelerating demand for credit in the late 1820s and early 1830s increased the pressure for more banks. The question recurred why the pre-1822 general incorporation statutes continued to operate while bank charters were individually passed on a highly political basis. At the end of the 1834 legislative session, a test was arranged, which came at the same time the *New York Evening Post* editorially supported the passage of a free banking statute. An amendment was submitted to the 1811 general incorporation statute for manufactories that sought to increase the number of counties where leather manufacturers could incorporate. An opinion on its constitutionality, if it should be passed by a two-thirds vote, was asked of Attorney General Greene C. Bronson,[15] who wrote a history of general incorporation statutes in New York and explained why they continued to be used after the adoption of the Constitution in 1822.

Bronson said that the intent of the two-thirds clause was to check the increase in the number of corporations because thier charters conferred special privileges. He said, "The construction which more certainly than any other will attain this end, is that which requires the legislature, in cases not already provided by law, to act directly on every question of this description."[16] This construction was not entirely consistent with the inclusive wording of the two-thirds clause, but it was probably in agreement with the intent of the framers, as indicated by the debates of the Convention, and with the 1825 Report of the Regents.

From 1822 to 1834, Bronson estimated that over 500 religious congregations had been incorporated; the Regents had chartered one college, six academies, and two Lancaster schools; eighty-four manufacturing corporations had filed charters; and he estimated that over one hundred libraries had been incorporated. This was a very considerable load lifted from the legislature. The framers of the Constitution, Bronson said, were not ignorant of these general incorporation statutes. They specifically referred to them at the Convention in language that assumed they would continue to operate, and because of this, it was impossible to suppose the two-thirds clause was intended to supersede them.

Bronson said that the amendment to the 1811 statute, which would increase the number of counties where leather manufacturing corporations would incorporate, was perfectly constitutional. This was not a covert attempt to extend the scope of the statute into classes of businesses that were not authorized prior to 1822. What then was the proper interpretation of the two-thirds clause in the Constitution as applied to all classes of corporations? In Bronson's opinion, the existing general incorporation statutes could be amended, but not in such a way as to extend their scope into businesses or public services not provided before 1822. The existing general incorporation statutes were not abrogated because "corporate bodies, save such as are authorized by existing laws, can only be created by the legislature itself, acting directly upon each particular case"; however, in all other cases, the legislature could create only one specific corporation by one statute, naming each corporation by its legal title.

Therefore, the Regents' interpretation of the two-thirds clause given in 1825 was correct, and they could continue to incorporate

educational institutions. Furthermore, the legislature had been constitutionally correct in rejecting the creation of obituary societies
by a general incorporation procedure in 1828, because "it went the
whole length in asserting the right of the legislature to pass general
laws for the creation of corporations in the mode which had been
practiced previous to the adoption of the present constitution." The
revisers had been wrong, said Bronson, although their opinions
must bear considerable weight. "It is believed . . . that the assent
of two-thirds of the members to a bill, under which an indefinite
number of corporations may spring into existence, does not answer
the requirement of the Constitution, but that such assent must be
given to a bill creating one or more corporations in particular." The
political significance of this recitation is found in the words, "in
particular." Bronson believed that the legislature could not pass a
general incorporation statute for banks or any other class of corporation, even if two-thirds of the elected members of the legislature approved. Each act of incorporation, except for the pre-1822
general incorporation statutes, must specifically name the corporation that was created.

It was a very able exposition of the meaning of the two-thirds
clause, but it was an interpretation that was conservative of Regency
power as embodied in the party caucus, because it strongly confirmed the legislature's power to charter each bank individually
while at the same time denying the constitutionality of a free banking law. Bronson's interpretation followed the literal intent of the
Convention, which believed that the maintenance of a sound banknote currency was facilitated by making banks difficult to charter
because a difficult chartering procedure would separate banking
from partisan politics. Only those few banks that everyone agreed
were necessary would receive the two-thirds vote necessary for incorporation.

Bronson's legal opinion was a timely bulwark of Governor
Marcy's political position because late in 1834 Marcy had defended
the Regency's bank policy when it was attacked by a dissident
group of New York City Democrats.[17] Both Marcy's and Bronson's
defense of the Safety Fund system was taken with the full
knowledge that the legislature was using the two-thirds clause
directly contrary to its intent. Under Regency leadership, the in-

fluence of banks in politics increased because the Democratic party's legislative majority increased the number of country banks that specialized in circulating paper money.

Van Buren and Marcy both agreed that the ten million dollar bank was politically undesirable because it would make a more efficient "monopoly" out of the Safety Fund system. Marcy objected because it threatened to upset a smoothly working party organization. He wanted to let things alone as long as there was prosperity. Van Buren objected because it would have whelped on the state level a monster similar to the one Jackson had just slain on the national level. Changes ought to be made in the system but in the direction of making the allocation of charters less political. One of Van Buren's correspondents who kept him informed about New York City politics wrote him in December 1834: "I incline to believe that this anti-monopoly warfare will extend—and if it extend, I cannot imagine that there can be any doubt of the issue in favor of those who contend for an overthrow of the present system of corporations." Ten months later, Van Buren's lieutenant in the United States House of Representatives, Churchill C. Cambreleng, writing after the Locofoco revolt, implicitly condemned the excesses of the Regency's bank policy. He said, "I do not say what will be done, as long as the legislature can make money by the charters of their own creation or prominent men can get the salaries of presidents or cashiers by enlisting in the ranks of Democracy."

By the end of 1836, even a leading member of the Regency was expressing doubts about the party's bank policy. Comptroller Azariah C. Flagg wrote privately in October, "repeal the restraining law, refuse all banks unless their stock is sold at auction and those who trade upon legislation (the honorable lobby) will be blown sky high: and the scene of log-rolling and corruption would be replaced by a decent regard to moral and official purity and a reasonable attention to the public business and general welfare."[18] Flagg publicly stated this position in December in an unsigned editorial in the *Albany Argus*. He understood the importance of the Locofoco revolt in 1835 and came to the conclusion that the Democracy's bank policy was self-defeating. There was too great a gap between the public professions of the party, claiming to be the true guardian of equal economic opportunity, and the practice of the party's leaders in splitting the banking melon among themselves. Flagg and others might be critical of the party's bank policy, but they could not control it because they could not control the log-rolling tactics of the caucus.

THE LOCOFOCO REVOLT

A rapidly growing faction within the Democratic party (called Locofocos) militantly opposed increasing the number of Safety Fund banks. This opposition was heavily concentrated in New York City. These men were mostly tradesmen and mechanics engaged in urban construction, who were likely to be small entrepreneurs. They were frequently led by Thompsonite physicians who shared with them the economic hardships of a highly discounted paper currency.

Inflation and a discounted currency tended to reduce their standard of living and prevent them from accumulating enough capital to purchase property, which not only threatened their economic well-being but also, in their opinion, was a threat to a viable urban democracy. They felt threatened because their wages were often paid in discounted banknotes from distant banks that were used by unscrupulous employers to meet their payrolls or pay off contractors. Banknote inflation defrauded them from part of their pay. These men believed that a person, in order to enjoy true liberty, had to possess property, and any government that passed laws that favored the accumulation of wealth in the hands of a privileged few or pursued monetary policies that hindered the democracy from acquiring wealth, was bad government. A viable urban-industrial democracy required that opportunities for business profits had to be equalized. This required laws of general application. Particularly, it required a law that equalized the opportunities to obtain credit. A general incorporation statute for banks was the best way to obtain this end; and to make it work, it had to be combined with a stable currency. Only these conditions could create democratic business opportunities in an urban-industrial environment.[19]

For this reason, President Andrew Jackson's claim that only the Democratic party could preserve the values of the Old Republic found a strongly favorable political response in the urban areas of

New York. The greatest virtue of the Old Republic, when it was simple and agrarian, was that every individual had an equal opportunity to own farmland. This virtue could be preserved by expanding the agricultural boundaries of the nation to the Pacific Ocean. It also could be extended to the urban-industrial sector of the economy in two basic ways: facilitate the universal ownership of town lots by city mechanics, and provide for equal access to commercial credit by the new varieties of urban businessmen.

In New England, sound industrial enterprises required that about one-third of a business corporation's capital be liquid and that its management have very close relations with banks. This high liquidity and intimate association with banks largely contributed to the success of the largest New England and New York textile mills. In the initial stages of industrialization, liquidity (or working capital) was usually supplied by bank credit. Marvin Meyers sums up Joseph A. Schumpeter's observation when he says that the "bold creation of credit, for all its follies, was the key innovation, i.e. creative economic development." All New York City businessmen knew the value of having a line of bank credit to use as working capital. This was especially true for the small entrepreneurs like contractors and tradesmen (both of whom were called mechanics in the language of the time), because they had limited cash reserves and a little-known credit rating, which made them the greatest sufferers from an unresponsive banking system and an unreliable currency. They wanted equal access to bank credit on a par with established business, and they wanted it from nonpolitical banks sensitive to their needs. These small entrepreneurs, as well as the anti-inflationists, strongly opposed the creation of any more Safety Fund banks in relatively remote locations but would favor more specie-paying commercial banks in the larger cities.[20]

With the beginning of the inflationary spiral in 1834, New York City tradesmen began to organize unions to secure commensurate wage increases. When this movement met with vigorous opposition, they turned to political action. The extent of the inflationary squeeze they were caught in is revealed by the increase in the price of flour. In March 1835, a barrel of flour cost $5.62, but two years later, it had risen to $12.00. Other commodities followed a similar course. The Locofoco cure for banknote inflation was an exclusively metallic currency and an end of the Safety Fund system that gave charters to political favorites; or if this could not be secured, a fully backed paper currency. They recognized "that bank credit augmented the supply of money, diminished the value of the dollar, and raised the prices which they as consumers had to pay," or as they said, "as the currency expands the loaf contracts."[21] In a futile attempt to mollify this faction, the Bank Commissioners recommended in 1834 that no new charters be passed and that operating banks be encouraged to increase their capitalization. None were chartered in 1835, but the Regency did not attack the state banks, nor would Tammany Hall support the nomination of candidates opposed to the expansion of the Safety Fund system.

This combination of opposites (entrepreneurs who wanted more banks and anti-inflationists who wanted fewer banks of issue) spoke the same language of economic protest. They walked out of the New York City Democratic party convention in October 1835 and formed the Equal Rights or Locofoco party. The one thing they could agree on was that the state had a duty to provide a sound currency. These urban Democrats had not recognized that the Bank of the United States had exercised a national restraining supervision over the credit practices of state banks, which had created a stable currency, and when it ceased to function, inflation would follow because of the expansion of banknote credit.

Locofocos believed that all business corporations should be created under general laws in order to equalize the profit opportunities in corporate enterprises. This included banks if a general banking law were framed in such a way that the notes they circulated were fully redeemable for specie. They were believers in competitive free trade, and especially, competitive free trade in credit. They believed that individuals should be left free to invest their capital wherever they wished, including the opportunity to invest in banks, as long as the currency these banks circulated was fully secured. A free banking statute would prevent the state from creating pet banks to issue notes that were not backed by real capital and whose only asset was an individual charter obtained through political influence. A free banking system would also facilitate the extension of credit to smaller businessmen and to new classes of enterprises by stimulating a free competition in banking.[22] "The legal order should protect and promote the release of individual creative energy to the greatest extent compatible with the broad sharing of opportunity . . . to secure a man a chance to be let alone, free of arbitrary public or private interference while he showed what he could do. . . . The legal order should mobilize the resources of the community to help share an environment which would give men more liberty," and the main way to do this would be to equalize opportunities to gain individual or corporate wealth either through the acquisition of farmland or equalizing the terms of credit to all businessmen, but particularly to small urban businessmen.[23]

More banks were needed in the larger cities to provide the credit needed to establish small businesses and exploit new markets. If a general incorporation statute for them could not be obtained because of the two-thirds clause, then a general law could be passed for corporate partnerships or some other circumventing device. Whatever means was used, it was recognized that only general laws could give the even-handed justice and equal-rights opportunities that would restore government to the simplicity of the Old Republic. General incorporation laws would eliminate all privileges by opening the advantages of corporate entrepreneurship to all capitalists. The only exceptions to this policy might be large-scale franchise projects like canals and railroads, which would probably require individual consideration.[24]

The Locofocos began their assault on the Safety Fund system by challenging the constitutional basis of banknotes issued by state-chartered banks. They said that banknotes were unconstitutional because they were really bills of credit in disguise. They based this contention on Chief Justice John Marshall's opinion in *Craig* v. *Missouri* in 1830. The case involved the constitutionality of a Missouri statute authorizing the state to issue certificates of credit that were to be redeemed by the state. Marshall defined these certificates as another name for bills of credit, which the Federal Constitution prohibited the states from issuing. The decision did not directly impair the constitutionality of the banknotes circulated by state banks because the backing for them was shareholders' capital and not on the state's credit, even though the state, through the incorporating process, authorized them to circulate as money.

In 1832, Daniel Webster had recognized that the national government had little direct control over the nation's currency and credit structure except through the discounting practices of the Bank of the United States. He was striving to preserve this instrument of national authority. Justice Joseph Story, in his *Commentaries*, published in 1833, also recognized that the states had usurped the national power over currency, and he commented that it was probably too late for the national government to retrieve it. In 1834, a test of the constitutionality of state banknotes finally came before the Supreme Court, but the decision was postponed until 1837, because of illnesses and deaths. When the issue was finally decided, the Court was composed almost wholly of Jacksonians, presided over by Chief Justice Roger B. Taney, who had been one of the leaders in killing the Bank

Chief Justice Taney's opinion in *Briscoe* v. *Bank of Kentucky* removed almost all doubts of the constitutionality of banknotes issued by state-chartered banks.[25] At issue was the constitutionality of the banknotes by a bank in which the state was the sole stockholder. Taney's opinion said that the credit behind the banknotes was not directly that of the state, but that of the bank; thus, it was irrelevant whether the state owned the bank's stock or it was owned by private individuals.[26] The Court refused to pierce the corporate veil; thus, if the banknotes issued by a state-owned bank were not bills of credit within the meaning of the Constitution, presumably all banknotes circulated by privately owned state-chartered banks were also constitutional. This was a conservative decision, which protected a very large and powerful vested interest that supplied more than 90 percent of the nation's currency.

In the meantime, the New York Supreme Court buttressed the Regency's banking policy by favorable interpretations of two key laws: the restraining statutes and the two-thirds clause. In doing this, the Court chose not to interpret the law in terms of the grievance intended to be remedied but on the law's literal wording. The first judicial sanction of the 1804 restraining law took place in 1818 in *The People* v. *the Utica Insurance Company*, which was reenforced in 1824 in *New York Fireman Insurance Company* v. *Ely*, when the Court held that the 1818 law "had for its object the guaranteeing to banks a monopoly of the rights and privileges granted to them which had been encroached upon or infringed by private associations."[27] The language was not what the Regency desired, but it was a legal sanction. The Court's interpretation of the two-thirds clause aided the Regency. The clause was applied only to those businesses (and benevolent societies) that could not be organized under the provisions of general incorporation statutes that had been passed prior to the adoption of the Constitution of 1821. The only controversial business in this category was banks.

In the January term of 1835, Justice Samuel Nelson, who had been a member of the 1821 Convention, rendered a favorable opinion in *The People* v. *Morris*. The case involved the constitutionality of a statute prohibiting grocers from selling liquor by the glass. It was argued that this prohibitory statute did not apply to incorporated municipalities that had charters passed by a two-thirds majority because any statute that regulated an incorporated municipality was, in effect, a charter amendment, and charter amendments had to be passed by a two-thirds majority of all elected members of the legislature. The liquor law had not received the requisite two-thirds assent.

Justice Nelson said the two-thirds clause was directed against private corporations that "had multiplied to an extent that had attracted public attention, especially banking institutions." On the other hand, "the organization of communities, and investing them with the privileges of mere municipal jurisdiction and authority, were not at all in contemplation. . . . This wide distinction was well known to the members of the Convention, and shows that the clause in the Constitution may be fully satisfied by confining its operation to the cases of private corporations."[28]

THE NEED FOR MORE COMMERCIAL CREDIT

By the mid-1830s, the Regency's banking policy was anachronistic, which put it on an unstable economic foundation. It did not provide enough legitimate credit for urban entrepreneurs to promote maximum economic growth, and it channeled too much credit into highly speculative projects. In 1834, the Whigs condemned the system for these reasons, plus its extremely partisan administration; and in late 1835, the *New York Journal of Commerce* reached the same conclusion. It said that the first aim of the state's banking system should be to supply the credit needs of businessmen: "Keep the bandages from the infant Hercules—give him the free use of his limbs and he will become a giant."[29]

The first half of the 1830s had been a period of exceedingly rapid industrial and commercial growth, especially in New York City. Industrialization was accelerated by the application of steam power to factory production while, at the same time, the size of the markets tributary to New York was being enlarged by the growing canal networks in Ohio, Indiana, and Illinois and by steamboat service on the Great Lakes and interior rivers. Abundant bank credit was needed by entrepreneurs who wished to construct local improvements, exploit larger markets, or utilize new technologies. Businessmen were the best persons to judge the need for new banks and the credit they created, not the politicians who passed the charters.[30]

The politicians tended to give charters to themselves or friends, as a means of getting rich quickly, without regard to efficiently serving the needs of commerce. In 1829, Albert Gallatin, Jefferson's ex-Secretary of the Treasury and a Wall Street banker at the time, estimated that a sound volume of banknote credit would provide a circulation of about seven dollars per person. In 1832, New York was just under this theoretical figure (assuming a population of two million), but a large part of it was based on the watered capitalization of the country banks (See Table 1). In the same year (1832), the country banks had a total capitalizaiton of 8.3 million dollars, and they circulated 8.0 millions in banknote currency. They had already expanded banknote credit to the limits of safety at the time the Bank of the United States ceased regulating the credit practices of state banks. In comparison, the city banks had a capitalization of 11.9 millions but circulated only 4.2 millions in banknotes.

Assuming a population of 2.2 million persons in 1836, a safe circulation would have been 15.4 million dollars, instead of the actual 22.1 million. This was a highly inflationary level. The ratio between the total credit extended (loans plus banknote circulation) by the city banks in 1832 to their reserves (specie plus deposits) was 3.9 to 1, while that for the country banks was 6.9 to 1. In 1836, the ratio of credit to reserves in the city banks had actually declined to

Table 1
VOLUME OF BANKNOTE CREDIT (IN MILLIONS OF DOLLARS)

	THEORETICAL VOLUME BASED ON CIRCULATION OF $7 PER PERSON	ACTUAL CIRCULATION	COUNTRY BANK CIRCULATION	CITY BANK CIRCULATION
1832	14.0	12.2	8.0	4.2
1836	15.4	22.1	13.9	8.2
1838	16.1	17.7	13.3	4.4

SOURCES: Robert E. Chaddock, *The Safety fund Banking System in New York, 1829-1866*, 296-297. Alonzo B. Hepburn, *A History of Currency in the United States*, 122.

2.9 to 1, while the country banks had increased theirs to 8.1 to 1 (See Table 2). Thus, by 1836, it is clear that the city banks still provided sound credit but that the country banks had been profligate in expanding banknote credit.

Economic growth was best promoted by facilitating the orderly expansion of credit where it was needed instead of clogging the channels of commerce with a large volume of highly discounted banknotes. In 1832, the total banking capital in New York was 20.2 million dollars, of which 11.9 millions were located in New York City, but in 1836, when bank capitalization had been increased to 32.5 millions, it was almost evenly divided between New York City and the country banks (See Table 3). This indicates that the amount of credit available to New York City businessmen grew proportionally smaller, as measured by capitalization, although increased deposits overcame part of this deficit. Furthermore, the large number of new and inadequately capitalized banks in small towns created an unsafe situation without centralized restraints on their credit practices, which allowed deposits to be quickly converted into banknotes for spending.

By July 1836, most Safety Fund banks had very low reserves to cushion the sharp deflationary pressures of Jackson's specie circular. This abrupt change in national monetary policy caused three banks in Buffalo to fail early in 1837, and the failure of the Dry Dock Bank in New York City in May triggered the Panic. All state banks suspended specie payments, something the Democracy had boasted would never happen. When the first Safety Fund bank failed and its assets were put into receivership, it was found that the Fund could not be used until there had been an audit of the bank's assets and they were found inadequate to cover its liabilities. Such a situation was contrary to the intent of the Safety Fund. Its specific purpose was to guarantee the value of the notes a bank circulated immediately upon a bank's failure, so they would continue to circulate at par until they were redeemed. The Safety Fund statute was hastily amended to allow its immediate use upon a bank's insolvency, but the amendment failed to limit the liabilities for which the fund was made responsible by the term *debt*. As the statute stood, the Safety Fund had to pay off all of a failed bank's debts, including deposits.

Table 2
RESERVES AND CREDIT EXTENDED (IN MILLIONS OF DOLLARS)

	COUNTRY BANKS				CITY BANKS			
	Total Reserves	Specie Reserves	Total Credit	Reserve Ratio	Specie Reserves	Total Reserves	Total Credit	Reserve Ratio
1832	3.3	.5	22.8	6.9 - 1	1.3	6.4	25.0	3.9 - 1
1836	5.5	1.7	44.7	8.1 - 1	3.9	15.1	44.7	2.9 - 1
1838	5.9	1.5	43.6	7.4 - 1	4.4	15.2	34.4	2.3 - 1

SOURCES: Robert E. Chaddock, *The Safety Fund Banking System in New York, 1829-1866*, 296-297. Alonzo B. Hepburn, *A History of Currency in the United States*, 122.

Table 3
CAPITALIZATION (IN MILLIONS OF DOLLARS)

	COUNTRY BANKS	CITY BANKS	TOTAL
1832	8.3	11.9	20.2
1836	15.9	16.6	32.5
1838	15.8	16.6	32.4

SOURCES: Robert E. Chaddock, *The Safety Fund Banking System in New York, 1829-1866*, 296-297. Alonzo B. Hepburn, *A History of Currency in the United States*, 122.

New York's banking statistics of 1838 are remarkably similar to those of 1836. This is because the over-extended country banks tried to stave off insolvency by carrying their bad debts as assets. This was difficult to do and eleven banks failed in rapid succession from 1840 to 1842. The Safety Fund was bankrupted. Only after the Fund was hopelessly insolvent was the word *debt* replaced with *circulating notes*.[31] Chaddock's description of the causes of insolvency is a litany of speculative loans made to bank officers who were, in many cases, politically powerful. This pattern of irresponsible management was repeated in most states. In 1837, the nation plunged into a depression, which bottomed in 1843. In that year, the circulation of the country banks was reduced to 5.5 million dollars, about what it had been in 1830 but their specie reserves were about twice what they had been in 1831. The noteholders of bankrupt Safety Fund banks lost an average of 20 to 25 percent of their value. The fiscal dislocations directly attributable to speculative banking were especially harmful to New York and other industrially advanced states.

The causes of the inflationary spiral of the mid-1830s and the panic-depression that followed were mostly beyond state control. This is true in spite of the basic flaws in the Safety Fund system: (1) its poor economic management; (2) its excessive liability for debts; (3) the failure of the Regency to create a state central bank; and (4) the loose operation of the free banking statute in its early years.

These fiscal uncertainties, in conjunction with the failure of the state's recently constructed branch canals to yield an adequate revenue, carried New York to the verge of bankruptcy in 1843. Under similar circumstances, Pennsylvania went over the brink.

A principal cause of the depression was President Jackson's destruction of the Bank for the national political advantages that would accrue to the Democratic party, especially in the South but also in large sections of the North and West. Van Buren approved of Jackson's action because its popularity furthered his presidential ambitions; and there is little doubt that, on the whole, it was a popular political act. The Bank's destruction accentuated three major distortions in the national economy: it strongly contributed to runaway inflation, it produced a congeries of unreliable state currencies, and it disrupted the orderly creation and allocation of credit.

The continued existence of the Bank would probably not have been able to prevent some sort of recession. Too many state banks were chartered in too short a time for it to adequately superintend their credit practices. Even the Suffolk Bank could not cope with the avalanche of notes circulated by the seventy-eight new banks chartered in Massachusetts between 1830 and 1836. Early in 1836, the Suffolk Bank's corresponding banks were overdrawn by more than $600,000, and it was not in a position to force them to reduce their overdrafts.[32] The Suffolk system did not save New England from suspension nor Massachusetts from numerous bank insolvencies, but it did facilitate a return to a stable currency and a sound credit structure, and it did survive the depression. If the Bank of the United States had existed, it could have restrained credit expansion in the mid-1830s, as it had done in the past, and it could have increased the amount of credit available during the depression. These central banking functions would have helped smooth the boom-bust cycle of 1834–1843. The Bank's destruction left a vacuum in this important sector of national power.

After the Bank's destruction, the national government had greatly reduced power to regulate the pulse of economic growth, and these powers were sporadically and haphazardly applied: the tariff (which steadily declined after 1833), land grants to certain internal improvement projects, river and harbor appropriations, mail subsidies, and military surveys. Some of these aids were of considerable value, but frequently there was an insufficient allocation of credit to effectively exploit the government's initial work. The lack of an effective national policy of economic growth, as well as the lack of an effective means of regulating the growth that was taking place, meant that the Federal Courts alone exercised some degree of continuing supervision over some of the forces that were vastly increasing the volume of interstate commerce. However, the Court's effectiveness was largely negative; that is, it prevented the erection of flagrant barriers to the interstate movement of goods and services. This power, however, was increasingly threatened by the slavery issue, which prevented the exercise of any effective supervision by Congress.

The Safety Fund system was also on an unstable political foundation in spite of being buttressed by the restraining statutes and a friendly court's interpretation of the two-thirds clause. Democratic control of the legislature was increasingly threatened by Locofoco and entrepreneurial opposition. It did not matter that the opposition tended to go in two directions, one in favor of more banks and the other advocating fewer banks of issue. They could both agree that the political management of the Safety Fund was a political evil and if they gained control of the legislature, they would destroy the Safety Fund system.

The close connections between entrepreneurs and banking is best documented in Massachusetts. From the beginning of industrialization, New England textile manufacturers had close business relationships with banks, especially those textile manufacturers that had transferred large blocks of capital from foreign commerce into cotton textile manufacturing and who already possessed experience in the use of finance capital.[33] The banking-manufacturing relationship was greatly facilitated by Massachusetts' bank policy. The Massachusetts legislature granted any legitimate application for a bank charter regardless of the political affiliation of its promoters. This policy was never changed, because by 1830, the state's one percent tax on banking capital was the largest single source of general revenue, and more banks meant more revenue. Massachusetts' liberal policy of chartering new banks made the banking business essentially nonpolitical. The nonpolitical character of

Massachusetts' banking meant that new banks could readily be chartered to aid the growth of new industrial or commercial ventures. Each sizable community had at least one bank and perhaps several, so that there was effective competition. In the larger cities, banks could be chartered that specialized in meeting the credit needs of one branch of commerce or industry. Their major weakness was their low capitalization, but communities willingly accepted this in order to have a local source of credit.[34]

By the end of 1836, Massachusetts, with a smaller commercial and industrial base than New York, had approximately 160 banks in operation (about one-quarter of the banks in the nation) with an aggregate capitalization of 38 million dollars. In contrast, New York had ninety banks, but only 32.5 million dollars in bank capital; and nearly half of the capitalization belonged to the country banks that specialized in circulating banknotes.

New York entrepreneurs wanted to duplicate Massachusetts' bank policy by forcing the Regency to adopt a policy of chartering all legitimate applications for bank charters or, if that failed, overthrow the Safety Fund system and initiate a free banking policy. In 1836, ninety-three new charter applications were submitted to the legislature—enough to double the number of banks in the state. The applications came in a presidential election year with New York's favorite son seeking the Presidency. The Democracy was placed on the horns of a dilemma: should it support the Locofocos and refuse to charter any more banks, or support the entrepreneurs and charter many more banks. The Regency compromised and approved charters for only twelve new banks.

A free banking bill does not appear to have been introduced in this election year, but a general incorporation bill for mutual insurance corporations, or associations, was. It came before the Senate Committee on Banks and Insurance. The Committee reported that it did "not mean to be understood as expressing a decided opinion against the constitutionality of a general law; they consider the point unsettled. . . . The Committee does not believe it expedient for the legislature to enact a general law authorizing the formation of mutual insurance companies."[35]

The Regency's stratagem of using the Bank War to shift attention away from the Safety Fund system had worked for a while—long enough to elect Van Buren President, but the reckoning was at hand. The New York legislative election of 1838 resulted in a permanent shift of power. A major reason for this shift was the Regency's inflexible bank policy in the previous six years. The triumphant Whigs passed a free banking law in 1838, which had the effect of seriously impairing the Regency's effectiveness. In the next eight years, the Democratic party was in office only half of the time, compared with its dominating position in the previous twenty-two years. What the banking issue began, the slavery issue completed: the destruction of the Regency. In the sixteen years between 1846 and 1862, the Democrats won the governorship for only one two-year term.

NOTES

1.   *Albany Argus,* April 14, 1828. See also William L. MacKenzie, *The Life and Times of Martin Van Buren,* 85–86.

2.   *Messages from the Governors of New York,* Vol. 3, 240–244, Jan. 6, 1829, Martin Van Buren.

3.   *New York Laws,* Ch. 94, 1829, 167. Bray Hammond, *Banks and Politics in America from the Revolution to the Civil War,* 549, 561–563. The substitution of *debts* for *banknotes* appears to have been unintentional. The general regulatory statute for banks passed by the Massachusetts legislature in 1829 (Ch. 96) made bank stockholders personally liable for the redemption of banknotes only.

4.   Robert E. Chaddock, *The Safety-Fund Banking System in New York, 1829–1866,* 261–273. Carter Goodrich, *The Government and the Economy: 1783–1861,* 337–350. Fritz Redlich, *The Molding of American Banking: Men and Ideas,* Vol. 2, Part 1, 191–194. Walter Hugins, *Jacksonian Democracy and the Working Class,* 188.

5.   In the same year, the Massachusetts legislature passed a general regulatory statute for banks on the assumption that every legitimate application for a bank charter would be passed, like the New York policy toward turnpike corporations. This statute authorized the governor to appoint a temporary three-man commission to inspect each newly incorporated bank to see if 50 percent of its specie capitalization was in the bank's vault before it opened for business. *Mass. Laws,* Ch. 96, 1829, 144.

6.   Robert E. Chaddock, *The Safety-Fund Banking System in New York, 1829–1866,* 267–269. *The People* v. *The Manhattan Co.,* 1832, 9 Wendell 351.

7.   Frank O. Gatell, "Sober Second Thoughts on Van Buren, the Albany Regency, and The Wall Street Conspiracy," *Journal of American History*, Vol. 53, 1966, 27-35. Frank O. Gatell, "Money and Party in Jacksonian America: A Quantitative Look at New York City's Men of Quality," *Political Science Quarterly*, Vol. 82, 1967, 245-247. Bray Hammond, *Banks and Politics in America from the Revolution to the Civil War*, 351-358. Frank O. Gatell, "Spoils of the Bank War: Political Bias in the Selection of Pet Banks," *American Historical Review*, Vol. 70, 1964, 44, 48-49. John M. McFaul, "The Politics of Jacksonian Finance," University of California Dissertation, 35-38.

8.   Jean A. Wilburn, *Biddle's Bank: The Crucial Years*, 48, 93, 99-103, 116, 129. Robert E. Chaddock, *The Safety-Fund Banking System in New York, 1829-1866*, map on 274, 283, 296-297. *Assembly Documents 1834*, No. 69, 4; *1835*, No. 74, 20-22.

9.   James R. Sharp, *The Jacksonians versus the Banks: Politics in the States After the Panic of 1837*, 297-299. *Assembly Documents 1833*, No. 89.

10.   William L. MacKenzie, *The Life and Times of Martin Van Buren*, 88.

11.   Davis R. Dewey, *State Banking Before the Civil War*, 8-26, 59-60. Robert E. Chaddock, *The Safety-Fund Banking System in New York, 1829-1866*, 285-287. Jabez D. Hammond, *The History of Political Parties in the State of New York*, Vol. 2, 447-449. Bray Hammond, *Banks and Politics in America from the Revolution to the Civil War*, 574. Ivor D. Spencer, "William L. Marcy Goes Conservative," *Mississippi Valley Historical Review*, Vol. 31, 1944, 213-215. Ivor D. Spencer, "William L. Marcy and the Albany Regency," *Brown University Dissertation*, 243-244. *Senate Documents 1834*, No. 47; 64; 89; 94. William L. Marcy subscribed to share in the Lockport bank and a bank at Oswego where a branch canal also supplied surplus water to flour mills. Marcy's total bank investment was $3,000 to 1832. Attorney General Greene C. Bronson invested at least $16,000 in the stock of six banks and his successor, Samuel Beardsley, invested at least $5,500 in three banks.

12.   Bray Hammond, *Banks and Politics in America from the Revolution to the Civil War*, 351-357, 419-421, 429-430, 438. Walter B. Smith, *Economic Aspects of the Second Bank of the United States*, 160-165. Fitzwilliam Byrdsall, *The History of the Loco-Foco or Equal Rights Party*, 27, 39-40, 68, 76, 99-102. *Senate Documents 1834*, No. 105; *1835*, No. 25. *New York Laws*, Ch. 130, 1834, 160.

13.   Nathan Miller, *The Enterprise of a Free People*, 116-129, 158-164, 224-227, Appendix I and II. Jabez D. Hammond, *The History of Political*

Parties in the State of New York, Vol. 2, 428–430. *New York Laws*, Ch. 286, 1831, 256.

14.   Jean A. Wilburn, *Biddle's Bank: The Crucial Years*, 100.

15.   Bronson owed his advancement to the Regency. He served as Attorney General from 1829 to 1836 and as a Supreme Court justice from 1836 to March 1845, when he was appointed Chief Justice, replacing Samuel Nelson who was appointed to the United States Supreme Court. Under the Constitution adopted in 1846, the Court for the Correction of Errors was replaced by the Court of Appeals as the highest judicial tribunal in the state. In the first judicial election, Bronson was elected one of the Appeals Court justices.

16.   This quote and the next three quotations come from Hiram E. Sickels, ed., *Opinions of the Attorneys-General of the State of New York*, 59–63. See also *Senate Documents 1835*, No. 4.

17.   Committee of Democratic Republicans to Marcy, Oct. 6, 1834; Marcy to the Committee, Oct. 11, 1834 (Marcy papers) from Ivor D. Spencer, "William L. Marcy and the Albany Regency," Brown University Dissertation, 247.

18.   Sedgwick to Van Buren, Dec. 29, 1834 and Cambreleng to Van Buren, Nov. 2, 1835 (Van Buren papers) from John M. McFaul, "The Politics of Jacksonian Finance," University of California Dissertation, 210–214. Flagg to Hoyt, Oct. 3, 1836, from William L. MacKenzie, *The Lives and Opinions of Benjamin F. Butler and Jesse Hoyt*, 117. Azariah C. Flagg, *Banks and Banking in the State of New York from the Adoption of the Constitution in 1777 to 1864*, #7.

19.   Jabez D. Hammond, *The History of Political Parties in the State of New York*, Vol. 2, 462–463, 477, 489–492, 502. Fitzwilliam Byrdsall, *The History of the Loco-Foco or Equal Rights Party*, 187. Richard Hofstadter, "William Leggett, Spokesman of Jacksonian Democracy, *Political Science Quarterly*, Vol. 58, 1943, 586–587. William Trimble, "Diverging Tendencies in the New York Democracy in the Period of the Locofocos," *American Historical Review*, Vol. 24, 1919, 407.

20.   Marvin Meyers, *The Jacksonian Persuasion*, 12–21, 83–90, 102–105, 146–154 (quote from page 86). Joseph A. Schumpeter, *Business Cycles*, Vol. 1, 294–295. Joseph Dorfman, "The Jackson Wage-Earner Thesis," *American Historical Review*, Vol. 54, 1949, 298–306. Edward Pessen, "The Workingmen's Movement of the Jacksonian Era," *Mississippi Valley Historial Review*, Vol. 43, 1956, 431–440. Rondo Cameron, *Banking in the Early Stages of Industrialization*, 36–41, 52–56. George S. Gibb, *The Saco-Lowell Shops*, 58–62. George R. Taylor, ed., *The Early Development of the American Cotton Textile Industry*: Nathan Appleton, "Introduction of the Power Loom and Origin of Lowell," Samuel Batchelder,

"Introduction and Early Progress of the Cotton Manufacture in the United States," xxvii, 30. Walter Hugins, *Jacksonian Democracy and the Working Class*, 183, 191–198.

21.   Bray Hammond, *Banks and Politics in America from the Revolution to the Civil War*, 494.

22.   Arthur M. Schlesinger, Jr., *The Age of Jackson*, 78, 192–199, 218–220. Carl. N. Degler, "The Locofocos: Urban Agrarians," *Journal of Economic History*, Vol. 16, 1956, 324–330. Richard Hildreth, *The History of Banks*, 137–139.

23.   James W. Hurst, *Law and the Conditions of Freedom in the Nineteenth Century United States*, 6, 17 (quotation on page 6).

24.   Joseph L. Blau, ed., *Social Theories of Jacksonian Democracy*, XXIV; 75 (William Leggett, Nov. 21, 1834, editorial in the *New York Evening Post*); 215–218 (John W. Vethake, Oct. 21, 1835, editorial in the *New York Evening Post*); 222–223 (Theodore Sedgwick, Jr., *What Is a Monopoly? Or Some Considerations Upon the Subject of Corporations and Currency*, 1835), 231–233.

25.   *Craig* v. *Missouri*, 1830, 4 Peters 410. Joseph Story, *Commentaries on the Constitution of the United States* (1833), Vol. 3, 19-20. *Briscoe* v. *Bank of Kentucky*, 1837, 11 Peters 257.

26.   Chief Justice John Marshall had said as much in 1824. It was "a sound principle that when a government becomes a partner in any trading company it divests itself, so far as concerns the transactions of that company, of its sovereign character, and takes that of a private citizen." It took only a slight extension of this reasoning to apply it to a bank wholly owned by the state: *Bank of the United States* v. *Planters Bank of Georgia*, 1824, 9 Wheaton 904. Edwin M. Dodd, *American Business Corporations Until 1860*, 40.

27.   *New York Fireman Insurance Company* v. *Ely*, 1824, 2 Cowen 711. See also *The People* v. *Utica Insurance Company*, 1818, 15 Johns 366. Bray Hammond, *Banks and Politics in America from the Revolution to the Civil War*, 566–570, 577.

28.   *The People* v. *Morris*, 1835, 13 Wendell 336–338.

29.   *New York Journal of Commerce*, Oct. 30, 1835 from John M. McFaul, "The Politics of Jacksonian Finance," University of California Dissertation, 118, 211–214.

30.   Rondo Cameron, *Banking in the Early Stages of Industrialization*, 94–99. The very rapid industrialization of Scotland had been immeasurably facilitated by a competitive banking system relatively free from politics. Walter Hugins, *Jacksonian Democracy and the Working Class*, 191. Stuart Bruchey, *The Roots of American Economic Growth, 1607–1861*, 147–150. Richard Hildreth, *The History of Banks*, 78, 89–91.

31. *New York Laws*, Ch. 380, 1837, 381; Ch. 247, 1842, 306.

32. Robert E. Chaddock, *The Safety Fund Banking System in New York, 1829-1866*, 6-7, 25-27, 304-322, 228, 351-359. Davis R. Dewey, *Financial History of the United States*, 225, 260. William G. Sumner, *A History of Banking in the United States*, 23-25, 233-234. Alonzo B. Hepburn, *A History of Currency in the United States*, 119.

33. Barbara Vatter, "Industrial Borrowing by the New England Textile Mills, 1840-1860, A Comment," *Journal of Economic History*, Vol. 21, 1961, 217-221. Lance E. Davis, "The New England Textile Mills and the Capital Markets: A Study of Industrial Borrowing, 1840-1860," *Journal of Economic History*, Vol. 20, 1960, 1-30. Lance E. Davis, "Stock Ownership in the Early New England Textile Industry," *The Business History Review*, Vol. 32, 1958, 204-222.

34. Paul B. Trescott, *Financing American Enterprise: The Story of Commercial Banking*, 5-9, 31-37. Richard Hildreth, *The History of Banks*, 126-137. Rondo Cameron, *Banking and the Early Stages of Industrialization*, 311-313. J. Van Fenstermaker, *The Development of American Commercial Banking, 1782-1837*, 77-80.

35. *Senate Documents 1836*, No. 25, 2.

6

The Free Banking System, 1838-1846

THE FREE BANKING STATUTE

Comptroller Azariah C. Flagg, writing anonymously in December 1836 in the *Albany Argus*, finally had the opportunity to put the Regency on public record as favoring the creation of free banks, provided they came under the provisions of the Safety Fund. "The [restraining] law as it now exists abridges the fair business rights of individuals, discountenances the free use of capital, and is detrimental to trade and commerce." Along with a free banking statute, he strongly supported the repeal of most of the provisions of the restraining laws, so that individuals could open offices to receive deposits and discount banknotes. When the legislature assembled in January 1837, Governor Marcy, in his annual message, favorably mentioned restricting the scope of the restraining laws.[1]

Two free banking bills were introduced in the 1837 legislature: one was for banking associations and the other was for limited partnerships. The one for associations authorized these businesses to engage in all aspects of banking, including issuing notes. They would be taxed the same as incorporated banks, and all of the regulations that applied to incorporated banks would apply to them, including the Safety Fund. The principal difference between associations and incorporated banks was in law suits. All suits involving associations were to be filed in the president's name or directed against the president.

When Attorney General Bronson was elevated to the bench, his successor Samuel Beardsley was presented with the same question

Bronson had faced in 1834. The legislature asked him about the constitutionality of the two bills that would create an unlimited number of banks by calling them something different than corporations, namely, associations and limited partnerships. In Beardsley's opinion, the associations had all the common law attributes of corporations, and none of the attributes of unincorporated associations. "The bill was manifestly designed to confer on banking associations . . . every essential attribute of a corporation." Therefore, in Beardsley's opinion, the associations were corporations, no matter what one called them, and the bill was unconstitutional because it created an indefinite number of corporations.[2]

Beardsley also submitted an opinion on the constitutionality of the second bill, which would have created an indefinite number of limited partnerships having all banking privileges except the right to issue notes. The partners were to have limited liability once all shares were fully paid-in but, until such time, shareholders had the full liability of a general partner; nor would the death of one of the limited partners dissolve the partnership. Beardsley said this bill was unlike any statute then in force, and the attributes conferred on the partnership made it a "body corporate, in the constitutional sense of the term." It in no way resembled either a co-partnership or a limited partnership; and since it sought to create an unlimited number of corporations, it was unconstitutional.

The legislature did not pass either free banking bill because the Senate refused to act, but the Assembly's Committee on the Two-Thirds Law believed that the bill for banking associations did not require a two-thirds majority in spite of the Attorney General's opinion. The legislature did, however, restrict the scope of the restraining laws.[3] Individual brokers were allowed to open offices of discount and deposit, but they could not issue evidences of debt that could circulate as money. The privilege of creating banknote credit was still reserved to the chartered banks. Restricting the scope of the restraining laws accomplished the substance of what the limited partnership bill proposed to do. It allowed discount-deposit brokers to organize as individual proprietors or partnerships but without limited liability or the power to create banknote credit.

Although the party made a strategic retreat by repealing most features of the restraining laws, it held fast to the policy of protecting the exclusive power of the chartered banks to create banknote credit. The 1837 report of the Bank Commissioners backed this policy by urging the legislature not to enact a free banking statute. The report of the Senate Committee on Banks and Insurance also stressed the need to limit the number of banks issuing notes. The Committee was also of the opinion that associations and partnerships had too many built-in defects to provide a stable currency, and all other quasi-corporate devices had been labeled unconstitutional.

The Committee, however, did make four recommendations. The first would require all Safety Fund banks to redeem their notes at par in New York City, and the second would give the state the power to regulate the intrastate discount rate. In effect, this was a proposal to make the state's chief bank of deposit (The Mechanics Bank of Albany) a state central bank to restrain the banknote credit practices of the Safety Fund banks. The third recommendation would have prohibited state banks from receiving as collateral the stock of any other state bank. This had become a problem because many bank investors had borrowed money to pay the first call for capital on their stock, then when the stock was placed in their hands they used it as collateral for loans, often from the same bank. The Bank Commissioners had been recommending this change since 1835. Finally, the Committee recommended that the mode of distributing the stock of newly chartered banks be changed. Only the last of these recommendations was enacted into law.

Almost immediately, the Panic came and the legislature authorized all banks to suspend specie redemption of their notes. The suspending law also restricted the volume of banknotes each bank could issue, since banks were no longer required to redeem them. Suspension was authorized for a year; otherwise, under the provisions of the revised statutes, all suspending banks would lose their charters and the state's credit system would be in danger of liquidation.[4] Inflation, the Panic, and suspension led to an overwhelming Whig election victory in the autumn legislative election of 1837. The Whigs interpreted their victory as a mandate to overturn the Safety Fund system. They were determined to pass a free banking statute, free from the semi-monopoly requirement of a special charter of incorporation.

Governor Marcy made an eleventh hour attempt to retain Democratic control of the state: he proposed two measures he believed would restore public confidence in banking and secure his re-election in the fall. In his annual message of 1838, he recommended passing a free banking statute: "I am inclined to the opinion that the legislature have the power to pass such a law; but the spirit of the Constitution requires that it should be passed as a two-thirds bill." Even though he publicly favored a free banking law, in private he strongly objected. He realized that it would undercut the party's economic base, as well as undermine public confidence in the Safety Fund system. In an effort to restore public confidence in the state's banking system, he recommended, in a special message, that the legislature authorize the issuance of six or eight million dollars worth of canal bonds to finance future construction, but until this work began, the Commissioners of the Canal Fund would deposit the money in Safety Fund banks to help them resume specie payments at the earliest possible date. The Whig-controlled legislature ignored Marcy, and specie payments were resumed in May 1838 without state aid.

Marcy's full about-face, in advocating a free banking statute, was triggered by the introduction in Congress in September 1837 of President Van Buren's sub-treasury bill. The sub-treasury bill, when it was finally passed, completed the radical separation of the national government from all banking corporations, a policy begun by the Bank veto in 1832. Van Buren's national policy forced the New York Democratic party to advocate, as a matter of principle, the separation of partisan politics from the banking business. A free banking statute was the only acceptable solution.

Marcy thought the corporation was the best means of organizing banks, but if the legislature had constitutional scruples, then limited partnerships could be made to do. He had his doubts about repealing the provisions of the restraining laws that prohibited individuals from issuing notes that could circulate as money; however, if ample security could be provided, he would approve even this. Marcy further recommended that free banks be required to keep a specie reserve of 15 or 20 percent for the day-to-day redemption of their notes, but he said nothing about bringing them under the provisions of the Safety Fund.[5]

Van Buren's attempt to rally Locofoco and entrepreneurial

support with his sub-treasury bill was a failure, as was Marcy's deathbed conversion to the virtues of a free banking statute. "This rejection of him [Van Buren] by his own state within a year of his succession to the Presidency was sad business, but it was largely the result of the inflation of bank credit, stimulated by the overthrow of the federal Bank, which he as much as any one—perhaps more—had instigated in the interest of New York's banks."[6]

The Whig-controlled Assembly followed Marcy's lead and looked for a way to sustain the constitutionality of a free banking statute. The first step was to refute the opinions of past Attorneys General that had called such a statute unconstitutional. The Assembly's Judicial Committee quoted the 1834 opinion of Greene C. Bronson when he had said that amendments to the 1811 general incorporation statute for manufacturing corporations would be constitutional. The Whigs proposed to amend the 1811 statute to include silk manufacturing and mining, and in so doing, they discussed the extent of the legislature's power to amend corporation charters.

The Committee described all statutes that regulated business corporations as, in effect, amendments to their charters. If corporate regulatory statutes were conceived as charter amendments, they would have to be passed by a two-thirds majority of the legislature, according to a literal interpretation of the Constitution. Obviously, this was not the intent of the Constitutional Convention of 1821. It would be an intolerable situation. Statutes regulating the powers of private corporations had always been passed by a majority vote. The Supreme Court had confirmed this interpretation in 1835 in *The People* v. *Morris*. Using this reasoning, the report's drafters concluded that a statute that regulated the creation of business corporations (even an indefinite number of corporations) could be conceived as a corporation regulatory statute and be enacted by a majority vote. Constitutionally speaking, such a statute would be no different from those that regulated existing corporations and were passed by a majority vote. The argument was a sham, but it provided a legal fig leaf for action the Whig majority was determined to take. The Whigs proceeded to pass a free banking statute, but it was enacted by the vote of two-thirds of the legislators present, not those elected.[7] The backers of the statute ignored Governor Marcy's suggestion that they use the corporation and trust that the courts would sustain its constitutionality. They called the free banks "associations" because they lacked a two-thirds majority of all elected members.

In preparation for passing the free banking statute, the Whigs repealed the Democratic-sponsored statute of 1835, which forbade banks from circulating notes of less than five dollars' value. Safety Fund banks were temporarily authorized to circulate lower valued notes (until 1841), but thereafter, the five-dollar limit went back into effect. The statute was worded in such a way that after 1841 the free banking associations would have the exclusive privilege of circulating banknotes under five dollars. This statute was passed for two reasons: during the Panic, there was a shortage of small coins to carry on commerce and the free banking statute would require all banknotes (regardless of denomination) to have securities backing them. When all banknotes had securities on deposit to guarantee their value, the circulation of low-value notes ceased being an issue.[8]

There were two major features to the free banking statute: a general incorporation procedure, and a method to guarantee the value of the paper currency these banks circulated. The Whigs abandoned the Safety Fund as collateral for banknotes. Instead, free banks were required to deposit 100 percent security for their banknotes. The securities could be the bonds of New York or the United States or of any other state approved by the Comptroller; or mortgages on unencumbered productive land in New York. They were to be held in trust by the Comptroller. All associations circulated a currency that was registered with the state, and they could circulate any amount as long as they placed securities of equal value in the hands of the Comptroller.

As part of the legal fiction of calling these banks "associations," the banknotes they issued were called "circulating notes"; and suits against them were commenced in the name of the president. The associations had a perpetual life and no upper limit of capitalization, but there was a minimum capitalization of $100,000. Any number of persons could form an association, including just one person. This characteristic, besides making the associations different from corporations, allowed the banknote brokers who had gone into the discount-deposit business after the repeal of the restraining statutes in 1837 to incorporate themselves and secure full limited liability. The fiction that associations were not corporations was further buttressed by inserting a reserve clause in the statute because the one in the revised statutes applied only to corporations; nor was the Bank Commission given jurisdiction over associations.

From 1838 to 1840, in spite of the deepening depression, the number of free banks increased immensely. In the first six months after its passage, over fifty charter applications were received, and before the end of 1839, a total of 134 certificates were filed. During the first three years of its operation, 167 charters were filed, but 78 of these never went into operation and of the first 80 that opened for business, 20 failed within three years. From 1838 through 1855, there were 438 charters filed, of which 231 either never went into operation, voluntarily closed, or failed. "It was a great thing politically. It was all things to all men. It promised more business opportunities, more banks, and more money, and protection for the public."[9] Free banks were strongly desired by entrepreneurs, particularly corporate entrepreneurs who wanted to enter new types of businesses or expand existing ones. Free banks offered the opportunity to create larger amounts of long-term credit by persons who pledged real property as part of the assets required to give 100 percent backing to the currency the banks circulated. Many of the early investors pledged mortgages, but in return they insisted on loans being made to them.

The conservative city bankers foresaw its speculative use and immediately organized to restrain its influence. The officers of the larger commercial banks in New York and Boston organized the Bank of Commerce, a free bank. The Bank of Commerce was a banker's bank designed to sustain the integrity of the notes of participating banks through a clearinghouse system of redemption—in the same way the Suffolk System worked in Massachusetts and the Mechanic's Bank of Albany could have operated if the Regency had desired. The Bank of Commerce regulated the banknote credit practices of associated banks through re-discounting. It was a successful use of the free banking statute to bring some order out of the fiscal uncertainty it created.

During the depression, from 1838 to 1844, the legislature was faced with the difficult task of trying to sustain public credit. This unhappy situation was further complicated by the bankruptcy of the Safety Fund and the imperfect operation of the free banking system. The Safety Fund system and the free banking system did not easily mesh because the Whigs insisted that banking associations were legally different from banking corporations; therefore, the laws that regulated the chartered banks did not apply to free banks. The weaknesses became evident in 1839 when the first free banks began business.

Free banks began purchasing their own notes at a discount, as well as the notes of country banks. They found that they could make a handsome profit by shaving notes, especially since some of the country banknotes were being discounted as high as 6 percent. This high discount rate was the result of the refusal, after the Panic, of the city banks to accept country banknotes at face value. Thus, the earliest free banks used a considerable portion of their capital for speculative purposes and not to provide needed commercial credit. Furthermore, since many of the free banknotes were unfamiliar to the public, there was often a high discount on them. The irregular discount rates worked a heavy burden on the orderly flow of commerce.

In 1840, the legislature followed the recommendations of the Comptroller and the Bank Commission on the method to end this abuse. All state banks (chartered and free) were required to keep an office or agent in New York City or Albany to redeem their notes at a maximum discount of one-half of one percent. All banks were given permission to set up a pooling arrangement to clear their notes, such as the city banks had done when they organized the Bank of Commerce. In effect, the law forced all state banks to form a mutual state central bank to restrain any excesses of banknote credit with the object of keeping the currencies of both banking systems at par. The law was highly successful because it achieved its objective within a year.[10]

Another defect in the free banking statute was the security of its notes. The law gave the Comptroller discretionary authority to accept or reject securities and mortgages to back the currency. When the law first went into operation, he accepted at market value the bonds of other states, as well as those of New York. The high rate of failure among the early free banks caused many of these securities to be sold soon after they had been deposited, and it was found that they had heavily depreciated. For example, Indiana and Illinois bonds sold for only 49 percent of their face value, while New York bonds retained 92 percent of their value during the worst stringencies of the depression. Mortgages fared little better. Because of these imperfections, the noteholders of insolvent free banks before 1845 lost nearly 39 percent of their value when presented for redemption. In 1840, the legislature required the Comptroller to accept only New York bonds as collateral for free bank currency. This created a large captive market for New York securities during the depths of the depression, which was a considerable aid in sustaining the state's credit.[11]

Even in spite of the poor redemption rates on the notes of insolvent free banks during the first few years of its operation, the law remained popular. "Banking ought to be free. Every man who wishes should be at liberty to engage in it."[12] There was, however, general agreement that there should be some further liability for bank stockholders to redeem their notes in case of bankruptcy. Double liability was frequently mentioned. Condy Raguet, one of the most influential supporters of a precious metal currency, was also a strong supporter of New York's free banking statute because he believed that the currency issued by them represented real capital that could not be inflated.[13]

When recovery was under way in 1844, the Comptroller was authorized to accept United States bonds as backing for the currency circulated by free banks, and individual free bankers were allowed to circulate banknotes if they deposited only $50,000 in securities with the Comptroller. With the return of prosperity in 1848, the Comptroller was again authorized to accept mortgages on unimproved, unencumbered land in New York, exclusive of buildings, but such mortgages could not be for more than $5,000, nor could they represent more than 40 percent of a property's assessed value. It had been especially difficult during the depression to sell mortgages larger than $5,000, and the sale of all mortgages had yielded an average return of only 63 percent. These liberalizations (acceptance of mortgages and being able to enter the banking business with a $50,000 deposit) encouraged the formation of many new banks, especially in smaller communities. The credit they created was available to help finance the 1850s boom in branch line railroad construction.

From the point of view of capitalist investors and entrepreneurs, the free banking statute was the means of equalizing the opportunities for creating and using credit and for participating in the profits of commercial banking. This was achieved by severing the link between politics and the process of securing a bank charter. It was the key law in the development of laissez-faire doctrine in New York because it opened the sensitive business of providing currency and credit to public participation with few restraints. In the end, most Locofocos were satisfied with a fully backed currency and a national government that paid its debts in specie; and most businessmen were satisfied because no restraints were placed on the creation of new banks or the use of deposit credit. The use of deposit credit grew rapidly after 1850 in the commercially mature states.[14] In the meantime, the constitutionality of the free banking statute was being vigorously challenged in the courts.

THE FREE BANKING STATUTE IN THE COURTS

The constitutionality of the free banking statute was immediately challenged. Its opponents used the arguments Attorney General Bronson had constructed in 1835. The first test was *Thomas* v. *Dakin*, decided in the October 1839 term of the New York Supreme Court.[15] The case arose when a free bank president, Anson Thomas, sued to collect a delinquent debt. Dakin, the debtor, argued that banking associations were corporations; the bill creating them had been passed by a majority of elected members of the legislature and not two-thirds as required by the Constitution; and any bill creating an indefinite number of corporations at the pleasure of individuals was unconstitutional. Therefore, banking associations could have no legal existence. The law suit was thus alleged to be the case of an unconstitutional bank suing to collect an illegal debt.

If the court agreed, then all of the contracts made by free banks would be in grave danger of becoming unenforceable because the legislature, by conferring essentially corporate powers on free banks was in effect overruling the two-thirds clause of the constitution. This the legislature could not do. Furthermore, if banking associations were not corporations, they were created in defiance of the restraining laws that forbade unincorporated banking. Any contract made by an unincorporated banking association would be void on one of two counts: they were constitutionally repugnant or they contravened the restraining laws. These contracts would violate one of the major premises of legal interpretation, that any contract must take into consideration the laws in force at the time it was made, and any contract that violated this principle was void from its inception.

In defense of its constitutionality, the free bankers said that free banking associations were not corporations because: (1) perpetual succession and limited liability were specifically bestowed on them, while these attributes were inherent in corporations under common law unless otherwise limited; (2) suits ran in the name of the association's president; and (3) the statute allowed individuals to be associations, which was an innovation. In addition, they claimed that the free banking statute was merely a total repeal of all restraining statutes. It was wholly in accord with the spirit of the Constitution because the two-thirds clause should be construed to strike a blow at monopoly, not to sustain one, and since associations were not corporations, a statute creating them could be passed by a majority vote of the legislature.

All three judges agreed that banking associations were corporations, no matter what the legislature called them, but a majority of the court held that these corporations were constitutional. Bronson, however, restated the interpretation of the two-thirds clause he had written as Attorney General, and dissented from his associates. He still thought a general incorporation statute allowing creation of an infinite number of corporations was unconstitutional. The majority, speaking through Chief Justice Samuel Nelson, held that the legislature had the power to create an infinite number of corporations by a general law, provided such a law was passed by two-thirds of the elected members of the legislature. Furthermore, they presumed that the free banking statute had been passed by the requisite majority because the statute was printed in the session laws. If it were passed by less than the requisite majority, this would require a new plea.[16]

Bray Hammond calls this decision "legalistic and reactionary in form but revolutionary in substance." It was revolutionary because it "put the corporate form of enterprise in a very new light . . . it exhibited the corporation as a democratic device, with which *laissez faire* was to accomplish more than it ever could otherwise."[17] This is true as it applied to the popular identification of corporate banking with privilege. By stubbornly identifying free banks as corporations, the old image of corporate privilege was shattered, but it did not create an entirely new corporate image. The general incorporation law for manufacturing enterprises had been functioning for twenty-eight years. This decision really belongs in the same category as *Briscoe* v. *Bank of Kentucky*, which legalized state banknotes, because it was a pragmatic legalization of a large percentage of New York's currency. Several similar cases were decided in the same way, and two were immediately appealed to the Court for the Correction of Errors. It is noteworthy that these appealed cases were decided by Senators voting as politicians and only incidentally as judges.

The two appealed cases were *Warner* v. *Beers* and *Bolander* v. *Stevens*.[18] Counsel for the debtors immediately went to the heart of the argument: "If, as the Supreme Court says, these associations are corporations and the legislature has the power to pass general incorporation statutes by the requisite two-thirds majority of all elected members of the legislature, then the whole case hinges on the actual majority which passed the statute." He charged that "this court ought to, and will, as the Supreme Court should have done, take judicial notice, without plea, by what majority the act . . . was passed." The lack of a two-thirds majority was "well known as matter of law or fact"; therefore, the whole "act is void for the want of assent of two-thirds of all the members elected to each branch of the legislature."[19]

Chancellor Reuben Walworth, speaking for the court, gave the authoritative interpretation of the Constitution. He denied that the court was authorized to look beyond the printed statute book; however, he did "not intend to express any definitive opinion, as it has never been brought before the Supreme Court in such a manner as to give the judges of that court an opportunity to express an opinion." He declined to overrule a law that had been assented to by two-thirds of those members present and signed by the Governor. It was a delicate political issue that was best left untouched by the courts.

Walworth had to find a rationale for sustaining the law. He went back to the intent of the two-thirds clause. "This language," he said, "is not in all cases to be construed literally; but it is to be construed according to its spirit and intent, so as to carry into effect the will of the convention, and of the people by whom this fundamental law of the state was framed and adopted. . . . It is proper for the court to . . . contemplate as they did, the evil to be remedied. . . . It is known to us as a matter of public history, that previous to 1821, great complaints had been made in relation to the granting of corporations with exclusive rights and privileges. . . . Such complaints had been made, particularly in relation to corporations with banking powers." It is certain that neither the convention nor the people who ratified the Constitution ever contemplated judicial rejection of a law granting equal right to every inhabitant in the state to associate for profit as long as these associations were at all times under the control of the legislature.

> This general law does not create monopolies, nor does it grant privileges to any individual which may not be enjoyed by any other, nor are any of these groups, even temporarily, beyond the control of the legislature. . . . For this reason, though I have no doubt that some of the powers given to the associations . . . are strictly corporate powers, so as to constitute such associations bodies politic corporate . . . I do not think the law comes within the spirit and intent of this restrictive clause of the Constitution, so as to require a two-thirds vote either to pass the law, or to alter or modify the provisions thereof.[20]

The Supreme Court's judgment was affirmed allowing free banks to recover their debts. The vote was 22 to 1. The court then resolved that the free banking law "is valid and was constitutionally enacted, although it may not have received the assent of two-thirds of the members elected." The vote was 23 to 1. It also resolved that free banking associations "are not bodies politic or corporate within the spirit and meaning of the Constitution." This was adopted 22 to 3.[21]

These decisions and the resolutions threw the whole legal profession into confusion. Were the associations corporations? And if they were, to what extent? In the same year, 1840, in *Delafield* v. *Kinney*, the Supreme Court, with Justice Bronson speaking, clarified a matter of procedure regarding suits against banking associations. They were corporations, and the provision in the statute by which they were to be sued in the name of the president was another method of bringing suit, but not the only way. The procedure in the revised statutes, whereby the name of the corporation was used, was equally good.[22]

At the end of 1840, there was a judicial impasse. One court insisted that associations were corporations, but refused to go behind the statute book to ascertain if the law had been constitutionally enacted. The other said they were not corporations "within the spirit and meaning of the Constitution." The free bank of Watertown decided to take advantage of this conflict. It refused to pay its capitalization tax. The case came before the Supreme Court in July, 1841, as *The People* v. *The Assessors of Watertown*. In this case, Bronson, again speaking for the court, explained some of the issues of *Warner* v. *Beers*, probably to head off a flood of litigation that would take advantage of this conflict between the courts. In doing so, he took some ironic swipes at his fellow judges on the Court of Errors:

> Senator Verplanck, who went further than anyone else towards denying their corporate capacity, concluded his opinion with the very cautious and guarded remark, that these associations under the banking law do not rightly fall within the true legal interpretation of the restraining clause of the Constitution, and still less within its spirit and design. This is far enough from saying that the free banks . . . are not corporations to every intent and purpose save that which related to the mode of creating them. True, the Constitution speaks of "any body politic or corporate," without limit or qualification; and although I have never been able to see how one class or description of corporations can be in, and another out of the provision, yet others have been able to make such a distinction. . . .

There is no ground for supposing that the other members of the court intended to deny the corporate capacity of these associations. The resolution which was adopted was carefully worded, so as to exclude any such inference. It does not affirm that the free banks are not corporations, but only that they are not such "within the spirit and meaning of the Constitution." . . . It would be highly derogatory to the court to assume that this qualified language was used without meaning. . . .

On the day or the day following the decision . . . in the case of *Warner* v. *Beers*, a resolution was offered by Senator Verplanck, affirming in direct and unqualified terms that these associations "are not bodies politic or corporate." Whether the mover was himself prepared to vote for such a resolution, or whether it was only offered for the purpose of collecting the sense of the members . . . I am unable to say. But that such a resolution could not have passed, is, I think, quite clear. It was laid on the table . . . and was not again taken up until 13 or 14 days later. When the consideration of the resolution was again resumed, it was immediately amended by unanimous consent— the mover himself, as I believe, not objecting to that course—by adding the very significant words, "within the spirit and meaning of the Constitution," and in that form was adopted. Now whatever may be inferred from simply reading the resolution as it finally passed, the history which I have given . . . renders it impossible to say that any member who voted for the resolution intended to deny that these associations are corporate bodies . . . I may add the further fact . . . that the Chancellor, who fully agreed with this court in the opinion that these banks were corporations, voted for the resolution as amended—indeed, I believe the amendment was proposed by him, and for the avowed purpose of meeting the views of those who agreed with him . . . that the free banks, though corporations were not such within the intent and meaning of the Constitution.

I have said this much much concerning the case of *Warner* v. *Beers* because . . . the bar seems to have fallen into the prevalent error of supposing that the court of last resort has held that our free banks are not corporate bodies. . . . It is high time the decision should be properly understood. What the Court for the Correction of Errors may hereafter hold upon this question, I will not undertake to determine, though I think there is very little probability that any court will ever say, in explicit terms, that these banks are not corporations.

Bronson went on to say:

> It may be true, as has been argued, that the legislature intended to
> make a legal being and give it all the essential attributes of a corporate
> body, and yet that it should not be a corporation. That, the legislature
> could not do. . . . Human powers are not equal to the task of chang-
> ing a thing by merely changing its name.[23]

Bronson concluded that banking associations were corporations for
purposes of taxation.[24]

What was the purpose of the collusion of both courts to agree in
substance while using opposed interpretations of the Constitution?
Both courts agreed that the free banking law was too popular to
void: the problem was to find a rationale to sustain it. The courts
could not harmonize this. Justice Bronson was a legal conservative.
He was alarmed at the potential growth of redundant and confus-
ing terminology that would rob accepted definitions of all meaning.
Bronson was saying, do not complicate the law by creating another
class of quasi-corporations. From this position, he and his fellow
Supreme Court justices refused to budge. Their remedy was to
change the Constitution, to bring the intent of the framers into harmony with the economic facts of the day. The Court of Errors, on
the other hand, was looking for a political face-saver, and was
more than willing to concede that associations were corporations as
long as the Supreme Court would let the fiction stand that they
were legally different. They wanted to allow the Constitution to
stand as it was, and to interpret it to fit the political realities of the
times, without giving a thought to what effect this action would
have on the structure of the law.

In April 1841, the case of *The People* v. *The Mayor of New York*
came before the court.[25] It involved a statute that had reorganized
the city's judiciary. A judge had been appointed to fill one of the
newly created vacancies and the statute directed the city to pay
him. The City Comptroller refused, not having been authorized by
the City Council, whereupon the unpaid judge applied to the
Supreme Court for a writ of mandamus. The city argued that the
judicial reorganization statute was an unconstitutional amendment
to a municipal corporation charter because it had failed to receive

the assent of two-thirds of all elected members of the legislature. Chief Justice Nelson, speaking for the court, said the distinction between private and public corporations was clear and well understood, and the two-thirds clause did not apply to public corporations. This opinion was a reaffirmation of *The People* v. *Morris*, but no constitutional issue was tested because Nelson said the writ applied for was the wrong one and the court could not accept jurisdiction.

In October of that year, the same issue reappeared before the court in *The People* v. *Purdy*. This time, there was an opportunity to judge the constitutional issue. The judicial reorganization statute had also annulled the right of aldermen to act as judges on the Court of General Sessions. This duty had been conferred upon them by the city's 1730 charter, and subsequently confirmed by the state legislature. Alderman Purdy used the same argument as above, that the statute had failed to receive the requisite two-thirds assent and was, therefore, unconstitutional.

The court majority reasoned otherwise. In the Court's opinion, the statute was constitutional because it did not abolish the office of alderman, which was an integral part of the city's charter, nor did it diminish the alderman's power. "The passing of the act of 1840 was not an attempt to alter a body politic or corporate, but the exercise of another legislative power entirely distinct—the power to take jurisdiction away from one court and transfer it to another."

Bronson dissented and said: "It has not been denied that the judicial tribunals of the state may, in some way, look beyond the printed statute book . . . ," which was an oblique way of saying, we can look if we want, or can refuse if we wish, just as the court had done in *Thomas* v. *Dakin*. In this case, Bronson denied that *The People* v. *Morris* was a valid precedent. The law involved in that case was a general statute applying to every citizen within the state, not just to one municipality. That sort of application was a legitimate exercise of the state's police power, and was only incidentally related to incorporated municipalities.

The wording of the two-thirds clause was meant to be inclusive. In fact, the exact issue now before the court had been anticipated at the 1821 convention. It had been asked whether the all-inclusive wording of the two-thirds clause was meant to apply to public as well as to private corporations. The reply had been yes, that "two-thirds would never be wanting to incorporate a village or a turn-pike." The clause was adopted unanimously. Therefore, "we have here the most unequivocal proof . . . that the framers of the Constitution meant precisely what they said."[26] Bronson believed the judicial reorganization statute was unconstitutional. The case was appealed and came before the Court of Errors in December 1842, as *Purdy* v. *the People*.

The Court of Errors overruled the Supreme Court by a vote of 13 to 11 because the majority was captivated by Bronson's minority opinion that this case had been exactly anticipated by the debates of the convention. It offered the Senators the opportunity of returning to the virtues of literal interpretation. Senator Paige, speaking for the majority, said: "Already have we, by lending too unguarded an ear to arguments in favor of a latitudinarian mode of interpreting the Constitution, struck out from the operation of the two-thirds clause, the identical corporations which are now admitted by everyone to be within the evil intended to be remedied. The case of *Warner* v. *Beers* consummated this judicial miracle."[27] The majority would follow this lead so long as it did not challenge the free banking interest. As long as this was not done, they could afford to be literal.

How did things now stand? The Court of Errors said free banks were not corporations within the "spirit and meaning of the Constitution," while the Supreme Court said they were identical to chartered banks; however, both courts agreed that the free banks were corporations for purposes of taxation. The Supreme Court said the two-thirds clause did not apply to municipal corporations, but the Court of Errors said it did.

In the years following 1841, the Supreme Court three times reaffirmed its opinion that free banking associations were corporations.[28] In the major case, *The People* v. *The Supervisors of Niagara*, 1842, a free bank resisted paying the corporation tax, but as we have seen in the *Watertown* decision, the bank sought to test the interpretation of the tax law rather than avoid paying the tax on constitutional grounds. In this case, Bronson affirmed the *Watertown* decision, that free banks and chartered banks were identical corporations and subject to the same corporate tax; however, the case was appealed to the Court of Errors on constitutional grounds, a major shift in emphasis from the original argument. The decision of the appealed case, *The Supervisors of Niagara* v. *The People*, was rendered in December 1844.

The obvious course was to affirm the decision in *Warner* v. *Beers* and declare that free banks were not corporations within the meaning of the tax law. This was done, but the favorable majority was only 11 to 8. The minority was almost entirely composed of those wishing to maintain the fictitious distinction between associations and corporations in order to guarantee the constitutionality of the free banking statute. Senator Bockee, speaking for this group, said:

> That learned Judge [Bronson] who delivered the opinion of the court professes that he is unable to comprehend how it can be that one class of corporations are within and another out of the Constitution. I confess that I labor under the same disability. To my vision, perhaps obtuse, but in this instance not more so than that of the learned Judge, it appears that the moment it is established that these institutions are corporations, it follows conclusively and irresistibly that they could not be constitutionally created by a bare majority of the legislature. I leave it to other minds more clearsighted than mine to discover how two propositions directly contradictory can both be true.

Senator Bockee went on to say:

> I have no doubt that these institutions ought to be taxed on their capital in the same manner as incorporated banks. . . . During the last two sessions of the legislature I have introduced bills in the Senate for taxing the free banks in the same manner as moneyed corporations. The passage of such bills was resisted on the ground that it would be unjust and inexpedient to make them so liable. I am not of that opinion. But believing that they are not corporations, I think they cannot be legally taxed as such until the legislature shall so provide.[29]

FREE BANKS AS THE CATALYST FOR A NEW CONSTITUTION

For the subsequent judicial history of the free banking law, it is necessary to consider the agitation that occurred preliminary to holding the Constitutional Convention of 1846. In 1844 and 1845, as in 1834, a bill came before the Senate to amend the 1811 general manufacturing statute. In 1844, the Judiciary Committee of the Assembly thought such an amendment would be unconstitutional, but in the next year an opinion was solicited form the Attorney General regarding the constitutionality of such an amendment. A bill had already passed the Assembly by a majority vote. The Attorney General, John Van Buren, did the best he could.[30] He affirmed the constitutionality of free banks, as matters then stood, but said there was another interpretation of the two-thirds clause recently given in *Purdy* v. *The People*, which extended the two-thirds clause to all public and private corporations. This made the amendment to the general manufactuing statute unconstitutional unless it received a two-thirds majority. The amendment died in the Senate. Three months later, the situation was thrown into utter confusion when the Supreme Court, in *DeBow* v. *The People*, invalidated the free banking law.

As long as the free banking system was not in direct jeopardy, the banking and corporation controversy was a dormant issue. Yet once the system was threatened, it became a major contributing factor toward holding a convention. If a convention were held, it would certainly embed the free banking system in the new Constitution. The major reason for holding a convention, however, was to limit the state's power to contract debts. During the depression, New York had had difficulty sustaining payments on the debts it had incurred to build canals and subsidize railroad construction. A large, powerful, and morally outraged part of the electorate wanted to write a debt ceiling into a new constitution and prohibit further state aid to private corporations.

Three other grievances generated support for a constitutional convention. Mob violence erupted in 1845, after an attempt was made to collect arrears in quit-rents on the Van Rensselaer Estate. A deputy sheriff was killed and Governor Silas Wright had been forced to declare one county in a state of insurrection in order to restore order. The tightly organized Van Rensselaer tenants wanted to make quit-rents unconstitutional. There was also a strong desire to revise the state's judiciary by increasing the number of judges and make them elective; and a vociferous minority of Locofocos was in favor of full Negro suffrage.

In 1844, the legislature received petitions from twenty-five counties praying for a referendum to call a constitutional convention. Governor Wright did not favor a convention and suggested that the legislature should pass the needed amendments. The legislature ignored his recommendation and, in May 1845, authorized a referendum in November. If it passed, delegates would be elected in April 1846, and the convention would assemble on the first of June. In the November 1845 election, 80 percent of the voters favored a convention.[31]

DeBow v. *The People* was the first case decided in the May 1845 term of the Supreme Court. The decision was rendered at the time the legislature was debating the advisability of holding a convention referendum. DeBow had been convicted of counterfeiting and passing the notes of a free bank. He challenged his conviction on the grounds of the constitutionality of the free banking law. If the law was not passed by the requisite majority, then the bank had no legal existence and his "crime" was nonexistent.

Bronson, now Chief Justice, speaking for the court, said the question of the validity of the statute "is directly and necessarily presented."[32] It was now known from looking at a copy of the engrossed bill in the office of the Secretary of State that it had not been passed by the requisite two-thirds majority. The obvious meaning of the Constitution was that a two-thirds assent was required for "every bill creating any body politic or corporate." The first exception was made in *The People* v. *Morris*. This exception rewrote the Constitution to read, "bills creating public corporations may be passed by a majority vote; and bills creating private corporations may be passed in the same way provided there is no monopoly, but if you wish to create a single private corporation which is a monopoly, then the assent of two-thirds of the members shall be required."[33] This was confirmed in *Warner* v. *Beers*, and reconfirmed in *The People* v. *The Assessors of Watertown*. However, in Bronson's opinion, this position was completely overthrown by the Supreme Court's decision in *The People* v. Purdy, which held that municipal charters had to be passed or amended by the requisite two-thirds majority.[34] The Court of Errors then took this position in *Purdy* v. *The People*. The Court of Errors, by upholding Bronson's opinion, discarded the authority of *Warner* v.

Beers. It was discarded because the Court had looked behind the statute book and found that the law amending New York City's charter had not received the requisite majority.

According to Bronson, "No judicial officer whether lawyer or layman, had ever yet ventured upon the unqualified assertion that these companies are not corporations," although in *Warner* v. *Beers,* two added resolutions denied that they were corporations "within the spirit, intent, and meaning of the Constitution." Bronson called these added resolutions an extra-judicial proceeding, entitled to great respect but not having the authority of a judicial decision; therefore, in *Purdy* v. *The People,* "the whole of this legal heresy was, as I humbly conceive, directly overruled. . . . The conclusion is obvious. Having examined and ascertained that the general banking law did not have the assent of two-thirds of the members of either house, it follows that . . . the banking companies which have been organized under it have no legal existence."[35]

It was not a coincidence that the decision in *DeBow* v. *The People* was rendered in the same month that the legislature was debating the calling of a constitutional convention. By undermining the free banks, Bronson was enlisting a powerful group in support of a convention, which would, of necessity, remove the two-thirds clause and embed free banks in the constitution.

Bronson as much as said so:

> The restraining law, which makes the monopoly, may undoubtedly be repealed by a majority vote; and I hope the day is not very distant when this, and other kindred laws which needlessly shackle men in their lawful pursuits, will either be greatly modified or wholly erased from the statute book. I am as firm a believer in the sentiment that the people are governed too much, as I am in the doctrine that where the Constitution speaks in unequivocal terms, and tends to no great evil or absurdity, it should be followed at all events—leaving the work of making amendments to the people, to whom it rightfully belongs.[36]

Bronson saw that the two-thirds clause was the greatest of the restraining laws, but because he placed a higher value on the integrity of legal terminology, he could not consent to interpreting it away. He did everything in his power to force its repeal by an amendment. He dramatized the issue at the most opportune time. He was now willing to come out into the open and declare the free banking statute unconstitutional, which it had been impolitic to do in *Thomas* v. *Dakin*, trusting that the case would be appealed and probably not acted upon until a new constitution was adopted.

A subsequent case, *Gifford* v. *Livingston*, decided on the precedent of the *DeBow* case, was appealed, and reached the Court of Errors in December 1845. This was one of the last cases to be decided by that court before it went out of existence under the new constitution. Practical political economy prevailed, and *DeBow* v. *The People* was overruled. Chancellor Walworth used *The People* v. *Purdy* to explain the Court's reasoning. The *Purdy* case had distinguished "between a general excise law extending alike to the whole state, and a law touching the charter of a single city. . . . That is precisely the distinction which I attempted to draw in the case of *Warner* v. *Beers*, between an act authorizing any association of individuals to exercise corporate powers for certain purposes, and that special legislation for the benefit of particular individuals . . . against which the Constitution was intended to guard. . . . If ever there was a case in which the principle of *stare decisis* should be applied to the decision of the court . . . this appears to be a proper . . . application."[37]

The opposition, with Senator Hand as its spokesman, said: "If as this court held in the case of *Purdy* v. *The People*, the constitutional provision under consideration embraces all corporations, public and private, and if it be also true that the institutions organized under the general banking law are corporations as was determined in *The Supervisors of Niagara* v. *The People*, it is difficult to see how the case of *Warner* v. *Beers* can be sustained. It seems to me there is no escape from the charge of irreconcilable inconsistency in our decisions."[38] He was right, but it depended on what interest group was being threatened. It was politically safe to apply the two-thirds clause to municipal corporations, but it would be economic and political suicide to overturn the free banking system. The Chancellor's opinion was accepted 15 to 7. The *New York Tribune* commented editorially on this decision as "most just and salutary," and felt congratulations were due, "that this long vexed question is at last put at rest."[39]

Thereafter, the new constitution abolished the Court of Errors and replaced it with the Court of Appeals. Chief Justice Bronson was elected a Justice of the new court. In *Gillet* v. *Moody*, which came before the new court in July, 1850, Bronson, in some *obiter dicta*, said of free banks:

> They are not corporations in a qualified sense, *as within the intent and meaning of some particular statute*, but are corporations to all intents and purposes. If anything can be settled by judicial decision this is settled. There was a difference of opinion between the Supreme Court and the Court of Errors on the question whether the Constitution applied to the free banks—the Supreme Court holding that it was applicable alike to all corporations, while the Court of Errors thought it applied only to corporations created by special charter. . . . But both courts were agreed that the free banks are corporations. If there was room for doubt on this point after the decision of the Court of Errors in *Warner* v. *Beers* . . . *The Supervisors of Niagara* v. *The People* removed all grounds for such a doubt.[40]

In short, the judicial conflict had served the important purpose of enlisting a powerful interest in favor of a constitutional convention, which of necessity revised the corporation clauses. Now, Bronson was for forgetting the whole issue.

NOTES

1. Robert Chaddock, *The Safety Fund Banking System in New York, 1829–1866*, 373–375. *Messages from the Governors of New York*, Vol. 3, 627–628, Jan. 3, 1837, William L. Marcy. *Albany Argus*, Dec. 19, 1836.

2. Hiram E. Sickels, ed., *Opinions of the Attorneys-General of the State of New York*, 78; *Assembly Documents 1837*, No. 303.

3. Hiram E. Sickels, ed., *Opinions of the Attorneys-General of the State of New York*, 78; *Assembly Documents 1837*, No. 304. *New York Laws*, Ch. 20, 1837, 14. *Assembly Journal 1837*, 1087, 1155.

4. Robert E. Chaddock, *The Safety Fund Banking System in New York, 1829–1866*, 278–279, 285–288, 301, 324–325. *Senate Documents 1837*, No. 38, 10–11. *New York Laws*, Ch. 235, 1837, 233. In 1834, Governor Marcy had suggested that commissioners be used to auction bank stock to investors, but the legislators had refused to end this source of personal reward.

5. Ivor D. Spencer, *The Victor and the Spoils, A Life of William L. Marcy*, 91. Ivor D. Spencer, "William L. Marcy Goes Conservative," *Mississippi Valley Historical Review*, Vol. 31, 1944, 221-223. *Messages from the Governors of New York*, Vol. 3, 654-656, 666, Jan. 2, 1838; 702-703, April 12, 1838, William L. Marcy. *New York Laws*, Ch. 450, 1837, 514.

6. Bray Hammond, *Banks and Politics in America from the Revolution to the Civil War*, 582: see also 496-499, and Ivor D. Spencer, *The Victor and the Spoils, A Life of William L. Marcy*, 91-94.

7. *Assembly Documents 1838*, No. 275; 277. *New York Laws*, Ch. 250, 1838, 245.

8. *New York Laws*, Ch. 46, 1835, 37; Ch. 51, 1838, 26. See Chapter 4, footnote 6.

9. Bray Hammond, *Banks and Politics in America from the Revolution to the Civil War*, 596.

10. Robert E. Chaddock, *The Safety Fund Banking in New York State, 1829-1866*, 305-307. Bray Hammond, "Long and Short Term Credit in Early American Banking," *Quarterly Journal of Economics*, Vol. 69, 1934, 95-96. William G. Sumner, *A History of Banking in the United States*, 313. Condy Raguet, *A Treatise on Currency and Banking*, 316-318. Franklin B. Hough, *New York Convention Manual, 1867*, Part 2, Statistics, 161. *Assembly Documents 1840*, No. 44, 5-12.

11. Robert E. Chaddock, *The Safety Fund Banking System in New York, 1829-1866*, 339-341, 446-448. Condy Raguet, *A Treatise on Currency and Banking*, 316-317. *Assembly Documents 1841*, No. 64, 6. *New York Laws*, Ch. 202, 1840, 154; Ch. 363, 1840, 306.

12. Anon., "Banking as it Ought to Be," *United States Magazine and Democratic Review*, Vol. 12, 1843, 425.

13. Condy Raguet, *A Treatise on Currency and Banking*, 205.

14. Bray Hammond, *Banks and Politics in America from the Revolution to the Civil War*, 594-599. *Constitutional Convention Documents of 1846*, No. 34, 5; Statement D. Davis R. Dewey, *Financial History of the United States*, 260. *New York Laws*, Ch. 41, 1844, 25; Ch. 281, 1844, 416. A similar statute was passed in 1846, allowing bankrupt Safety Fund banks to postpone the sale of real estate they owned, in order to avoid crippling losses when sold on a distressed market: *New York Laws*, Ch. 97, 1846, 100.

15. Bray Hammond, "Free Banks and Corporations: The New York Free Banking Act of 1838," *Journal of Political Economy*, Vol. 44, 1936, 197-205. *Thomas v. Dakin*, 1839, 22 Wendell 81.

16. *Thomas v. Dakin*, 1839, 22 Wendell 111-112.

17.   Bray Hammond, *Banks and Politics in America from the Revolution to the Civil War*, 586.

18.   *Warner* v. *Beers*, 1840, 23 Wendell 103; *Bolander* v. *Stevens*, 1840, 23 Wendell 103.

19.   *Warner* v. *Beers*, 1840, 23 Wendell 111–112.

20.   *Warner* v. *Beers*, 1840, 23 Wendell 125–128.

21.   *Warner* v. *Beers*, 1840, 23 Wendell 189–190.

22.   *Delafield* v. *Kinney*, 1840, 24 Wendell 347.

23.   *The People* v. *The Assessors of Watertown*, 1841, 1 Hill 617–620, 622–623.

24.   The same conflict occurred in Michigan, which also had a two-thirds clause in its constitution. In 1837, the Michigan legislature passed a free banking statute, which was a copy of the one defeated in New York in 1837. The interpretation of the two-thirds clause in Michigan's Constitution came before the Federal Circuit Court in 1840; Justice McLean sustained Michigan's free banking statute and accepted the New York Supreme Court's opinion in *Thomas* v. *Dakin* that associations were corporations. He said that the number of corporations created by any one law was a matter of policy, not of principle as long as the statute was passed by the requisite majority: *Falconer* v. *Campbell*, 1840, 8 McLean 195; West Publishing Co., Vol. 8, Case 4620, 963. The Michigan Supreme Court reversed this decision in 1844 (*Green* v. *Graves*, 1844, 1 Douglass 351), but it was never appealed to the United States Court for final arbitration. Four years later, the Michigan Supreme Court (*Brooks* v. *Hill*, 1848, 1 Mich. 118) held that all contracts made under the provisions of Michigan's free banking statute were void from the beginning. See Ronald E. Seavoy, "Borrowed Laws to Speed Development: Michigan, 1835-1863," *Michigan History*, Vol. 59, 1975, 41–52.

25.   *The People* v. *The Mayor of the City of New York*, 1841, 25 Wendell, 679.

26.   *The People* v. *Purdy*, 1841, 2 Hill 37.

27.   *Purdy* v. *The People*, 1842, 4 Hill 398.

28.   *Willoughby* v. *Comstock*, 1842, 3 Hill 389. *The People* v. *The Supervisors of Niagara*, 1842, 4 Hill 20. *The Matter of the Bank of Danville*, 1844, 6 Hill 370.

29.   *The Supervisors of Niagara* v. *The People*, 1844, 7 Hill 508. There was a whole series of statutes that applied the regulations covering chartered banks to banking associations. Chapter 130, 1841 applied bankruptcy procedures and Chapter 319, 1841 required associations to file financial reports similar to those of the chartered banks. All these statutes

attempted to bulwark the fictitious distinction between banking corporations and banking associations that had been made in *Warner* v. *Beers*.

30.   Hiram E. Sickels, ed., *Opinions of the Attorneys-General of the State of New York*, 129. *Assembly Documents 1844*, No. 162. *Senate Documents 1845*, No. 59.

31.   Charles Z. Lincoln, *The Constitutional History of New York*, Vol. 2, 9, 64, 102–103.

32.   The court consisted of Bronson, Jewett (a newly elected District Judge), and Samuel Beardsley. Beardsley had been Bronson's successor as Attorney General and had followed Bronson's reasoning in giving an opinion that the free banking bill was unconstitutional, when it was being considered by the legislature in 1837.

33.   *DeBow* v. *The People*, 1845, 1 Denio 13.

34.   This was not quite true. Bronson's argument in *The People* v. *Purdy* was a dissent.

35.   *DeBow* v. *The People*, 1845, 1 Denio 17–19.

36.   *DeBow* v. *The People*, 1 Denio 12.

37.   *Gifford* v. *Livingston*, 1845, 2 Denio 386–388.

38.   *Gifford* v. *Livingston*, 1845, 2 Denio 394.

39.   *New York Tribune*, Jan. 3, 1846: from Bray Hammond, *Banks and Politics in America from the Revolution to the Civil War*, 591.

40.   *Gillet* v. *Moody*, 1850, 3 Comstock 385–386.

7

Corporation Policy
and the Constitution
of 1846

CORPORATION POLICY

The main reason for calling a Constitutional Convention in 1846 was the burden of public debt. After the depression, public opinion was overwhelmingly in favor of preventing the accumulation of future state debts. Most of New York's public debt had been acquired in the 1830s when the state built or underwrote the construction of many large-scale internal improvement projects. Most of the projects were canals, but later in the decade, several railroads received state subsidies. New York's experience with revenue derived from the Erie Canal was used as a selling point to secure public approval for these massive expenditures. Extravagant claims were made for the earning potentials of these projects in order to convince the public of the necessity of building them, either with public funds or by lending the state's credit to private corporations.[1] It was claimed the income from these projects would be sufficient to make them self-supporting and allow the state's property tax to be lowered or ended.

The people were eager for the economies of cheap overland transportation, and these selling points were very attractive in the easy-money years of 1830–1837. Canal building was undertaken on a vast scale in New York, Pennsylvania, Ohio, and elsewhere, and in the final two or three years before the depression, many states committed themselves to railroad projects as well. Since these projects were to be self-liquidating, their financing was usually shaky.

New York began a large-scale internal improvement program in 1835 by starting the enlargement of the Erie Canal and undertaking the building of an extensive network of feeder canals. It also subsidized the construction of one private canal company and twelve railroad corporations. By 1842, the state debt had reached $28 million, of which the vast bulk had been incurred to build canals. In that year, the legislature stopped all public expenditures on internal improvements without explicit legislative approval and levied a one-mill state property tax to sustain the state's credit. All future projects were restricted to those that could be financed out of current revenues.[2] This violent retrenchment was pushed through the legislature by fiscally conservative Democrats. On the basis of the new land tax, sufficient bonds were floated to meet the insufficient revenue from the feeder canals. The Common School Fund, the Free Bank Deposit Fund, and all banks were authorized to invest in these bonds.[3]

During the depression, five of the subsidized railroads went bankrupt, throwing the burden of paying their bonded debts on the state. The defaulted railroad debts totaled $3,515,700, of which $2.7 million was attributable to the New York and Erie Railroad, while the rest came from the Catskill and Canajoharie and the Ithaca and Owego Railroads. Two other railroads with a combined debt of $200,000 continued to make interest payments but ceased paying into the sinking fund. The other seven railroads and the canal company, with debts totaling $1.7 million, continued to make both interest and sinking fund payments.

The state could have acquired title to the bankrupt railroads for a small expenditure at a bankruptcy sale; however, when the state foreclosed on the Ithaca and Owego in 1842, the Comptroller declined to bid on the railroad's assets. Only one bid was made, for $4,500, and it was accepted.[4] The state did not want to get involved in managing any more internal improvement projects, which is why the state refused to foreclose on the New York and Erie Railroad when it defaulted and continued in default until after the 1846 Convention. The state hoped the New York and Erie would regain its solvency. The state's hands-off policy was designed to preclude New York from ever having to rescue any railroad corporation with a further public subsidy.

During the depression, most states had difficulty remaining solvent. Some repudiated their debts, some negotiated partial settlements, some deferred interest payments, and some barely managed to maintain interest payments by levying higher land taxes. Most states adopted policies of stringent restraints on capital expenditures. The state constitutional conventions held between 1842 and 1855 generally locked the door against further debt creation by forbidding new debts beyond certain low limits without a referendum, and forbidding the state to loan its credit to private corporations.[5]

This was a logical response to the failure of the inflated promises that were made at the time the states built the internal improvements; therefore, the states got out of the internal improvement business. It is not true, as some have said, that the state constitutional conventions held between 1842 and 1855 put the business corporation on trial.[6] What was on trial was the proper relationship of business corporations to the state, especially businesses like banks and railroads that affected the welfare of the whole state.

Prohibiting states from subsidizing any project undertaken by a private corporation was one aspect of the controversy involving the proper relationship of business corporations to the state. State loans that had been defaulted by business corporations had been responsible for a substantial portion of the state's debts, and the public demanded an end to all subsidies. The second aspect in the controversy over the proper relationship of business corporations to the state involved their creation. There was strong popular support for a policy of opening the opportunities for corporate profits equally to all entrepreneurs, which was, in turn, inseparably linked to the demand for a general incorporation statute for banks because free banks would provide the maximum amount of credit for entrepreneurs. The passage of the free banking statute, after the Regency-led Democratic party had been voted from office, indicated the direction of future corporation policy. Business corporations would be non-political at the time of their creation, and if certain classes of businesses required regulation, regulation would be based on the banking experience.

The policy of corporation creation under general laws was not a political issue at the 1846 Convention for two reasons: an over-

whelming majority of the delegates voted to embed the free banking statute in the Constitution, and the state was drastically limited
in the kinds of aid it could give to private business projects.
Limiting state aid to business corporations, particularly internal
improvement projects, implemented the greater policy of preventing the state from contracting future debts and removed any reason
for government favoritism, for or against, one class of business corporation. The great depression of 1837–1844 was the watershed in
the development of the modern American business corporation
because the state constitutional conventions held after 1840 almost
always contained provisions that effectively separated corporate
business opportunities from state politics; although, local franchises like gas light and omnibus companies continued to be
secured through local political influence.

The free banking statute made banking a nonpolitical business
because its general incorporation procedure opened banking to all
entrepreneurs who possessed the requisite capital, not just to those
who had political connections. Once the creation of banks was
thrown open to general capitalist participation, on the basis of sufficient prior regulation to protect the value of the currency, other
classes of businesses had little difficulty getting the same privilege.
The free banking statute marked a permanent shift in the state's
business policy; it cast the development of laissez faire business
doctrine into corporate form. This was the attitude of the 1846
Convention when it adopted, without much dissent, a provision to
allow general incorporation statutes for all business corporations.

General incorporation statutes satisfied some very powerful
social and economic interests. Local municipalities hungered for the
twin benefits of abundant credit and cheap, all-weather transportation, which banks and railroads promised. Railroad promoters
wanted free access to sources of capital and credit, as did the
municipalities they served, while fiscal conservatives dreaded the
growth of the state debts. These interests and the depression experience combined to crystallize the doctrine of laissez faire: the
radical separation of the state from corporate business enterprises
and the adoption of general incorporation statutes. As much as
anything else, general incorporation statutes kept the state governments from bestowing economic advantages on one group at the

expense of another; they opened the opportunities for corporate business profits to all individuals with initiative, capital, or technical skills; and capital contributions could be made in small quantities, were voluntary, and based on the investor's own judgment. A species of latter-day Jeffersonian doctrine was used to justify this position: "Government itself, abstractly considered, is a necessary evil, and our theory is to limit its actions within the narrowest bounds permitted by its necessity."[7] This was summed up by the Jacksonian phrase, "The world is governed too much," which was the core of laissez faire doctrine.

The constitutionalizing of laissez-faire doctrine came at a crucial period in the technological development of railroad transportation, when New York and the nation were on the threshold of enormous economic growth. General incorporation laws helped sustain an entrepreneurial momentum after the state and national governments abdicated economic leadership by refusing to participate in further internal improvement projects. They left promotion, construction, and management of railroad enterprises in private hands at a time when there was an enormous demand for railroads and an enormous desire on the part of individuals and municipalities to invest in them. The demand for railroad service created an equivalent need for credit to aid construction and take advantage of the new business opportunities that grew out of enlarged markets.

It is no accident of timing that the demand for free banking statutes coincided with the coming of the railroad age. Of the eighteen states (of thirty-two) that passed free banking statutes before 1860, sixteen were passed after 1849 when railroads began to carry large volumes of freight and earn high profits. Free banking systems were one of the more efficient means of meeting the need for more credit, and allocating it to towns and cities that underwent rapid growth with the coming of railroads, a situation that often eclipsed older centers of population based on river and canal commerce. New York's free banking statute of 1838 anticipated the railroad age because of the rapid commercial growth that had taken place in the previous ten years along the route of the Erie Canal. Free banks greatly expanded one of the most important functions of local development banks under the Safety Fund system—supplying considerable long-term credit to factories by constantly renewing short-term loans. By doing this, free banks helped to equalize the opportunities for individuals to make high profits and for communities to obtain long-term social benefits.[8]

General incorporation statutes for railroads and other classes of businesses opened these investment opportunities to the democracy. In the broadest policy sense, general incorporation statutes allowed corporation creation with all of the legal favors state governments could bestow, but without actually contributing capital. These statutes granted perpetual succession, single legal entity, self-incorporation at any time without political influence, concentration of management, limited liability for the investor, easy access to the courts, and a competitive access to all sources of capital and credit. General incorporation statutes for business enterprises were a major economic aspect of the social and political forces that democratized American society during the Age of Jackson, 1825–1855.

THE CONSTITUTION OF 1846

Fiscally conservative Democrats controlled the 1846 Convention, and the policies they favored were restrictions on state investments in internal improvement projects, low land taxes, and economy in government. Their election pledge had been safety in state finance, which meant preventing the state from undertaking further internal improvement projects or aiding their construction until the whole of the canal debt was paid. They made it mandatory (Article 7) for the legislature to extinguish the canal debt from canal revenues, and they limited future state indebtedness to one million dollars, except for the twin contingencies of repelling invasions or suppressing insurrections. Any future bond issue in excess of the one million dollar ceiling had to be approved by a statewide referendum, which had to include in it a tax provision to fund the bonds.[9] Furthermore, $200,000 per year was earmarked from the Canal Fund's net income to support the general government, and after the canal debt was paid, up to $672,500 per year could be taken from the canal's annual net income to defray the costs of the general government. The canal system was going to be made to yield direct financial benefits instead of being a potential source of fiscal weakness.

There were two sections of the new constitution that applied to all business corporations except banks; Article 8, Section 1, and Article 7, Section 9:

> Corporations may be formed under general laws; but shall not be created by special act, except for municipal purposes, and in cases where in the judgment of the legislature, the objects of the corporation cannot be attained under general laws. All general laws and special acts passed pursuant to this section may be altered from time to time or repealed.
>
> The credit of the state shall not, in any manner, be given or loaned to, or in aid of any individual, association, or corporation.

The convention believed that most business corporations should be created by general incorporation statutes, but this policy was not made mandatory because some members of the convention thought there might be circumstances where special acts would be needful or desirable; therefore, special charters for purposes other than banking were not entirely forbidden. The legislature retained some discretionary power to deal with unusual corporate situations, like the chartering of large cities, and this discretionary power was re-enforced by the adoption of a reserve clause. However, the intent of the convention was clear: wherever possible, corporations were to be created under general laws.

The section that forbade the state to loan its credit to any corporation or individual greatly restricted state aid to all business corporations engaged in building internal improvement projects, especially railroads. The restriction on state aid was further enforced by Article 1, Section 9, which required the assent of two-thirds of the elected members of both houses for every appropriation of public money or property for local purposes, but state aid was not entirely forbidden.[10] The legislature might still aid railroad construction by donations of land or money or by waiving taxes. The effect of these sections, however, was to reverse the earlier state policy of actively encouraging the construction of internal improvement projects; these sections completed the radical separation of the state government from all business corporations, first begun by the general incorporation statute for manufactories of 1811 and strongly confirmed by the free banking statute of 1838.

Similarly, Article 8, Section 9, was designed to curb municipal governments from pledging their credit resources: "It shall be the duty of the legislature to . . . restrict their [cities and villages] powers of taxation, assessment, borrowing money, contracting debts, and loaning their credit. . . ." Many municipalities, like the state, had borrowed money to aid railroad construction. In many cases, this debt had been a heavy burden during the depression. However, the advantages of all-weather railroad transportation were compelling, and every town of any commercial importance wanted rail communications as soon as possible. The debt provisions ensured that work on lengthening and doubling the locks and widening and deepening the channel of the Erie Canal would nearly stop, a policy that would endanger the whole investment because the canal could not yield its full return until the whole project was completed. The work was not completed until 1862, by which time railroads were highly competitive in carrying freight. The forces against debt creation were righteous, insistent, and overwhelming.

Three classes of corporations received special treatment because of their relation to the public welfare in matters of debt creation. They were municipalities, banks, and utility franchises. Municipal corporations were not an issue. It was the nearly universal opinion that the the legislature should curb the debt-contracting powers of municipal governments and also make it "the duty of the legislature to provide for the organization of cities and incorporated villages . . ." (Article 8, Section 9). The implication was that some classes of municipal governments should be organized under general incorporation statutes.[11]

Banking was one of the biggest issues of the convention, but the major difficulties were already solved. The free banking statute had survived a constitutional challenge in the courts and had retained its popularity through the depression. There was little opposition to it and it was wholly embedded in the Constitution in Article 8, Section 4. This section read, "The legislature shall have no power to pass any act granting any special charter for banking purposes, but corporations or associations may be formed under general laws." Banks had to be created under a general incorporation law, a mode of creation not required of any other class of corporation.

The public did not always make a distinction between liability for bank stockholders and liability for stockholders in other classes of business corporations, and the convention reflected this. There was a powerful minority who wanted personal liability for stockholders of banks of issue, to ensure that no noteholder was ever defrauded whenever a bank became insolvent. In late June, soon after the convention was organized, a delegate on the Committee of Banks and Banking said: "The Committee unanimously agreed that all persons authorized by the government to issue paper for circulation as the representative of coin should, in addition to other securities, be personally responsible for the certain redemption of such paper. This regulation of the currency was emphatically demanded by our constituents."[12]

Many members of the convention wished to go one step further and make all corporate investors fully liable. The Committee on Incorporations other than Banks agreed with this position in its report submitted on July 2. It contained an ambiguous liability section that is difficult to interpret, but the Chairman explained it. The committee felt that all corporate investors should be subject to personal liability because it was only democratic that shareholders who hoped to gain an equal share of the profits should bear an equal share of the losses; however, internal improvement corporations were so essential to the well-being of society that they should be excepted from this rule.

At the same time, there was a clear recognition of the great contribution that all classes of business corporations made to society, provided there was an equality of opportunity to participate in them.

> They viewed them as very useful institutions for the employment of capital, the development of enterprise, and to carry on the businesses which requires greater capital than individuals or limited partnerships can conveniently furnish. . . . It made no difference . . . whether a business was to be carried on by corporators or others so long as the business was legitimate. . . . But this system [of general incorporation laws] should allow men of small means to come in and unite in carrying on business. The principle was democratic; but when these privileges were limited to the few . . . it was opposed to every principle of democracy.[13]

The controversial issues of banking and incorporations were then postponed until near the end of the convention, after other less controversial issues had been settled. On succeeding days, beginning on September 25, the reports of the Banking Committee and the Committee on Incorporations were discussed. The early meetings of the Incorporation Committee had framed a very awkward section requiring stockholders of bankrupt corporations to be proportionally liable for corporate debts to the amount of the stock they owned. The ensuing debate showed that there was strenuous opposition to proportional liability. One delegate pointed out that, "if you continued this system of individual liability you would drive small capitalists away from these investments and none but John J. Astor would have any control of this matter. If that was democracy, to enrich the rich against the poor, then he [the delegate] would have nothing to do with it."[14] Another said, "One of the objects for incorporated associations was to bring private capital into uses for public benefit; this would be accomplished only to any considerable extent by authorizing citizens of moderate means to contribute to a limited extent."[15] In spite of these arguments, proportional liability for corporation stockholders was adopted by the close vote of 49 to 45 and confirmed by a second vote of 44 to 42 when an attempt was made to exempt stockholders of utility corporations.[16]

In the meantime, on September 21 and 25, petitions against unlimited liability were received, which led to an extension of the debate and contributed to the adoption of contradictory amendments. The whole liability issue was in utter confusion, and a special committee was appointed to resolve the conflict. During this pause, the banking sections were considered. Noteholders were given first preference to the assets of bankrupt banks, and bank stockholders, after 1850, became doubly liable but only if their banks circulated banknotes. The few banks that did not circulate notes retained the limited liability of the revised statutes.[17]

With the banknote controversy settled, the pressure for personal liability was partially vented and the convention could make some needed distinctions. It adopted the discretionary section (Article 7, Section 2) that allowed the limited liability of the revised statutes to remain in force unless otherwise altered by the legislature: "Dues [debts] from corporations shall be secured by such individual liability of the corporators . . . as may be prescribed by law."[18]

After constitutionalizing the free banking statute and acquiescing to the continued operation of corporate limited liability, the convention could look at other classes of corporate businesses. Some extremely useful public functions were performed by franchise corporations; they had to be protected and encouraged; and the opportunities for profits in them had to be equalized. This could best be achieved by following the banking example and creating them under general laws, but with a minimum of state involvement in their management policies.

Franchise corporations primarily meant railroads, and the major controversy was the expediency of the state lending its credit to build them. Controversy arose because in the immediate past, several railroad corporations had defaulted on their interest and sinking fund payments and had burdened the state with paying them. The largest defaulter was the New York and Erie Railroad. The convention was of the opinion that all of the state's ties with the New York and Erie should be severed, so that the state would never again be obligated to support its debt structure. This policy would require the state to foreclose on the railroad and then look for private buyers; in the meantime, the state would be burdened with the railroad's management. This was to be avoided at all costs. It would be better for the state to forgive the Erie's debts, as eventually was done, than get involved in a situation that might lead to further public debts. The convention followed a hands-off policy and adopted a permissive section, Article 7, Section 4, which left to the legislature the expediency of foreclosing or extending the time to collect these debts, but laid down the policy that the debts should be "fairly enforced and not released or compromised."

A second controversy over franchise corporations dealt with the expediency of granting them the power of eminent domain. The taking of private land by private corporations was a big factor in the popular desire to regulate franchise corporations. Many persons who believed railroads should be created by general incorporation statutes also believed that the power of eminent domain should be granted to each applicant by an individual act. They felt that eminent domain was the ultimate expression of sovereign power because it infringed on individual property rights; therefore, its use ought to be jealously guarded.[19] The convention was very sympathetic to this attitude and attempted to remedy this grievance by adopting a major clause from the 1807 turnpike regulatory statute (Article 1, Section 7), which provided that whenever private property was to be taken for public use, the value of the land and damages were to be determined by three state-appointed commissioners.

Railroad rate structures were not a big issue until after the Civil War, except insofar as railroads competed with the state-owned canals for the available freight traffic. This was not a serious problem in 1846.

Finally, in order to avoid a recurrence of the shameful fight between the Supreme Court and the Court of Errors over the constitutionality of the free banking statute, Article 8, Section 3, defined corporations "to include all associations and joint-stock companies having any of the powers and privileges of corporations not possessed by individuals and partnerships. And all corporations shall have the right to sue and shall be subject to be sued in all courts in like cases as natural persons." Although not a very precise definition, it made clear the convention's opposition to the legislative device of calling a corporation something else in order to avoid a constitutional limitation.

NOTES

1.   Lending the state's credit took the following form: state certificates of indebtedness (bonds) were issued to the corporation, which had to auction them within a specified time, usually three months. Premiums on the selling price went into the School Fund. The benefiting corporation set up a sinking fund to repay the state and the state took a first mortgage on the company's assets.

2.   Carter Goodrich, *Government Promotion of American Canals and Railroads, 1800–1890*, 52–58. *Documents of the Constitutional Convention 1846*, No. 47. *New York Laws*, Ch. 114, 1842, 79.

3.   Lee Benson, *The Concept of Jacksonian Democracy*, 68. Ronald E. Shaw, *Erie Water West, A History of the Erie Canal, 1792–1854*, 335, 351–352. The state did everything possible to provide a market for its bonds. Prior to the bankruptcy of the Safety Fund in 1841, it had bought large quantities of Canal Fund bonds. All the other state-administered funds made substantial investments, including all newly organized free

banks. By 1846, the free banks had deposited over $4 million worth of New York bonds with the Comptroller (out of a total of nearly $7.5 million), with which to back over $6.5 million of paper currency they circulated. *Documents of the Constitutional Convention 1846*, No. 34, 4; 40, 3.

4.   William G. Bishop, William H. Attree, reporters, *Report of the Debates and Proceedings of the Convention, 1846*, 845–855. Harry H. Pierce, *Railroads of New York: A Study of Government Aid, 1826–1875*, 17. The state had also foreclosed the Catskill and Canajoharie Railroad, but construction of it had not begun.

5.   Carter Goodrich, "The Revulsion Against Internal Improvements," *Journal of Economic History*, Vol. 10, 1950, 156. A. James Heins, *Constitutional Restrictions Against State Debt*, 3–10. Guy S. Callender, "The Early Transportation and Banking Enterprises of the States in Relation to the Growth of Corporations," *Quarterly Journal of Economics*, Vol. 17, 1902, 113–114, 129–131, 159–162.

6.   John W. Cadman, *The Corporation in New Jersey, 1791–1875*, 107–110.

7.   *Senate Documents 1847*, No. 63, 2.

8.   Hugh Rockoff, "The Free Banking Era: A Reexamination," *Journal of Money, Credit, and Banking*, Vol. 6, 1974, 150, 163. Albert Fishlow, *American Railroads and the Transformation of the Ante-Bellum Economy*, 52–77, 171–181, 263–269, 306–311. Harold F. Williamson, "Money and Commercial Banking, 1789–1865," in Harold F. Williamson, ed., *The Growth of the American Economy*, 139–240. George D. Green, "Louisiana, 1804–1861," in Rondo Cameron, ed., *Banking and Economic Development: Some Lessons of History*, 215–220, 227–231. Erling A. Erickson, *Banking in Frontier Iowa, 1836–1865*, 79, 83–93, 96–99.

9.   This provision was probably borrowed from the New Jersey Constitution of 1844 (Article 4, Section 6) where it was a device to protect the monopoly position of the Joint Companies in transportation between New York City and Philadelphia, and thus guarantee the state an income from this source.

10.   Harry H. Pierce, *Railroads of New York: A Study of Government Aid, 1826–1875*, 17–18.

11.   William G. Bishop, William H. Attree, reporters, *Report of the Debates and Proceedings of the Convention 1846*, 463.

12.   William G. Bishop, William H. Attree, reporters, *Report of the Debates and Proceedings of the Convention 1846*, 183.

13.   William G. Bishop, William H. Attree, reporters, *Reports of the Debates and Proceedings of the Convention 1846*, 223.

14.   William G. Bishop, William H. Attree, reporters, *Report of the Debates and Proceedings of the Convention 1846*, 976–977.

15.   William G. Bishop, William H. Attree, reporters, *Report of the Debates and Proceedings of the Convention 1846*, 977.

16.   William G. Bishop, William H. Attree, reporters, *Report of the Debates and Proceedings of the Convention 1846*, 974, 978, 980.

17.   The double liability section used almost the exact words of the 1811 general incorporation statute for manufacturers, which the courts in *Briggs v. Penniman* 1826 had interpreted to mean double liability. The legislature passed double liability legislation in 1849 (Ch. 226), which was tested in *U.S. Trust Co.* v. *U.S. Fire Insurance Co.*, 1858, 18 N.Y. 199. The court pointed out: (1) (209), because of the reserve clause, this statute was not in violation of the obligation of contract clause in the United States Constitution; (2) (218) the meaning of the New York Constitution was obviously double liability because it followed language used by the courts before the adoption of the Constitution. See also *The Matter of Oliver Lee and Company's Bank*, 1860, 21 N.Y. 13-20, for a concise account of bank liability under the Constitution of 1846 and how general incorporation statutes, with a reserve clause, transformed corporation charters from contracts into enabling acts.

18.   William G. Bishop, William H. Attree, reporters, *Report of the Debates and Proceedings of the Convention 1846*, 1005-1006, 1020-1022. *Convention Documents 1846*, No. 42; 125; 126; 127.

19.   William G. Bishop, William H. Attree, reporters, *Report of the Debates and Proceedings of the Convention 1846*, 118, 222, 966-967, 1021.

8

Implementing
the Constitution

NEW YORK ADOPTS GENERAL INCORPORATION AS ITS SETTLED POLICY

The general incorporation statutes passed from 1847 to 1855 were mostly for business corporations, particularly those that undertook internal improvement projects, but the legislature also passed general statutes for villages and a wide variety of benevolent public service organizations. The class of business that made the greatest long-term use of self-incorporation was manufacturing, and the manufacturing statute of 1848 served as the model for all general laws for business corporations. The statutes for local internal improvement projects, like bridges, generally delegated broad regulatory powers to local governments, while the state retained jurisdiction over larger projects. The following is a list of general incorporation statutes passed from 1847 to 1855:

1847	Villages	1848	Manufacturing, Mining, Mechanical, and Chemical Corporations
1847	Rural Cemeteries		
1847	Plank Roads and Turnpikes		
		1848	Gas Light Corporations
1848	Benevolent, Charitable, Scientific, and Missionary Societies	1848	Telegraph Corporations
		1848	Railroad Corporations
		1849	Insurance Corporations
1848	Toll Bridges	1850	Railroad Corporations

1851	Proprietary Schools	1853	Building Erection Corporations
1851	Building, Mutual Loan, and Accumulating Fund Associations	1853	Ferry Corporations
		1854	Societies to Establish Free Churches
1852	Ocean Steam Navigation Corporations	1854	Private and Family Cemetery Corporations
1853	Union School Districts	1854	Associations for Improving the Breed of Horses
1853	Proprietary Libraries		
1853	Medical Colleges		
1853	Agricultural and Horticultural Societies	1854	Stage Corporations in the City of New York
1853	Fire Insurance Corporations	1854	Navigation Corporations for Lake George
1853	Life and Health Insurance Corporations	1854	Lake and River Navigation Corporations

The characteristics of these laws were: investors almost always retained double liability until shares were fully paid-in; thereafter they had limited liability; and investors were usually required to pay-in half of the authorized capital within one year and the remainder within two. Railroads were the major exception because of the length of time it took to build them and because of their enormous cost. Corporations had a minimum life of twenty years, but more frequently it was fifty years. An indefinite life was usually granted benevolent and municipal corporations and telegraph and railroad companies. A mechanic's lien was placed in all statutes that created corporations that would employ a large number of hourly paid employees, like railroads. In many of these statutes, there was a provision that encouraged individually chartered corporations to recharter under the general law.

Most statutes had no upper limits of capitalization, but most franchise corporations had minimal requirements. In the case of railroads, the limit was $1,000, and later $10,000, per mile to ensure that construction did not begin until there was enough capital to see useful work done. Directors of business corporations usually incurred personal liability as a penalty if they failed to comply with some regulations placed elsewhere in the statute. All promoters had to publish their intent to incorporate in one or more local newspapers several weeks before they applied for incorporation, and all corporations had to file copies of their articles of incorporation with one or more public bodies. Local benevolent corporations, like rural cemeteries, had to file only with the county clerk, but business corporations participating in regional or statewide markets had to file a copy with the county clerk and some state agency, usually the Secretary of State. All corporations, whether benevolent public service organizations or statewide franchises, had to file an annual financial report with some state agency and usually with the nearest local government. Each share had one vote.

General incorporation legislation was not one of the major items of business in the legislative session of 1847. The Constitution sanctioned free banks without the need of enabling legislation, so the legislature devoted its time to more pressing needs; however, it found time to pass three general statutes. Two others, for manufacturing and railroads, were defeated. It was not until 1848 that the constitutional policy of enacting general incorporation statutes for business corporations was actively pursued. Even then, the legislative habit of passing special acts was not abandoned. In 1850, Governor Hamilton Fish vetoed four special charters that could have been incorporated under a general law. He said the legislature did not possess the power to pass these special charters because general incorporation statutes were available; therefore, the charters were unconstitutional. Fish's vetoes were sustained. In 1851 and 1852, Governor Washington Hunt vetoed several special charters for the same reason and he was sustained. In 1853, the Democrats took control of the legislature and elected Horatio Seymour as Governor. The party needed all the favors it could bestow to stay in office, and he allowed nearly 300 special charters and charter amendments to become law without his veto, but no general incorporation statutes were repealed and several new ones were enacted. The flood of special charters continued in 1855. This splurge of private acts clogged the legislature and was not halted until 1856, in the second year of Governor Myron Clark's administration.[1]

MANUFACTURING, MINING, MECHANICAL, AND CHEMICAL CORPORATIONS

Governor John Young recommended passage of general incorporation statutes in his 1847 message. He interpreted Article 8, Section 1, as imposing a duty on the legislature to pass general incorporation statutes because there was "scarcely any subject of legislation to which the public is looking with more interest than that which relates to corporations for manufacturing purposes."[2]

The 1847 bill was based on an 1830 Massachusetts general regulatory statute and New Jersey's 1846 general incorporation statute. It penalized stockholders with full liability until the full par value of every share was paid-in. It passed the Senate, but many members of the Assembly had strong reservations about making stockholders fully liable under any circumstances because of the outcry raised by New Jersey businessmen after the passage of their 1846 law; consequently, the bill was not enacted in 1847. The New Jersey law had generated controversy because it required full stockholder liability. The Democratic party had feared that limited liability of any kind posed a threat to political equality. The New Jersey Whigs were more favorably disposed toward business promoters and urged businessmen to come to the legislature for better terms contained in individual charters, which they did but at considerable expense. New York politicians were more sympathetic to the needs of businessmen and, when the general incorporation statute for manufacturing companies was passed in the following year, limited liability for corporate investors was essentially a nonpartisan issue.[3]

The 1848 law was passed after Governor Young declared that New York's future prosperity "should look primarily to the encouragement of industry. But this object can only be obtained under laws that will invite the investment of capital.[4] This was the first general incorporation statute for business corporations passed under the new Constitution. It was essentially the same bill proposed in 1847, except that double liability was substituted for full liability until shares were fully paid-in. Three or more persons could organize a corporation, and the management structure was purposely left undefined so it could fit a large number of situations.

Corporations could only own sufficient real estate to carry on their business, and they were forbidden to own stock in other corporations or make loans to their own stockholders. In an attempt to prevent watering of stock, persons were prohibited from purchasing stock with anything but money. The useful device of exchanging stock for property was overlooked, but in 1853, this was specifically authorized provided such stock was fully paid-in.

In the same year (1853), business corporations were made to bear a fairer share of taxation. Corporations holding a cash surplus greater than 10 percent of their legal capitalization (meaning banks) had to pay taxes on the surplus, and manufacturing and marine insurance corporations could no longer commute all of their taxes by paying a 5 percent tax on their net earnings, if they earned less than 5 percent profit on their capitalization. This statute allowed local governments to increase their tax on banks and insurance corporations and, for the first time, to tax the lands and buildings of many manufacturing corporations. Manufacturing and marine insurance corporations were no longer infant or sick industries.

By 1852, the United States had developed a wide variety of industrial skills, which were concentrated in factories. Factory production had largely displaced the household manufacture of textiles, leather goods, and the fabrication of most wood products. New York's policies of low taxes on corporate manufacturing, adopted in 1825, and the ease of incorporation for manufacturing enterprises had been real stimuli in aiding New York's rapid industrialization and a concomitant increase in private and public wealth.[5]

The 1848 general incorporation statute for manufacturing enterprises continued this policy and was highly successful. From 1848 through 1855, there were 685 incorporations under it and over 4,700 through 1866, including over 1,000 for the production and refining of petroleum. As happened under the 1811 statute, the definition of manufacturing was continually broadened. In 1851, businesses that raised vessels or other heavy objects were allowed to incorporate; in 1855, companies that cut, stored, and shipped ice were comprehended; and in 1857, printers, publishers, and newspapers were added.[6]

GAS LIGHT CORPORATIONS

The gas light business was a type of municipal internal improvement enterprise, like aqueducts, that had no unincorporated competition to delay the passage of a general incorporation statute. The first gas light corporation was chartered in 1823 to serve New York City. Six more were chartered by 1848. The statutes for gas light and manufacturing corporations were nearly identical and were passed on successive days. The only significant differences between them allowed gas light companies to dig up the streets of any municipality if the local government consented, and authorized local governments to exempt their facilities from property taxes for three years. The legislature assumed these corporations would improve street lighting and provide illumination for the interiors of public buildings. In 1854, these corporations were authorized to issue bonds up to one-third of their paid-in capital, at no more than 7 percent interest for as long as twenty years.[7] Fifty-one of these corporations were chartered between 1848 and 1855.

TELEGRAPH CORPORATIONS

The success of long-distance telegraphy was demonstrated in 1839, when Samuel F. B. Morse strung forty miles of wire between Washington, D.C. and Baltimore. In 1845, the New York legislature authorized the owners of the Morse telegraph patents, whose attorney was Amos Kendall, to string lines anywhere within the state. This statute was not an act of incorporation but an enabling act that allowed any Morse-licensed company to use public highways as rights-of-way. The telegraph companies were licensed by territory, and the licensees paid from $25 to $100, or the equivalent in fully paid-in stock, as royalties for every mile constructed.

The first commercial telegraph line in the United States was built from New York City through Baltimore to Washington, D.C., and was completed in January 1846. In June 1845, the New York, Albany and Buffalo Telegraph Company was organized but not incorporated. It completed stringing lines in September 1846. The trans-New York line was the second completed line. The proprietors of Morse's patents, however, were not the only owners of workable telegraph patents. After some major technical difficulties had been overcome, competing lines, using one or two rival patents, were rapidly constructed into all commercial villages because they wanted telegraphic communications as soon as possible, just as they thirsted for railroad transportation.

The fifth general incorporation statute passed during the 1848 session was for telegraph companies. The statute encouraged the tremendous expansion of the telegraph network then taking place by specifically authorizing any existing telegraph company to reincorporate under its provisions. Like the plank road-turnpike statute, the companies organized under this act had to specify their routes, but they were not granted power of eminent domain, although they could purchase, hold, and convey property necessary to their business. A procedure was set up, however, whereby persons who had poles placed on their property could seek compensation.

Stockholders were liable to the amount of the par value of their shares plus 25 percent. This was a compromise of the controversy debated at the constitutional convention over the proper liability for franchise corporations. Because railroads took land and made fixed improvements on a large scale, they were granted full limited liability. It was an absolute necessity in order to attract capital. Because telegraph companies were allowed to use the rights-of-way of public highways and invested far less capital per mile than railroads, they did not receive full limited liability. All companies incorporated under this statute and doing business in New York had to receive dispatches from other telegraph corporations and transmit them in the order in which they were received for the usual charges. Special arrangements, however, could be made with newspapers for dispatching public news.

The provisions relating to the transmission of messages were probably passed at the instigation of Kendall because, when he licensed companies to construct telegraph lines, he envisioned that branch lines would be equally entitled to use trunkline facilities. The trunkline operators, however, were dissatisfied with the revenue-splitting arrangement. The franchise contract was vaguely enough worded so that a contrary interpretation was possible—the trunklines saw an opportunity to buy up feeder lines at reduced prices if they denied them the right to transmit their messages at regular fees and in the order in which they were received.[8]

In 1851, telegraph corporations were permitted to extend their lines to connect or unite with any other company's lines, provided two-thirds of the capital interest of both corporations approved. *Unite* was interpreted to mean *merge*, so that this was a legal authorization to tie the nearly bankrupt western telegraph corporations to the New York trunklines, and to bring some order out of the cut-throat competition between the various parallel lines operating under competing patents. The statute was substantially an enactment of the charter of the New York and Mississippi Valley Printing Telegraph Corporation, organized on April 1, 1851, under the 1848 general incorporation statute. The company was controlled by Rochester interests and was relatively highly capitalized. Besides hoping to end cut-throat competition, this company wanted to gain control of the western telegraph companies centered around the Great Lakes and feed their traffic through a Buffalo connection to New York City.

The first fruits of this legislation were the mergers of competing lines along the major trunkline routes: New York City–Boston; New York City–Washington, D.C.; and New York City–Buffalo. The merged companies proved highly profitable; consequently, the building of competing lines along these routes was encouraged. This created a situation that would later be repeated with railroads. After 1855, however, favorable contracts with railroads to dispatch trains gave the companies that had strung lines along railroad rights-of-way such a competitive advantage that competing lines built along public highways were no longer attractive investments.

In 1853, the legislature passed a very liberal statute to help New York financial interests gain control of financially weak telegraph companies chartered by states in the Great Lakes and Ohio Valley regions. Favorable legislation was a necessary first step in creating a national telegraphic network tributary to New York City. Several major consolidations of western franchises had already taken place and the focus of these networks was toward Philadelphia. Consolidation appeared to be the most effective means of constructing a system advantageous to New York, and the 1853 statute gave New York capitalists a decided advantage in securing western connections.[9]

The general incorporation privilege was extended to all telegraph corporations that had lines wholly within or partially outside the state, and the companies could own any interest, up to total ownership, of any in-state or out-of-state corporation. The statute thus enabled New York capitalists to form holding corporations that could be operating companies as well. In many respects, it was a legalization of what had already taken place on a smaller scale through cash purchase, stock exchange, and long-term leasing. Long-term leasing was a device borrowed from railroads and was the most common way of creating a system. New York telegraph companies were also granted the power of eminent domain, and shareholders were granted full limited liability. Their shares were also taxed at the same rate as other business corporations, which, in reality, was a tax exemption because telegraph companies, like railroads, had nearly all of their capital invested in fixed facilities.

At the same time that New York investors secured the advantage of holding companies to facilitate building interstate telegraph systems, the holders of the Morse patents were attempting to harmonize the interests of the companies they had licensed. The first American telegraphic convention was held in Washington, D.C. on March 5, 1853, but it demonstrated, as much as anything else, that there was little long-term basis for harmony short of consolidation. In 1856, the two largest telegraph networks in New York merged and the resulting company had lines into the Mississippi Valley.

RAILROAD CORPORATIONS

Between 1826 and 1833, the New York legislature chartered forty-one railroad corporations. All but one of these pioneer railroads were short lines connecting interior cities or linking them with navigable water. Most were built with local capital. If the legislature thought one would compete with the canal system in carrying freight, a clause was inserted in its charter making it pay canal tolls during the months the canal was not frozen.

The New York and Erie Railroad was the only trans-New York trunkline, and its route was as nearly noncompetitive with the Erie Canal as a railroad could be. It ran from the Hudson River at the border between New York and New Jersey, through the mountainous southern tier of counties to the town of Dunkirk on Lake Erie. It was granted a huge subsidy when the state lent the company its credit; that is, the state guaranteed to pay the interest and principal of its bonds if, for some reason, the company should fail to generate sufficient revenues to do it. It followed the route of a turnpike that Governor DeWitt Clinton had recommended the state build in 1825 but whose construction had been defeated in 1827 by the votes of fiscal conservatives and representatives from counties along the canal.[10] The financial success of the Erie Canal in the 1830s provided much of the bonding power that allowed the state to lend its credit to aid the construction of railroads and feeder canals. The people craved them and were sold on the idea that they would be as profitable as the trunkline canal. Railroads and feeder canals were urged upon the public as self-liquidating.[11]

New York and Pennsylvania pursued a similar policy in regard to internal improvements. Both states financed construction of two transportation systems, while Massachusetts, which lacked the financial resources of these two states, prudently bided its time and then chose to subsidize a trans-state trunkline railroad. New York weathered the depression from 1838 to 1844 by abruptly stopping all expenditures for internal improvements in 1842 and levying a state property tax at a time when property owners could least afford to pay it. For the next ten years, the state's fiscal policy aimed to maintain the state's credit and reduce its debt. Pennsylvania adopted the same policy, but its debt-revenue structure was such that it failed to sustain its credit.

In both New York and Pennsylvania, there was a tremendous popular reaction against the state building or subsidizing internal improvement projects by incurring long-term bonded debts.[12] New York's Constitutional Convention of 1846 strongly reflected this position. The rigid fiscal limitations it imposed left the state with no alternative but to adopt a laissez faire economic policy that radically separated business enterprises from state participation in almost the same way that the 1784 general incorporation statute for religious congregations had excluded the state from interfering in religious matters.

The railroad business was on the threshold of immense profitability due to technological improvements and the economies that would result from merging the upper New York short lines into a trunkline route that could capture the rapidly growing volume of freight coming from the west. Capitalist investors saw an opportunity for railroads to skim off the Erie Canal's high-value freight, especially after 1847 when the Erie Canal carried more freight originating in the west than from within New York. There would be especially high profits and large capital gains if canal tolls were also removed. Beginning about 1847, capitalist investors who were mainly the directors of the existing railroads began purchasing the shares of small investors whose risk capital had built the railroads. The director-investors wanted the profit opportunities of trunkline railroading for themselves and accepted the constitutional provisions that excluded future state participation in internal improvement projects, just as bank promoters had previously succeeded in excluding the state from participation in the banking business. At this point, the policies of railroad investors and fiscally conservative Democrats coincided. It was: keep the state from subsidizing any more canals or railroads.

By excluding the state from participation in all internal improvement projects, railroad managers were in a position to initiate unrestricted competition with their chief New York rival, the state's canal system, and have a free hand to construct trunkline systems across state boundaries. They also wanted complete freedom to erect a rate structure for freight and passengers that would favor through-traffic from the west, often at the expense of in-state, short-haul shippers; and they wanted the freedom to compete for western traffic with the trunkline railroads that served Philadelphia and Baltimore.

In their desire to compete, railroad managers had the full support of the powerful import-export interests in New York City and part of the state's manufacturing interests. Railroad managers thought in terms of restructuring the national marketing pattern. They sought to tie the markets of the trans-Appalachian states to the eastern seaboard cities and to break the commercial linkage of the interior with New Orleans via the Mississippi, Ohio, and Missouri Rivers.[13] After the perfection of the railroad as a long-distance means of carrying freight, around 1845, the Erie Canal was no longer adequate to guarantee New York City's position as the preferred port of entry into the west. The vastly enlarged volume of domestic trade that the railroads promised to generate, made it absolutely necessary for New York City to have its own trunkline into the west.[14] This need for a trunkline railroad west, and all that it promised, was a concept considerably broader than that of most state officials, who thought only in terms of paying off the state's debts and serving those business interests within the state that could bring political pressure to force the equalization of intrastate freight rates.

RAILROAD LEGISLATION

Railroad legislation began in New York in 1839, with a statute allowing "any railroad corporation to contract with any other railroad corporation for the use of their respective roads, and thereafter to use the same in such manner as may be prescribed in such contract." The idea of allowing one railroad to lease the franchise of another was probably borrowed from a Massachusetts statute of 1838.[15] This statute helped weak railroads avoid bankruptcy during the depression and encouraged the formation of railroad corporations that could operate without state financial aid. As soon as recovery from the depression began, the state acted to protect canal revenues from railroad competition by delegating to the Canal Commissioners the power to collect tolls from all railroads that paralleled or competed with the state's canals. Statutes to this effect were passed in both 1844 and 1847.[16]

After 1846, the volume of railroad legislation rapidly increased. Laws were needed to incorporate railroads, enforce safety standards, control financing, and regulate competition. For example, Troy and Albany were competing to become the eastern terminus of the upper New York railroad system. In 1847, the Troy-based Schenectady and Troy Railroad broke an 1843 passenger interchange agreement between it and the railroads serving Albany. In order to restore orderly public service, the legislature compelled all competing railroads that crossed one another to grant each other equal interchange privileges. The statute also authorized the appointment of three temporary commissioners to arbitrate any interchange disputes and to issue judgments binding on all parties for two years. The Commission's decisions were subject to review by the state Supreme Court. This regulation was probably borrowed from Massachusetts, which had faced a similar problem in 1845.

The legislature also compelled certain operating roads to lay heavier iron rails (fifty-six pounds per yard) by January 1848, to replace dangerous strap-iron rails. This legislation was inspired by the horrible safety records of the operating roads, in large part caused by the rapid decay of the longitudinal wooden stringers on which the strap-iron rails were nailed. When the stringers decayed, the flimsy strap-iron rails worked loose, curved around the train's wheels, and penetrated passenger cars like spears. Railroad corporations were also authorized to double their tracks, relocate grades, straighten curves, and make other capital improvements, such as improving the drainage of existing roadbeds, building permanent stone bridges, increasing the size of cars, and purchasing heavier and more powerful engines. To finance these improvements, the legislature allowed the operating roads to increase their bonded indebtedness to $10,000 per mile. These improvements, plus telegraph dispatching, led to a marked increase in the efficiency of railroads during the decade from 1845 to 1855; but just as important, there was an increase in the size of rail systems under one management, and management increased its efficiency in gathering information and allocating resources.[17]

A general incorporation statute for railroads was passed in 1848, after having failed passage of 1847 because the legislature was reluctant to grant powers of eminent domain to railroad corporations.[18] The railroad committee said they were not sure railroads were public highways in the same sense as turnpikes, although the courts and earlier legislative sessions had believed differently. Safety regulations formed about a quarter of the statute's provisions; however, the penalties for safety violations were not severe and there was no provision for state inspection. Before a railroad could begin constructing its right-of-way, the company's stockholders had to subscribe $1,000 per mile for its proposed distance, and 10 percent had to be paid-in. Only then could the corporation elect directors and register its articles of incorporation with the state.

Stockholders were made fully liable for paying the wages of the company's employees if it went bankrupt, and railroad contractors had to deposit some form of security with a railroad company to ensure the payment of their employees' wages. The maximum rate for fares was set, but the legislature reserved the power to reduce fares without the corporation's consent if the company's earnings exceeded 10 percent on its paid-in capital. Land belonging to the state could be granted to a railroad for compensation (which could be very little), and roads that paralleled canals had to continue to pay canal tolls. The state also reserved the right to purchase the railroad after ten years and within fifteen years for the corporation's total investment. A similar provision had been included in the turnpike statute of 1807, but neither option was ever exercised.

The power of eminent domain, however, was not granted to railroads. The Senate committee that favored the 1847 railroad general incorporation statute believed that this "sacred and important trust" should be in the hands of a public authority, not a private corporation. The same report contended that if a general statute were to authorize an indefinite number of corporations to take property without legislative consent, a general scramble would ensue "and the right of private property would soon be less respected here than under any despotic government in the Christian world."[19] This policy accurately reflected the sentiment of the Constitutional Convention of 1846 where a substantial minority had fought for further controls over railroad corporations, especially their power to take private land, but did not exactly know how to go about it.

Some committee members advocated that all franchise charters be passed by a two-thirds vote, but this method had been discredited by the experience with Safety Fund banks. It also ran counter to the powerful public sentiment that all corporations should be created by general statutes. Some degree of added stockholder liability in franchise corporations was also rejected as inconsistent with the state's policy of encouraging rapid railroad construction, but some additional reserve power was thought necessary. Practically the only regulatory device left was for railroads to return to the legislature, after they had met all other requirements for incorporation, and request a separate grant of eminent domain.

To meet such an objection and to obtain an unfettered right to eminent domain, advocates of the general incorporation statute proposed the appointment of a tribunal, which would certify that a projected railroad was a public utility. Certification would carry with it the right of eminent domain. The legislature, however, deemed eminent domain too important a power to be delegated with the result that railroads were required to return to the legislature to secure it. This made the legislature's joint committee on railroads into a de facto railroad regulatory commission with considerable power to prevent the construction of new railroads that might compete with the canal system or an established turnpike or railroad. In 1849, the Railroad Committee held hearings on the request of the Syracuse and Rochester Railroad, already incorporated under the 1848 general statute, that it be declared a public utility and given the power of eminent domain. The direct route of the Syracuse and Rochester Railroad would compete with both the Auburn and Syracuse and the Auburn and Rochester roads, and these two lines contended that the competition would bankrupt them.

The short lines said that there was an implied contract between them and the state because the state had loaned them its credit, and because they had relaid their road with heavy iron rails as required. They claimed their roads had pioneered rail transportation, and by the nature of the railroad business, they had a large fixed investment that could not be converted to an alternate use, such as could easily be done upon the bankruptcy of a manufacturing corporation. They believed that the state was obligated to protect the existing roads from potential bankruptcy. They claimed that their 8 percent profit had not been excessive, especially since they had paid high improvement costs.

The promoters of the direct line ignored the argument that financially strong railroads without competition were in the public's best interest. They quoted the doctrine of the *Charles River Bridge* case and showed how railroads had driven stage lines and turnpikes out of business, all for the public good. Railroad competition, they contended, would be a great public benefit. Although the Assembly voted to grant the power of eminent domain to the Syracuse and Rochester Railroad, the Senate rejected it. Later in the session, an amendment was introduced repealing the eminent domain section of the 1848 statute, but it was overwhelmingly defeated. The legislature was not yet willing to open the railroad business to unregulated participation. Some degree of restraint was thought necessary to protect the public interest.

In 1850, the general incorporation statute for railroads was rewritten and the 1848 statute repealed. The main change exempted newly incorporated railroads from returning to the legislature for an individual grant of eminent domain. Governor Hamilton Fish had recommended this because it would take from railroad corporations "every ingredient of exclusive privilege" by putting land acquisition by eminent domain procedures under general laws. The recent lobby battle of the Syracuse and Rochester Railroad Corporation was not mentioned. In polite words, Fish said that such a change would remove a great burden of time-consuming administration from an already-burdened legislature, and would end a great speculative influence upon its orderly functioning. He really meant that the change would relieve the legislature of a tempting opportunity to corrupt itself. Fish saw no reason why eminent domain should not be granted to all railroads because it worked very well when granted to turnpikes and plank roads.[20] The statute removed a major obstacle to unrestricted railroad construction and competiton, which was probably preferable to leaving discretionary regulatory powers in the hands of a venal legislature.

Rewriting the general incorporation statute for railroads offered the opportunity to increase the minimum capitalization to $10,000 per mile, of which 10 percent had to be paid-in before construction could begin. As a palliative, the state land office was authorized to make outright gifts of state-owned land to those railroad corporations requiring it. Gifts to private corporations had not been forbidden by the Constitution of 1846.

SOURCES OF RAILROAD CAPITAL

All the early New York railroads, except the New York and Erie, were built with American capital. There were three main sources: local investors who purchased a few shares of common stock, short-term credit that was continually renewed by local banks, and state subsidies prior to 1842. Most investors bought shares in anticipation of profits, but many invested for improved transportation facilities that would increase local land values, in much the same way local residents had invested in turnpikes.[21] The earliest New York railroads were not attractive investments for large capitalists because they preferred more remunerative investments in banks and western lands. Capitalist investors did not make large purchases of railroad securities until 1845–1850 when technological improvements in railroad equipment made the long-distance movement of freight possible. These improvements created an opportunity for large capital gains.

From the beginning, the New York legislature had pursued a contradictory railroad policy. The state's financial policy was to protect its canal revenues in order to amortize the canal debt, but at the same time, it was good politics to actively aid railroad construction. Cities and villages were eager to enjoy rapid, all-weather transportation. The earliest railroads seemed to offer little competition with canals in carrying freight because their flimsy construction allowed them to carry only people. By the time of the 1846 Convention, advances in railroad technology had made this situation obsolescent. Only if the flow of public credit to railroads were stopped and canal tolls imposed could the earning capacity of the Erie Canal, and the credit structure it supported, be protected from aggressive railroad competition. This was tried and failed.

Although state credit to railroads was prohibited by the 1846 Constitution, local government credit was not. By 1850, it was a commercial necessity for major towns to have railroad connections, and trunkline railroads and some branch lines had become highly profitable businesses, or potentially so. Railroad promotion and construction became a way to get rich quickly, and entrepreneurs turned with increasing success to local municipalities for financial support. After 1850, many branch lines were built almost wholly by the sale of municipal bonds and unsecured bank loans. The construction of branch lines was a mirror recurrence of the pressure in the 1830s to build feeder canals.

Many branch lines, with their limited traffic, could only be built if the municipalities through which they passed purchased stock. In many cases, there were only limited prospects that this stock would pay sufficient dividends to return the investment, but this was the price a village had to pay in order to get a railroad built to it. State subsidies and local bank credit had facilitated the building of canals, the rapid expansion of river steamboat transportation, the financing of industrial enterprises, and finally, the initial construction of railroads. When banks could no longer supply enough credit to satisfy the demand for new railroads, and the state withdrew its resources, railroad promoters tapped a new source of credit: local municipalities. The credit was available because there was often great popular interest in building a railroad, and communities would heavily tax themselves to see it built. Many of these roads also had high initial earnings, especially if one was built in a heavily settled area where there was no competitive water route, and also because little provision was made for equipment depreciation or roadbed maintenance.[22]

Railroad promoters (especially of branch lines) sold stock, not bonds, to municipal governments. The money to purchase stock was raised by selling municipal bonds, with the money to pay off the bonds coming from tax receipts that the village pledged for the next fifteen or twenty years. The municipal bonds or bonds sold by the railroad companies themselves were more attractive than stock to capitalist investors because bonds had first call on a corporation's earnings and municipal bonds had tax receipts to sustain their value. Bonds tended to hold their value better during periods of financial difficulty.

Unscrupulous promoters or overly eager communities abused municipal bonding power by incurring larger debts than they could fund. In 1853, the legislature acted to limit municipal sources of credit, which the Constitutional Convention of 1846 had indicated ought to be done. Municipal corporations were forbidden to contract a funded debt greater than 8 percent of the aggregate assessed valuation of their taxable real estate, and no debt could be contracted unless it was for "a specific object to be expressly stated in the ordinance proposing the same, unless such ordinance shall have been passed by two-thirds of all members elected to the common council . . . and shall have been submitted to and approved of by a majority of tax payers . . . at a special election . . . nor unless the legislature shall by law have ratified such ordinance. . . ."[23] Nor could municipal corporations lend their credit to any individual, association, or corporation.

The modest restraints the legislature placed on municipal credit were more than compensated for by other action. In 1851, Governor Washington Hunt noted in his annual and special messages that the Erie Canal was strangled with traffic and would continue to be congested until it was fully enlarged. He emphasized that the state's investment in the partially enlarged canal would not yield its anticipated revenues until the project was completed. He believed that railroad competition was tending to undercut canal traffic, which in the long run would reduce canal revenues and jeopardize the repayment of the canal debt. The only means of ensuring that the canal debt could be repaid out of canal revenues was the immediate completion of its enlargement. He seemed to suggest that a fully enlarged canal could move bulk commodities at a cost low enough to keep rail rates under control. He added that the time was past when railroads needed state subsidies.

Acting on this advice, the legislature did two things: it repealed the canal tolls for railroads, and authorized the issuance of $9 million of canal revenue certificates, in spite of the constitutional ban on the state incurring this amount of new debts.[24] The removal of canal tolls was the first step in the emergence of New York railroads as competitive freight carriers. They immediately engaged in cut-throat competition which forced the state to lower the canal rates. This had the effect of threatening the fiscal structure of the canal—and of the state—but the commercial interests of New York City were greatly pleased with the increased competition among the transportation arteries into the west. It gave them a great competitive advantage in exploiting the rapidly growing western market.

In the meantime, in 1852, the New York Court of Appeals declared the issue of canal revenue certificates unconstitutional because they merely called debts by another name in order to circumvent the Constitution's limit on indebtedness.[25] The Court's action forced the state to seek a constitutional amendment allowing the state to float bonds to complete canal enlargement; otherwise, the constricted canal could not hope to meet railroad competition and the canal would become a revenue-absorbing burden.

Increasing the state's debt was very unpopular with fiscally conservative Democrats. Just raising the issue precipitated the protest resignations of twelve Democratic legislators and the calling of a special election to fill their seats. Most of the vacant seats were won by friends of canal enlargement, and in a special legislative session, they passed a constitutional amendment authorizing the issuance of the necessary bonds. The next Governor, Democrat Horatio Seymour, favored the amendment and it was ratified by referendum in February 1854. Like ex-Governor Hunt, Governor Seymour doubted that railroads would take traffic away from an enlarged canal, but this prediction was almost immediately proven wrong. Canals were poor competitors with technologically advanced, well-managed railroads, and the revenues of the canal system continued to decline until the advent of the Civil War. An attempt was made in 1854 to halt this decline by re-imposing canal tolls but it failed, mainly because of a lavish publicity campaign by the railroads.[26]

The second key measure that allowed railroads to become competitive freight carriers was the consolidation of the fragmented upstate, short-line railroads into a single trunkline route from Albany to Buffalo. The consolidation was accomplished by a special act of incorporation passed in 1853.[27] The situation was the exceptional one foreseen by delegates to the 1846 Constitutional Convention who declined to write a requirement into the constitution that all classes of corporations had to be created by general laws. The act legalized a consolidation already arranged so the actual merger was promptly completed, to give birth to the first New York Central Railroad.[28] It was as great a financial success as the Erie Canal had been in its earlier years.

In 1855, the legislature allowed any New York-chartered railroad to lease any other railroad franchise, including franchises in other states, and exchange the stock of leased railroads for stock in the parent corporation in order to simplify the capital-management structure. This law extended to railroads the same advantages granted to telegraph corporations in 1853, so railroad managers could create interstate systems reaching into the west.[29] Previously, the state had authorized specifically named operating railroads to purchase shares in other roads. In the case of the Lewiston Railroad, it was allowed to merge with the Buffalo and Niagara Falls Railroad, while another statute allowed any New York-chartered railroad to purchase shares in the Great Western Railroad, up to the value of 5 percent of its capitalization, provided it located its eastern terminus somewhere along the Niagara River.[30] The Great Western was planned to run through Canada West (Ontario) to the Detroit River. At Detroit, it would connect with the Michigan Central Railroad then approaching its western terminus in Chicago. A similar object was the goal of the Buffalo and State Line Railroad to be built along the south shore of Lake

Erie to connect with the Michigan Southern and Northern Indiana Railroad, then approaching a Chicago terminus.[31] The process of consolidation, which began in 1839 when railroads were allowed to lease other railroad franchises, rapidly accelerated in the 1850s when New York's trunklines reached out to capture a large percentage of the rapidly growing western market, just as the Erie Canal had previously done.

In 1855, New York reconsidered its policy of the radical separation of the railroad business from state control. In that year, the legislature established a three-man railroad commission. It was based on the 1829 Banking Commission even to the point of including a directly elected representative of railroad management on it, plus the state engineer-surveyor and an appointee of the Governor. It was given broad powers of investigation but no independent powers of enforcement. It had to work through the Attorney General to remedy the abuses it found. It was empowered to investigate railroad accidents and inspect newly built rights-of-ways before allowing them to be opened to the public. It could also examine railroad managers under oath, especially in fiscal matters, and require special reports from any railroad. In exercising these powers, the Commission combined the reasons that had led three New England states to establish railroad commissions: Rhode Island in 1839 to facilitate connections between competing lines and mesh their service; New Hampshire in 1844 to supervise eminent domain powers; and Connecticut in 1853 to enforce safe operating and maintenance procedures.

The first report of the Railroad Commission described its efforts to increase passenger safety by inspecting bridges and roadbeds. It urged the adoption of a standard system of bookkeeping, and a uniform operating code in the interests of greater safety and greater public information on railroad financial practices.[32] Its doom was sealed, however, because it criticized the railroads for increasing revenues without regard to profits, often soliciting new business at cost. In order to end this cut-throat competition, the Commissioners recommended that the state enforce a pro-rate schedule between long-and short-haul shippers. Rates would be proportional to the distance traveled and the speed of the train. The Commissioners' object was twofold: to enhance the competitive position of intrastate shippers, and to protect canal revenues. The trunkline railroads had been charging little more for traffic originating in the western states than for local traffic. By forcing the trunkline roads to charge more for fast freight, the Commissioners hoped to protect canal revenues, so that funding the canal debt would not be endangered to the point where it might become a charge upon the public revenue.

From its inception, the Commission indicated it would act positively, and the railroads objected. The railroads feared that the Commission's plan to protect canal revenues would amount to the re-imposition of canal tolls, and this action would hinder the formation of an interstate rail system that could effectively compete with Philadelphia's and Baltimore's trunkline connections to the west. A bill was introduced in 1856 to abolish the Commission, but it was rejected by the Senate because the Senate was of the opinion that the legislature had to retain supervision over railroads to maintain the rights of those who contributed to a railroad's construction, and the traveling public who contributed to its maintenance. The same bill was re-introduced in 1857 and passed. It appears that bribery was involved. After 1857, there was little interest in reviving the Commission. Apparently, the public was not ready to accept commission regulation to safeguard its interest because it wanted the economies of railroad transportation on just about any terms. After the Commission's dissolution, the state was left with only one major weapon of railroad regulation, the chartering of competing lines. The constant threat of competing lines was an uneasy policy to live with, but railroad management did so for thirty years, until forced to seek a national solution. In 1887, railroad companies acquiesced to the establishment of the Interstate Commerce Commission.

THE SYMBIOSIS OF RAILROADS, BANKS, AND MANUFACTURING

The groundwork for the extraordinary growth in United States industrial production in the 1850s was laid in the canal era, and in this growth, New York was the leader. Canals and steamboats radically reduced long-distance transportation costs and called into being the first large regional markets, but canal construction was limited by geography, and the efficiency of canals was further hindered by slow speeds and winter freeze-up. The more flexible railroads brought the advantages of cheap distribution into almost all corners of the state, operated the year around, and by speeding deliveries, lessened the need and cost of maintaining large inventories.

The completion of the trunkline railroads into the interior had an accelerating impact on New York's economy in much the same way that the Erie Canal had previously catalyzed the state's economic growth. Between 1810 and 1855, upper New York was transformed from a pioneering economy into an early industrial society, while at the same time New York City became the largest commercial city in North America. The extraordinary transformation of New York's economy in so short a time was due, in large part, to the rapid completion of trunkline transportion arteries that were soon fleshed out by feeder lines, which further enlarged the regional market created by canals.[33] New York was the first region of the nation to have competing transportation systems, and it had this advantage well in advance of other sections of the nation.

The Constitutional Convention of 1846, by forcing the state to restrict capital expenditures, left the legislature with little alternative to passing general incorporation statutes for all classes of corporate businesses if a rapid exploitation of the state's resources was to be achieved. This constitutionalization of a laissez-faire corporation policy put corporate business opportunities in the hands of men who would use the policy most efficiently. It especially encouraged rapid railroad construction without political favoritism, such as the Regency had practiced in banking.

However, rapid railroad construction depended on more than the general law. It was greatly helped by the state's mature banking system, which supplied abundant credit, as well as by numerous other favorable laws designed to enhance the competitive position of New York's commercial and industrial interests. Most of these laws in the 1850s related to railroads: (1) the state did not foreclose on the New York and Erie Railroad when it became insolvent, which allowed its private management to construct a system into the midwest; (2) in 1851, ten short-line railroads in upper New York were authorized to merge into the New York Central trunkline route; (3) the formation of other railroad systems was facilitated by retaining the 1839 statute allowing long-term leasing of railroad franchises; (4) in 1851, several railroad corporations were allowed to purchase shares in other railroads, and in 1855, any state railroad was authorized to merge with any other in order to simplify their capital structures; (5) canal tolls on railroads were removed in 1851, which had the effect of giving New York City competitive arteries of trunkline transportation into the west; (6) the Erie Canal was enlarged over violent political opposition; (7) the Railroad Commission was dissolved when it attempted to equalize long- and short-haul rates; (8) a new general incorporation statute for railroads was passed in 1850, which granted railroads unrestricted use of eminent domain; (9) the very favorable tax ruling in *Mohawk and Hudson Railroad Company* v. *Clute* (1834) was allowed to stand without legislative alteration; and (10) in 1853, the legislature authorized the formation of telegraph holding companies that could cross state lines, thereby facilitating the assemblage of regional systems that would aid New York businesses in competing for western markets.

By 1855, the impact of railroads on New York's economy had initiated self-sustaining industrial growth. Self-sustained industrial growth is achieved when the industrial sector of the economy generates enough internal savings to meet most of its new capital requirements, as well as maintain existing operations at a technologically efficient level. By 1855, the industrial sector of the economy was large enough so that these savings and investments were, more or less, automatically made. Railroading was the key industry that accelerated industrial growth into the self-sustaining stage. Railroads lowered overland distribution costs of manufactured goods by speeding their delivery to consumers, and as a result, there was a rapid increase in the size of the regional market tributary to New York. The enlarged market meant that factories within it could increase in size, which markedly lowered unit costs. Railroads and the larger manufacturers, particularly the producers of textiles, also stimulated the demand for heavy and light engineered products, as well as encouraging improvements in high-pressure steam engines and innovations in metal casting and machining technology. Without the development of sophisticated metalworking and steam power technologies, it would have been difficult for any nation to achieve self-sustained industrial growth in the nineteenth century.[34]

All of these industries needed credit to take advantage of the opportunities for rapid expansion. The liberal creation of credit was probably just as important as lowered long-distance overland transportation costs in achieving the point of take-off into self-sustained industrial growth. This is usually not recognized. Credit was absolutely essential in the capital-deficient United States. Credit was provided by banks. There were no vast aggregations of inherited wealth, so that the richest had but recently acquired a moderate capital surplus, largely through their own efforts and probably by the intelligent use of credit. At a remarkably early date, the United States had an extensive and well-developed banking-credit system that magnified the limited capital resources of the nation. These banks were often inadequately regulated, but this was not a fatal weakness.[35]

New York contained a large number of men who were trained in the use of credit and were willing to venture it on large-scale enterprises, as well as on local businesses. These men lived in a society where political equality had become a reality and where small amounts of capital were very widely held. What was needed was a method of mobilizing the capital and credit resources of an economic and political democracy, while at the same time preserving an equality of opportunity to initiate and participate in an increasingly large number of potentially profitable business opportunities suddenly made available by more efficient distribution and other technological innovations.

General incorporation statutes for banks and railroads were major devices to mobilize and allocate the state's capital and credit resources to new classes of business, especially to railroads. This legal encouragement occurred at a time when banking and railroad investments, taken together, had an enormous cross-fertilizing effect, which yielded high private profits and the highest social returns. These two general incorporation statutes were highly successful and were extensively copied by other states, particularly in the west, where they encouraged the rapid construction of trunk-line routes that joined onto the New York systems; but in New

York itself, the general railroad law was most frequently used to construct feeder lines. From 1849 to 1855, eighty-one railroads were chartered under its provisions.

ADJUSTMENTS IN THE STATE'S BANKING SYSTEM

After the bankruptcy of the Safety Fund, a series of statutes attempted to reduce the depreciation of the system's banknotes that were still unredeemed. The one-half of one percent tax on the capital of participating banks was continued indefinitely, the banknotes held by solvent banks were allowed to be exchanged for New York bonds, and the sale of assets in the hands of receivers could be delayed to avoid ruinous sacrifices.[36] There was also a major setback. In an act of shortsighted economy, the Governor, in 1843, gave his tacit approval to ending the Bank Commission because it had not prevented the failure of the Safety Fund system. This was promptly done because it cut down his patronage power, and bank regulation was placed in the hands of the Comptroller. This same statute also provided for the registration of all Safety Fund banknotes, as was required of all notes circulated in the free banks.[37]

After adoption of the new constitution in 1846, the state tried to encourage Safety Fund banks to re-incorporate under the free banking statute. The Safety Fund banks rejected this policy because they would have to deposit securities as collateral for their notes. The legislature did not force the Safety Fund banks to do this, nor did it use the radical remedy of the reserve clause to force the Safety Fund banks to merge with the free banking system. In the next year, however, a comprehensive bank liability statute was passed, implementing the constitution. After January 1, 1850, stockholders of all banks of issue, whether Safety Fund or free, were made doubly liable for all the bank's debts and a year later, Governor Hunt requested that regulation of banks be taken from the Comptroller and vested in a special bank department. The Superintendent of the Bank Department was given all the powers that had been exercised by the Comptroller and the defunct Bank Commission.[38]

INSURANCE CORPORATIONS

Life insurance was not a significant business until after 1840. In that year, the New York legislature passed a statute allowing a married woman to receive the benefits of policies, free from the claims of her husband's creditors, to an amount of coverage that could be bought for an annual premium up to $300. The demand for life policies rapidly increased and, in 1842, the city's leading businessmen organized the New York Mutual Life Insurance Company. The life insurance business prospered and other states soon copied the law in order to encourage the organization of local life insurance corporations.[39]

Even more important than expanded coverage was the need for strong companies in the older fields of insurance. The chief weakness of most insurance companies was their lack of real capital and liquidity. An 1848 statute tried to promote liquidity of mutual corporations by requiring them to collect 20 percent of their premiums in cash, with the remainder being secured with negotiable notes. This ratio between the cash premiums and negotiable assets was about what the stronger mutuals were charging; however, there was no provision for enforcing the ratio, nor was there any way to prevent the company's management from paying back to its policyholders the surplus cash premiums at the end of each year.

In 1849, the whole fabric of insurance regulations was remodeled by the passage of a general incorporation statute that comprehended both mutual and stock corporations.[40] Corporations organized under it could underwrite one of three categories of risks: marine; fire and inland navigation; and life and health. The latter class of corporations had the added privilege of selling annuities. No insurance corporation could underwrite risks outside of its field and all corporations could make re-insurance. The principal aim of this statute was to secure minimum capitalization such as had been required for banks under the free banking statute.

All fire insurance companies doing business in the high-risk area of New York City were required to have a higher capitalization. For example, stock companies had to have a minimum capitalization of $150,000 if located in New York City, but only $50,000 if located elsewhere in the state. Stock life insurance companies incorporated under the provision of this statute could not begin operations until they had a safety fund, called an unearned premium fund, that had $100,000 actually paid-in and invested in approved securities. Foreign life insurance corporations doing business in New York had to have this fund held in trust by New York citizens. The state was trying to guarantee a sound life insurance industry by requiring stock life insurance corporations to guarantee the value of their policies in the same way that a stable currency had been achieved by requiring free banks to fully back their their banknotes with approved assets. Mutual corporations were also authorized but not compelled to accumulate a fund of surplus earnings to pay claims without calling on the pledged negotiable securities deposited with the company by its policyholders. The other classes of stock insurance companies (fire and marine) were also authorized but not compelled to invest their surplus capital in an unearned premium fund of approved securities.

Insurance companies could make loans on all varieties of real estate provided the appraised value of the land was at least twice the mortgage's value. A mortmain clause was also included whose aim was to prevent real estate from accumulating in the hands of insurance corporations where land was commonly used as collateral. Furthermore, unless the Comptroller issued a certificate of exemption, the real property a company acquired through foreclosure, or had conveyed to it to satisfy debts, or land it purchased to satisfy a judgment, could be held for only five years. Agrarian fear of corporate ownership of land was still strong.

Agents of all out-of-state and foreign fire insurance corporations had to be licensed by the Comptroller and, in a supplementary statute, they were required, if selling policies in New York City, to post a $1,000 bond with the City Treasurer or with the local fire department but only a $500 bond if located elsewhere in the state; and the corporation they represented had to be as highly capitalized as New York corporations. Foreign fire insurance corporations also had to pay a 2 percent tax to the treasurers of local fire departments on all annual premiums collected. Two years later, in 1851, all life insurance corporations (stock and mutual) then doing business in the state were required to deposit an unearned premium fund of $50,000 in approved securities with the Comptroller, but if organized under the general incorporation statute of 1849, they had to deposit $100,000; and the Comptroller was granted broad investigatory power over the financial affairs of all insurance corporations, especially life insurance corporations. He was authorized to preside over their bankruptcy, and agents of all out-of-state life insurance corporations were brought under comprehensive regulation.[41] These regulatory procedures were closely based upon banking experience. In effect, the Comptroller was authorized to set up a semipermanent regulatory commission for insurance corporations and enforce their public service responsibilities in a similar way as had been done for banks.

The comprehensive general incorporation statute for insurance corporations of 1849 was partially replaced in 1853 by two separate general incorporation statutes, leaving only marine corporations that could be chartered under the 1849 statute. The first of these statutes authorized stock corporations to insure life, health, and livestock and the second comprehended mutual and stock corporations to underwrite fire risks. This statute was necessitated by the loose operation of mutual fire insurance companies organized under the 1849 law.

The 1849 general law had invited mass frauds by allowing mutual fire insurance companies to incorporate by merely subscribing $100,000 in secured notes. Not one dollar in cash had to be contributed and even the property that was represented by the $100,000 of notes could be grossly overvalued. Furthermore, the promoters were allowed to withdraw these notes as soon as bona fide notes were pledged from persons who desired real insurance protection. A second weakness was the practice of paying agents a straight commission instead of a salary on the policies they sold. This encouraged them to write policies without any attempt to classify them on the basis of risk. A third weakness was the competition between unsound companies, which caused the cash portion of the premium to be lowered to hazardous levels.

The 1853 statute for fire insurance corporations greatly aided the organization of sound mutual companies because it forced them to increase their capitalization and liquidity. All notes deposited with a mutual company at its organization had to remain with the company until it had accumulated sufficient surplus capital to equal the capitalization of stock companies. Their surplus capital could be invested in a broad variety of securities that included railroad stocks and bonds. In addition, mutual companies were required to have a larger number of initial subscribers who had to put up many low-value notes as collateral. This gave stock companies a competitive advantage in insuring large commercial and industrial buildings. In 1854, mutual fire insurance corporations that tried to compete in urban areas were allowed to reorganize as stock companies.

Between 1849 and the passage of the 1853 statute, fifty-four mutual companies were chartered, but the recession of 1852 bankrupted all of the weak and fraudulent companies. The 1853 statute closed the door to further mass frauds. By 1860, only seven of these fifty-four companies were still in business. The average loss to policyholders per bankruptcy was $50,000.[42]

Mutual fire insurance corporations were relegated to rural areas where they could be started with little capital and where they insured low-risk buildings. These corporations were essentially local, nonprofit, public service organizations, which Massachusetts had encouraged to incorporate in 1835 by enacting a general regulatory statute. New York did not make a distinction between rural public service corporations and urban-commercial companies until 1857 when a general incorporation statute was finally passed for township fire insurance companies.[43] In 1859 insurance regulation was placed in the hands of an Insurance Department, similar to the Bank Department.

The 1850s was a period of very extensive regulation of insurance corporations. Massachusetts appears to have led the way, but New York was not far behind. The regulations were nearly always in the direction of providing security for policyholders by regulating corporate investment and financial practices. These regulations were adopted with the approval of the stronger insurance corporations, in an effort to strengthen weaker, undercapitalized companies, and it took place at a time when the value of life insurance sales was rapidly increasing.[44]

PLANK ROADS AND TURNPIKES

New York's first plank road corporation was chartered in 1844. Its roadway was completed in July 1846, and it was immediately profitable. Its high profitability led to a great demand for charters at the 1847 legislative session. In order to prevent its time from being consumed by hearing each application, the legislature passed a general incorporation statute for plank roads and turnpikes. Plank roads were a new form of overland transportation first built in Upper Canada (Ontario) in 1834. They were usually short, from five to twenty miles in length, and radiated like spokes from market towns situated on canals or railroads. Plank roads were frequently called farmer's railroads because they performed the function of branch lines and because farm wagons could operate on them, which was impossible on conventional railroads.[45]

The 1847 law updated the 1807 turnpike statute to apply to both plank roads and turnpikes; however, as the price for obtaining legislation so soon after the Convention, while the issue of franchise corporations was still fresh in the public mind, investors were saddled with double liability. A minimum capitalization of $500 per mile was required, and County Supervisors had to approve of the project and then appoint a three-man commission to lay out a route that would best serve the public. Only then could the corporation acquire land via eminent domain proceedings. The same commission was also to certify that a minimum distance of five miles had been completed before allowing the company to collect tolls, and the maximum annual dividend rate was set at 10 percent. The road and its ancillary facilities were liable to local taxation.

By 1853, the defects of plank roads were obvious. Although they required little capital to build, they deteriorated very quickly and this more than offset their low capital cost. Shareholders applied to the legislature for relief and were granted an increase in tolls and exemption from all taxation if the corporation's net annual income did not exceed 5 percent on the paid-in capital. At the same time, existing turnpike corporations were deprived of the total tax exemption they had enjoyed under the revised statutes of 1828 and

1852, but if they earned less than 5 percent on their paid-in capital, they could still commute all of their local real estate taxes by paying 5 percent of their profits to the County Treasurer. In 1854, plank roads and turnpikes were authorized to abandon the whole or part of their roads or resurface their rights-of-way with gravel, but on doing so they could collect only turnpike tolls. From 1847 to 1855, only twelve turnpikes were chartered, while during the same period 347 plank roads were incorporated, but because of their great shortcoming, the plank road era ended abruptly in 1853.[46]

TOLL BRIDGE, FERRY, AND STAGECOACH COMPANIES

The demand for toll bridge charters was small and decreasing because the public wanted free bridges. For this reason, the general incorporation statute of 1848 granted county Boards of Supervisors the authority to issue building permits, regulate tolls, and defer construction until 25 percent of the shares had been subscribed and 5 percent paid-in. Only then could the articles of incorporation be filed with the County Clerk and State Engineer. In 1853, a general incorporation statute was passed for ferry corporations, and in 1854, one was passed for omnibus enterprises operating in New York City.[47]

NAVIGATION CORPORATIONS

In 1852, ocean steam navigation corporations were authorized to organize under a general incorporation statute. Such corporations could be capitalized at from $50,000 to $2 million, but once a corporation was established, its capitalization could be diminished or increased provided a reduction in capitalization did not fall below the corporation's debt. In 1853, the maximum capitalization was increased to $4 million. From 1853 through 1855, fifteen corporations were organized under the statute.

A general incorporation statute was enacted for steamboat corporations on Lake George in 1854. It was made subject to all the provisions of the ocean navigation statute, but capital limits were from $20,000 to $200,000. Later in the session, the general incorporation privilege was extended to all the state's navigable waters whether a company used steam or sail propulsion.[48] No corporation formed under this statute could own shares in any other, nor combine with any other corporation organized under its provisions, nor could railroads own shares in one, nor could such a corporation mortgage its property or have liens on it until the company's stock was fully paid-in. In 1854 and 1855, seven corporations were chartered under the statute's provisions.

BUILDING ERECTION CORPORATIONS

In 1853, a general incorporation statute was passed allowing five or more persons to form a corporation to erect buildings.[49] It is not clear whether this was a general incorporation statute for contractors who were in the business of erecting buildings or for investors who proposed to erect buildings, and own and manage them. The wording of the statute applies to both situations, but it was probably intended for investors intending to erect one particular building or group of buildings. Fourteen of these corporations were chartered between 1853 and 1856.

UNINCORPORATED COMPANIES

The legislature did not recognize a legal distinction between incorporated and unincorporated companies until 1849, although a Michigan case had made this distinction eighteen years earlier. Unincorporated associations or joint-stock companies (the terms are identical) were widely used in the import-export business, wholesale distributing, sail and steam navigation, the Erie Canal carrying trade, shipbuilding, tanning, printing, and in a large variety of other businesses. The two main features of unincorporated businesses were full shareholder liability and not being a single legal entity; but they often possessed some of the other attributes of unincorporated businesses, such as numerous shareholders, relatively high capitalization, and occasionally a paid professional management. Legally speaking, however, such businesses were no more than expanded partnerships.

The 1849 statute authorized suits against unincorporated companies to run in the name of the president or treasurer, which would include all of the shareholders or associates; and suits would not abate upon the death of one of the company's owners. Nothing in the statute, however, was to be construed as bestowing any corporate powers on unincorporated associations except the power to be sued in its collective capacity. In 1851, the use of this statute was more precisely defined. It could be used in situations where an association of seven or more persons held property in common.[50]

NOTES

1. *Messages from the Governors of New York*, Vol. 4, 515, April 1, 1850, Hamilton Fish; 574, April 5, 1851, Washington Hunt; 636–639, April 15, 1852, Washington Hunt. *New York Laws*, 1853, 1854, 1855, Index, "Corporations."

2. *Messages from the Governors of New York*, Vol. 4, 379, Jan. 5, 1847, John Young.

3. A. B. Johnson, "The Legislative History of Corporations in the State of New York, or, The Progress of Liberal Sentiments," *Hunt's Merchants Magazine*, Vol. 23, December 1850 in Carter Goodrich, ed., *The Government and the Economy: 1783–1861*, 403. John W. Cadman, *The Corporation in New Jersey, 1791–1875*, 149. *Senate Documents 1847*, No. 116; *Assembly Documents 1847*, No. 143; 240.

4. *Messages from the Governors of New York*, Vol. 4, 400, Jan. 4, 1848, John Young. *New York Laws*, Ch. 40, 1848, 54.

5. Douglas T. Miller, *Jacksonian Aristocracy: Class and Democracy in New York, 1830–1860*, 112–113, 116–118. D. L. Burn, "The Genesis of American Engineering Competition, 1850–1870," *Economic History*, Vol. 2, 1931, 307. An English observer in the 1850s was highly impressed by the legal encouragement that several state governments gave entrepreneurs by ease of incorporation for manufacturing operations, with limited liability for stockholders. *New York Laws*, Ch. 333, 1853, 705; Ch. 654, 1853, 1240.

6. Franklin B. Hough, *The New York Convention Manual, 1867*, Part 2, Statistics, 34–36. *New York Laws*, Ch. 14, 1851, 16; Ch. 301, 1855, 516; Ch. 262, 1857, 549.

7. *New York Laws*, Ch. 37, 1848, 48; Ch. 312, 1854, 665.

8. Robert L. Thompson, *Wiring a Continent, 1832–1866*, 66–68. James D. Reid, *The Telegraph in America*, 112, 300. *New York Laws*, Ch. 243, 1845, 264; Ch. 265, 1848, 392.

9. Robert L. Thompson, *Wiring a Continent, 1832–1866*, 194–202, 215, 262–272. *New York Laws*, Ch. 471, 1853, 931.

10.   Dixon R. Fox, *The Decline of Aristocracy in the Politics of New York 1801–1840*, 337. Jabez D. Hammond, *Life and Times of Silas Wright*, 84–85.

11.   The Erie Canal was always profitable, and this fact helped prevent the bankruptcy of the state in 1842. Only New Jersey appears to have made its internal improvement debts self-liquidating, and this was done by granting a monopoly to the Joint Companies (railroad and canal) and levying a transit tax on all passengers and freight between New York City and Philadelphia. After 1835, New Jersey received a steady and increasing revenue from this tax, and was not forced to levy a land tax until the exigencies of the Civil War. John W. Cadman, *The Corporation in New Jersey, 1791–1875*, 55–59.

12.   Pennsylvania got out of the internal improvement business from 1842 to 1859. Carter Goodrich, "The Revulsion Against Internal Improvements," *Journal of Economic History*, Vol. 10, 1950, 146–147, 161–164. Louis Hartz, *Economic Policy and Democratic Thought: Pennsylvania, 1776–1860*, 149, 161–165.

13.   Lee Benson, *Merchants, Farmers, and Railroads*, 9–18. Alvin E. Harlow, *The Road of the Century: The Story of the New York Central*, 70–74. John L. Ringwalt, *Development of Transportation Systems in the United States*, 148–149. Douglass C. North, *The Economic Growth of the United States, 1790–1860*, 105–111.

14.   Louis B. Schmidt, "Internal Commerce and the Development of National Economy before 1860," *Journal of Political Economy*, Vol. 47, 1939, 814–816. Stanley Lebergott, "United States Transport Advance and Externalities," *Journal of Economic History*, Vol. 26, 1966, 440–446.

15.   *New York Laws*, Ch. 218, 1839, 195. *Mass. Laws*, Ch. 99, 1838, 383.

16.   Frank W. Stevens, *The Beginnings of the New York Central Railroad*, 290. Henry V. Poor, *Sketch of the Rise and Progress of the Internal Improvement of the Internal Commerce of the United States* (1881), 40. *New York Laws*, Ch. 335, 1844, 518; Ch. 270, 1847, 298. In 1844, about 90 percent of the revenues of New York railroads came from passenger traffic. In 1854, the New York Central Railroad had $2,943,000 in freight revenue and $4,388,000 in passenger revenue. In 1855, passenger and freight revenues were nearly equal.

17.   Frank W. Stevens, *The Beginnings of the New York Central Railroad*, 288–300, 332–335. Harry H. Pierce, *The Railroads of New York: A Study of Government Aid, 1826–1875*, 60–72. David M. Ellis, *Land Lords and Farmers in the Hudson-Mohawk Region, 1790–1850*, 175–180. Alfred D. Chandler, Jr., "The Railroads: Pioneers in Modern Corporate

Management," *Business History Review*, Vol. 39, 1965, 17-25. Peter Temin, *Iron and Steel in Nineteenth-Century America: An Economic Inquiry*, 40-48. *New York Laws*, Ch. 222, 1847, 240; Ch. 272, 1847, 201.

18.   *New York Laws*, Ch. 140, 1848, 221. *Senate Documents*, 1847.

19.   *Senate Documents, 1847*, No. 64, 3-5.

20.   *Messages from the Governors of New York*, Vol. 4, 495, Jan. 2, 1850, Hamilton Fish. Lee Benson, *Merchants, Farmers, and Railroads*, 1-6. Anon., "Railroad Legislation in New York in 1849," *The Merchant's Magazine and Commercial Review*, Vol. 21, July-December 1849, 164-171. L. Ray Gunn, "Policital Implications of General Incorporation Laws in New York to 1860," *Mid-America*, Vol. 59, 1977, 184-185. *New York Laws*, Ch. 140, 1850, 211.

21.   In 1831, the court defined railroads as public improvement franchises and confirmed the power of the legislature to grant them the power of eminent domain; *Beekman* v. *Saratoga and Schenectady Railroad Corporation*, 1831, 3 Paige Chancery 75. The court had previously confirmed the state's power to grant eminent domain to turnpike corporations, *Rogers* v. *Bradshaw*, 1823, 20 Johns 742, which was based on an earlier opinion by Chancellor Kent, *Gardner* v. *Village of Newburgh*, 1816, 2 Johnson Chancery 162, which broadly construed the use of eminent domain powers for public improvements, provided there was just compensation.

22.   John L. Ringwalt, *Development of Transportation Systems in the United States*, 124, 147-148. Harry H. Pierce, *Railroads of New York: A Study of Government Aid, 1826-1875*, 8-12, 15-20, 27-29.

23.   *New York Laws*, Ch. 603, 1853, 1135.

24.   *Messages from the Governors of New York*, Vol. 4, 378, 451, 542. Jan. 2, 1851; June 10, 1851; Washington Hunt. *New York Laws*, Ch. 497, 1851, 972; Ch. 485, 1851, 911.

25.   *Newell* v. *The People*, 1852, 7 N.Y. 9. The canal revenue certificates were not guaranteed by the state's credit, except out of anticipated canal revenues. Judge Greene C. Bronson gave an advisory opinion in favor of the constitutionality of such certificates. He said they were secured by a fourth mortgage on the canal's revenue. Ronald E. Shaw, *Erie Water West, A History of the Erie Canal, 1792-1854*, 367-371.

26.   Don C. Sower, *The Financial History of New York State from 1789 to 1912*, 80-87. Herbert D. A. Donovan, *The Barnburners, 1832-1852*, 50. *Messages from the Governors of New York*, Vol. 4, 670-674, Jan. 4, 1853, Horatio Seymour.

27.   Harry H. Pierce, *Railroads of New York: A Study of Government Aid, 1826-1875*, 4-21, 26-27. *New York Laws*, Ch. 76, 1853, 110.

28.   Frank W. Stevens, *The Beginnings of the New York Central Railroad*, 350-360. Of ten companies, seven were in operation, and one

was under construction and nearly completed. Two had their routes laid out but construction had not yet begun.

29. *New York Laws*, Ch. 302, 1855, 517.

30. Frank W. Stevens, *The Beginnings of the New York Central Railroad*, 341–346. *Laws of New York*, Ch. 147, 1850; Ch. 117, Ch. 157, Ch. 275, 1851. There were two periods of intense railroad construction in New York. The first period was from 1848–1853, and the general incorporation statute for railroads was a major legal aid. The second was from 1868–1873. In the second period, there was twice as much money spent, and ten times as much municipal aid given. Feeder lines made up a very large percentage of construction during the second period; Harry H. Pierce, *Railroads of New York: A Study of Government Aid, 1826–1875*, Appendix, Charts 2 and 3.

31. The completion dates of the major trunkline railroads were: New York and Erie to Dunkirk, 1851; the Pennsylvania to Pittsburgh, 1852; the Baltimore and Ohio to Wheeling, 1853; the Hudson River and New York and Harlem to Albany, 1851; the Michigan Central to Chicago, 1852; and the Great Western to Detroit, 1853.

32. Edward C. Kirkland, *Men, Cities, and Transportation*, Vol. 2, 233–235. *Annual Report of the New York Railroad Commission, 1856; Assembly Documents 1856*, No. 12, Part 1, xx–xxvi, xxxix, xlii. *New York Laws*, Ch. 526, 1855, 960.

33. Gabriel Kolko, *Railroads and Regulation, 1877–1916*, 26–46. Thomas C. Cochran, *Railroad Leaders, 1845–1890*, 26. Lee Benson, *Merchants, Farmers, and Railroads*, 6–9, 204–209. Whitney R. Cross, *The Burned-Over District*, 55–73.

34. Stuart Bruchey, *The Roots of American Economic Growth, 1607–1861*, 148–150, 158–172. Walt W. Rostow, "The Take-Off into Self-Sustained Growth," *Economic Journal*, Vol. 66, 1956, 45–47. Peter Temin, "Steam and Waterpower in the Early Nineteenth Century," *Journal of Economic History*, Vol. 26, 1966, 188–189. David J. Jeremy, "Innovation in American Textile Technology during the Early 19th Century," *Technology and Culture*, Vol. 14, 1973, 40–48. D. L. Burn, "The Genesis of American Engineering Competition, 1850–1870," *Economic History*, Vol. 2, 1931, 299. H. J. Habakkuk, *American and British Technology in the Nineteenth Century: The Search for Labour-Saving Inventions*, 7–8, 32–34, 52–59. John E. Sawyer, "The Social Basis of the American System of Manufacture," *Journal of Economic History*, Vol. 14, 1954, 369–374. Nathan Rosenberg, "Technological Change in the Machine Tool Industry, 1840–1910," *Journal of Economic History*, Vol. 23, 1963, 418, 428–431. Merritt R. Smith, *Harpers Ferry Armory and the New Technology*, 284–292. The business of making machines used in industrial production

became identifiable as a separate industry about 1840 and was firmly established by 1855. The development of this industry indicates a high degree of technological sophistication.

35. Alfred D. Chandler, ed., *The Railroads, The Nation's First Big Business*, 43-45. Leland H. Jenks, "Railroads as an Economic Force in American Development," *Journal of Economic History*, Vol. 4, 1944, 7-8. Thomas C. Cochran, "The Entrepreneur in American Capital Formation," in Moses Abramovitz, ed., *Capital Formation and Economic Growth*, 345-347, 355-357. Joseph A. Schumpeter, *Business Cycles*, Vol. 1, 326-333.

36. Robert E. Chaddock, *The Safety Fund Banking System in New York, 1829-1866*, 326, 334-337. *New York Laws*, Ch. 18, 1840, 14; Ch. 292, 1841, 279; Ch. 114, 1845, 91; Ch. 97, 1846, 100.

37. Jabez D. Hammond, *The Life and Times of Silas Wright*, 358-359. *Messages from the Governors of New York*, Vol. 4, 33-34, Jan. 3, 1843, William C. Bouck. *New York Laws*, Ch. 218, 1843, 299.

38. *New York Laws*, Ch. 226, 1849, 340; Ch. 164, 1851, 309.

39. Shepard B. Clough, *A History of American Life Insurance, 1843-1943*, 29. *New York Laws*, Ch. 80, 1840, 59.

40. *New York Laws*, Ch. 205, 1848, 319; Ch. 308, 1849, 441. *Deraismes v. Merchants Mutual Insurance Company*, 1848, 1 Comstock 371, confirmed the power of mutual insurance companies to cash pledged assets when unexpectedly large losses occurred.

41. *New York Laws*, Ch. 178, 1849, 239; Ch. 95, 1851, 167.

42. Albert S. Bolles, *Industrial History of the United States*, 831-832. *New York Laws*, Ch. 463, 1853, 887; Ch. 466, 1853, 904; Ch. 551, 1853, 1029; Ch. 369, 1854, 771.

43. John Bainbridge, *Biography of an Idea: The Story of Mutual Fire and Casualty Insurance*, 88. Lester W. Zartman, ed., *Yale Readings in Insurance*, 24-25. *New York Laws*, Ch. 739, 1857, 574. *Mass. Laws*, Ch. 147, 1835, 529.

44. Shepard B. Clough, *A Century of American Life Insurance, 1843-1943*, 42. Marquis James, *Biography of a Business, 1792-1942: The Insurance Company of North America*, 145. In 1854, in Philadelphia, there were twenty-six insurance corporations. A local business publication classed nine as reliable, ten as having insufficient assets, one as unsafe, and six as fraudulent. In the Panic of 1857, fifteen of the twenty-six failed.

45. Joseph A. Durrenburger, *Turnpikes: A Study of the Toll Road Movement in the Middle Atlantic States and Maryland*, 144-145. Caroline E. MacGill, *History of Transportation in the United States before 1860*, 299-305. *New York Laws*, Ch. 210, 1847, 216.

46. Franklin B. Hough, *New York Convention Manual, 1867*, Part 2; Statistics, 33. *New York Laws*, Ch. 250, 1849, 374; Ch. 245, 1853, 535; Ch. 654, 1853, 1240.

47. T. S. Gillet, ed., *General Index of the Laws of the State of New York*, 110–124. Bridge construction with public funds became more frequent after 1820. *New York Laws*, Ch. 259, 1848, 375; Ch. 135, 1853, 213; Ch. 142, 1854, 325.

48. *New York Laws*, Ch. 228, 1852, 302; Ch. 124, 1853, 202; Ch. 3, 1854, 9; Ch. 232, 1854, 518.

49. *New York Laws*, Ch. 117, 1853, 179.

50. *New York Laws*, Ch. 258, 1849, 389; Ch. 455, 1851, 838. The legislature's intent to make unincorporated associations corporations for the limited purposes of being sued in a collective capacity was confirmed in *Corning* v. *Greene*, 1856, 23 Barbour 33. See also *Williams* v. *Michigan Bank*, 1831, 7 Wendell 542.

9

Later Benevolent
Public Service
and Municipal Corporations

CEMETERY CORPORATIONS

The first two general incorporation statutes enacted under the new constitution were passed in 1847. They were for rural cemeteries: one for individual organizers and the other for villages. The one for individuals was the same statute the revisers had tried to insert in the revised statutes in 1828, but which the legislature rejected as unconstitutional. The state's initial cemetery legislation had been passed in 1826 when townships were authorized to own burial grounds, a privilege extended to religious congregations in New York City and adjoining counties in 1842 and to all religious congregations in 1850. The 1847 cemetery statute for incorporated villages authorized them to establish a public burial ground if the voters approved, but the cemetery's title vested with the incorporated village and not with an independent governing body. In 1854, any number of persons were authorized to purchase up to three acres of land for use as a private or family cemetery.[1]

BENEVOLENT, CHARITABLE, SCIENTIFIC, AND MISSIONARY SOCIETIES

The general incorporation statute for all classes of charitable-scientific societies removed a routine burden from the legislature. From its passage in 1848 to 1855, a total of 265 societies were chartered under its provisions. Five or more persons could incorporate upon obtaining the approval of one of the justices of the

Supreme Court in the district where he lived. To prevent abuses by legacy seekers, only 25 percent of the value of all legacies (up to a limit of $10,000) could be received if the donor left a wife and children, and such bequests were wholly invalid if made within two months of death. In 1854, the state required charitable societies that wished to mortgage their real property to secure permission from the state Supreme Court. If the Court agreed, it had the power to direct how the money was to be used.[2]

SAVINGS BANKS AND BUILDING, MUTUAL LOAN, AND ACCUMULATING FUND ASSOCIATIONS

While studying the poor laws in 1810, a Scottish Presbyterian clergyman originated the idea for a savings bank. He organized one for his parish and publicized the idea so that by 1817 seventy-eight of them were operating in Great Britain. To ensure their integrity, he lobbied for legislation to bring them under government supervision. Protection was secured in 1817 with passage of a general organizational statute that placed the management of each bank in the hands of a board of trustees.[3]

New York incorporated its first savings bank in 1819, two years after Massachusetts had incorporated the first one in the United States, and three years after the first one opened in Philadelphia. An attempt had been made to secure incorporation in New York in 1817, but it failed because the promoters called it a bank. This involved it in the acrimony of the currency and credit controversy of that year.[4] In the following year, the same charter was reintroduced with its title changed to savings corporation, and Governor DeWitt Clinton recommended its passage in the same sentence in which he favored legislation to support orphan asylums, religious and moral societies, and free public schools. The New York Society for the Prevention of Pauperism sponsored it in order to encourage tradesmen and persons of modest means to make small regular savings. The depositors received the interest that was earned when their savings were invested in low-risk securities. The officers of the corporation were prominent citizens who served without pay.

The savings bank failed to receive a charter in 1818 because the promoters of a commercial bank tried to lobby their charter through the legislature in the guise of philanthropy, and the legislature was occupied in passing a new and stronger restraining statute. It was not incorporated until 1819. The only investments the bank could make were in United States and New York bonds, but in the next year, it was authorized to invest in New York City bonds, and later banks could invest in an enlarged variety of securities. The bank was an instantaneous success and soon was one of the larger financial institutions in the city. By 1821, it was the largest single investor in the bonds sold to build the Erie Canal. Later, it made large investments in the municipal bonds of New York City that financed the building of sewers, freshwater conduits, and other large-scale public health and public improvement projects.

From the beginning, the board of directors included men who were directors of commercial banks, and who voluntarily gave their time to operate the bank. Initially, the bank was open for business only six hours per week and at the end of each day, the net deposits were taken to a commercial bank for deposit. The organizers of later mutual savings banks were often directors of commercial banks who frequently allowed the savings bank to have a rent-free office in their building. When this occurred, the deposits made by the savings banks were added to the deposits of the commercial bank and thus increased their ability to make loans. The commercial bank had the use of these deposits until the directors of the savings bank invested accumulated savings in long-term securities.[5]

In the 1846 legislative session, during the controversy over holding a constitutional convention, a committee reported against the passage of a general incorporation statute for savings banks. Two years after the adoption of the constitution, however, another general incorporation statute was introduced and passed by the Assembly, but it was rejected by the Senate. A majority of the Senate believed that a general incorporation statute would vitiate public confidence in the integrity of savings banks because a special act implied that the state had examined the sponsors and found them to be honest and respectable men in whom the public could trust.

Another attempt to enact a general incorporation statute was made in 1850, but its opponents sought the opinion of the Attorney

General on its constitutionality. If savings corporations were really banks, they could be created under the existing free banking statute. If they were not banks, they required special charters, and the opponents of the general law had enough votes to defeat it. The Attorney General thought they were not within the meaning of the constitutional provision because they did not circulate banknotes. They were really savings institutions, popularly called banks.[6] He believed that if the legislature found it feasible to create them under a general incorporation statute, then any special charters would be unconstitutional under Article 8, Section 1.[7] Based on this opinion, which satisfied no one, the proponents of a general incorporation statute introduced a new bill in 1851. A majority of the Assembly's Judiciary Committee favored it and accused the directors of the existing savings banks of opposing a general law for fear of competition. Those who opposed the law raised the objection that the sponsors of nonprofit savings banks ought to be examined by the state. This was a responsibility that could not be safely delegated to local authorities because it would invite mass fraud. The bill was not passed, and New York did not get a general incorporation statute for savings banks until 1875.[8]

After the failure to enact a general incorporation statute for savings banks, the legislature passed a general incorporation statute for building, mutual loan, and accumulating fund associations. It was in the nature of a consolation prize. These associations resembled the modern savings and loan association. The first of these associations in the United States was organized in 1831 in Frankford, Pennsylvania, then an industrial suburb of Philadelphia. The principal founders were a group of millowners and workers, several of whom had immigrated from England where mutual building societies had been organized as early as 1780.

Like savings banks, their purpose was semi-philanthropic, to encourage urban workers and tradesmen to accumulate funds for "the purchase of real estate, the erection of buildings, or the making of other improvements on land, or to pay off incumbrances thereon, or to aid its members in acquiring real estate, making improvements and removing incumbrances."[9] Incorporation was of immense advantage. If the members were not incorporated and were not granted limited liability, they were partners at common law and would be fully liable for the debts of all the other members. This would be self-defeating. Both building and loan associations and savings banks were local self-help organizations that reflected the increasing urbanization and industrialization of the United States. They helped an urban democracy stabilize by aiding industrial workers to acquire a stake in society by becoming home owners. Great Britain protected these organizations by an act of Parliament in 1836, but Pennsylvania, in 1850, was the first state to provide encouragement when it amended its general incorporation statute for charities to include them. Between the passage of the New York statute in 1851 and January 1856, seventy-two of these associations were chartered.[10]

OTHER BENEVOLENT PUBLIC SERVICE CORPORATIONS

In 1851, a general incorporation statute was passed for proprietary schools, and in 1853, ones were passed for proprietary libraries, union school districts, agricultural and horticultural societies, and medical colleges. In 1854, general incorporation statutes were passed for religious congregations having rent-free pews and for corporations to improve the breed of horses. The purposes of these organizations had continuously received public encouragement since the late eighteenth century, and most of them had been granted individual incorporation at a very early date.[11] They were essentially noncontroversial and had been innocent victims of the two-thirds clause of the 1821 Constitution.

VILLAGES

A general incorporation statute for villages was passed in the special session in the fall of 1847, thus carrying out the convention's intention that villages should be created under a general law. Villages had to contain at least 300 persons, but if a village's area was greater than one square mile, it had to contain a population at the ratio of at least 300 per square mile. The application for incorporation was to be made before the County Court of Sessions, and after a hearing, the Court could declare the village a corporation.[12]

NOTES

1.   *New York Laws*, Ch. 67, 1826, 47; Ch. 153, 1842, 191; Ch. 133, 1847, 125; Ch. 209, 1847, 214; Ch. 112, 1854, 265.

2.   *New York Laws*, Ch. 319, 1848, 447; Ch. 50, 1854, 125.

3.   James H. Manning, *Century of American Savings Banks*, Vol. 1, 37-39. H. Oliver Horne, *A History of Savings Banks*, 39-53.

4.   Peter L. Payne, Lance E. Davis, *The Savings Bank of Baltimore, 1818-1866*, 15-24.

5.   Alan L. Olmstead, *New York City Mutual Savings Banks, 1819-1861*, 3-21. Weldon Welfling, *Savings Banking in New York State*, 4-16. Emerson W. Keyes, *A History of Savings Banks in the United States*, Vol. 1, 312-376, 387-400. Nathan Miller, *The Enterprise of a Free People*, 88. Stuart Bruchey, *The Roots of American Economic Growth, 1607-1861*, 143-144. Lance E. Davis, Peter L. Payne, "From Benevolence to Business: The Story of Two Savings Banks," *Business History Review*, Vol. 32, 1958, 386-393. *New York Laws*, Ch. 62, 1819, 66; Ch. 347, 1839, 320.

6.   Hiram E. Sickels, ed., *Opinions of the Attorneys-General of the State of New York*, 203. Bray Hammond, *Banks and Politics in America from the Revolution to the Civil War*, 194. *Assembly Documents 1846*, Jan. 5, 1846. As a result of this opinion, a statute was required (Ch. 136, 1857) to bring savings banks back under the regulation of the Banking Department.

7.   Three years later the courts said otherwise, and frequently thereafter they made the obvious interpretation that the legislature did not have to create all corporations by a general incorporation procedure. *Mosier v. Hilton*, 1853, 15 Barbour 663. *The People v. Bowen*, 1859, 30 Barbour 39.

8.   Emerson W. Keyes, *A History of Savings Banks in the United States*, Vol. 1, 400-411, Vol. 2, 39-40. *Assembly Documents 1851*, No. 39; 40.

9.   New York Laws, Ch. 122, 1851, 234.

10.   Henry M. Bodfish, ed., *History of Building and Loan in the United States*, 11, 25, 32, 79, 500-502, 547. Joseph H. Sundheim, *Law of Building and Loan Associations*, 3-30. Roy A. Foulke, *The Sinews of American Commerce*, 181-182.

11.   *New York Laws*, Ch. 269, 1854, 591.

12.   *New York Laws*, Ch. 426, 1847, 532.

10

The Development
of Corporation
Regulation

STATE REGULATION

By 1855, most commercial states had developed five devices to protect the public interest against unwise grants of power to business corporations. The two most primitive were a time duration of charters and unlimited liability. The time duration was usually twenty years or less. New York created few business corporations with full liability because this doctrine tended to retard investments in large-scale projects that had great social utility. The three more sophisticated limitations on corporate powers were: (1) narrow interpretation of charters; (2) a reserve clause that allowed the legislature to amend any charter at any time and for any reason; and (3) creation of independent regulatory commissions.

The New York legislature always granted some form of limited liability, usually double liability, to the shareholders of businesses that were organized as corporations. Double liability found its way into the 1846 Constitution for banks that circulated paper currency, but the extent of liability for other classes of business corporations was left to legislative discretion. This was usually limited liability: the shareholder being liable for only the fully paid-up value of each share owned. The distinction between those businesses that had always been organized as corporations and those that had always been organized as single proprietorships or partnerships (with full liability) slowly began to break down after 1855 when the general incorporation statute for manufacturing was amended to comprehend many types of businesses that had originally been organized as full liability enterprises but found the corporate structure more convenient.

In the early years of the republic, the popular concept of a business corporation was as a monopoly. It was a concept that died slowly because many of the early corporations had semi-monopolistic features. However, because many of the early business corporations performed socially beneficial functions, the courts at an early date protected them from what they considered to be democratic assaults on wealth, such as unilaterally repealing charters, discriminatory taxation, or unrealistic regulation. One of the major legal concepts that bulwarked the doctrine of vested rights was interpreting charters as contracts. James Kent, a Federalist who sat on New York's Council of Revision, favored this interpretation at an early date and he was supported by Republican governors. Kent believed that a charter was a privilege that was not to be granted except for a necessary public good; but once granted, it became a right that was to be protected as long as the corporation served the ends for which it was created. When the United States Supreme Court defined charters as contracts in 1819, in *Dartmouth College* v. *Woodward*, this concept was already familiar to New York lawyers.

Kent first wrestled with this problem in April 1804 when the legislature passed a statute altering the election procedure in the City of New York, contrary to the city's charter. It was a political act because the Federalist party was strongly represented in the city. Kent spoke as a Federalist partisan, although he used judicial language, and he did not make a distinction between public and private corporations. He said, "Where the ordinary process of law affords a competent remedy, charters of incorporation containing grants of personal and municipal privileges were not to be essentially effected without the consent of the parties concerned." He did, however, concede that such alterations would be justified by "some strong public necessity."[1] His opinion was overruled. A similar idea was expressed by the Massachusetts Court in *Wales* v. *Stetson* in 1806.[2]

Governor George Clinton's annual messages of 1801 and 1802 had recognized that turnpike charters did not reserve enough regulatory powers to the state, and in 1803, he cautioned the legislature at considerable length about the proliferation of these corporations. He specifically mentioned "the difficulties which occur in devising amendment to acts of this kind without invading corporation rights, which ought to serve as an admonition to great care and circumspection in framing future ones."[3] In 1806, the legislature put strong regulatory powers in the hands of county turnpike commissions, authorizing them to open the gates of any turnpike that was out of repair. Kent strongly objected on the grounds that such an act voided the charter-contract between the state and the turnpike corporation without a judicial hearing. Kent was again overruled.

In 1807, the legislature tried to alter the charter of Columbia College, contrary to the privileges confirmed in 1787. Kent wrote a veto opinion in which he again admitted that intervention of the legislature would be justified "by some strong public necessity, to which all chartered privileges may be deemed subservient"; however, he went on, "It is a sound principle in free governments . . . that charters of incorporation, whether granted for private or local, or charitable, or literary, or religious purposes, were not to be effected without due process of law, or without the consent of the parties concerned."[4] This veto was upheld.

Three days later, when the legislature passed a statute forbidding out-of-state insurance corporations from underwriting risks in New York City, Kent spoke against this shortsighted policy. He gave a very strong constitutional objection. This statute was "inconsistent with the second section of the fourth article of the Constitution of the United States which declared that the citizens of each state shall be entitled to all privileges and immunities of citizens of the several states. This inter-community of privileges secured to the citizens of the several states applies to their personal rights and immunities, and among others, to the free right to exercise trade and commerce." He further said: "It denies to the citizens of other states a right allowed to the citizens of this state, of making a contract of insurance by an agent. . . . This is unconstitutional discrimination."[5]

This is an extremely important generatlization. Kent applied the privileges and immunities of natural persons to business corporations, not only to New York-chartered corporations, but to all business corporations created by state legislatures. Furthermore, they could only be amended by due process of law—a test in the courts—not by legislative action unless consented to. This put business corporations on the same legal basis as incorporated benevolent public service organizations, which Kent had interpreted to be implied contracts, to be honored by the state.[6] When the *Dartmouth College Case* was decided in 1819, the concept of charters as contracts was quite familiar to New York lawyers and was embedded in New York Constitution of 1821, in Article 7, Section 14.

At the same time the charter-contract concept was being defined, two parallel limitations were emerging: one a court rule stating that charters of incorporation must be narrowly construed, and the other, the reserve clause embodied in a statute. The court rule emerged from the earliest litigation involving business corporations that came before the United States Supreme Court, where Chief Justice John Marshall had repeatedly stated the court's opinion that private corporations possessed only those powers closely related to the business authorized in the charter. This doctrine was a variation of the common law doctrine of municipal corporations. At common law, municipal corporations possessed only those powers necessary to perform the duties for which they were created. This was in sharp contrast to the common law as it applied to business corporations, which held that they could engage in any form of business not specifically forbidden in their charter. The American doctrine of limited corporate powers was best defined in the *Dartmouth College Case*, but by that time it had been recorded in many opinions by state courts and was generally accepted as a limitation on all private charters of incorporation.[7]

The major limitation on the charter-contract doctrine was the reserve clause, which gave the legislature total discretionary powers to alter or repeal any charter, at any time, and for any reason. In a concurring opinion in the *Dartmouth College Case*, Justice Joseph Story said, "If the legislature mean to claim such an authority [to repeal a charter without the consent of the corporation] it must be reserved in the grant."[8] The first explicit reserve clause in New York was placed in the 1806 general incorporation statute for county medical societies. The clause was designed to avoid the charge that either the New York Medical Society or a county medical society could act as a monopoly. Without this clause, the medical profession could have developed the idea of being a vested interest free from public control, especially since it had received corporate recognition by the state.

The first reserve clause for a New York business corporation was placed in the charter of the Commission Company in 1813 when the legislature reserved the right to amend its charter at any time after five years. The Commission Company was a wholesale corporation that promoted the production and facilitated the distribution of consumer goods made in New York during the commercial disruptions of the War of 1812 when imported manufactured goods were cut off. The reserve clause protected all retail and wholesale merchants, who possessed personal liability, from any unfair competition from a company whose stockholders possessed limited liability. The next reserve clauses were enacted in 1816, when they were inserted in two bank charters. In both cases, the clauses were placed in the last sentence of the charter and were in the nature of a radical remedy. The legislature retained the power to dissolve the banks at any time. The reserve clause was given its first widespread application in 1817, although the bank charters passed in that year did not contain it. It was not placed in the Constitution of 1821.

In 1824, the scale of bribery employed to secure a charter for the Chemical Bank made a mockery of the intent of the two-thirds clause. As a concession to securing the two-thirds majority needed for incorporation, a reserve clause was included. This raised the question of the expediency of making the reserve clause into a general statute. The Assembly passed such legislation, but the Senate had doubts about impairing all vested rights, although it was of the opinion that most private charters ought to have reserve clauses. The Senate was immediately questioned about the legal meaning of the clause, and by a near-unanimous vote adopted a resolution that the reservation of the right to alter or repeal a charter did not require a reason to be given. The exercise of that power was always a matter of legislative expediency.[9] In the next few years, the reserve clause was inconsistently inserted in charters until it was permanently enacted by the revised statutes of 1828.[10]

It was immediately tested in the courts. The New Jersey legislature had repealed the charter of a bank for stopping specie payments, and in an effort to collect some of the bank's assets, a Chancery suit was begun in New York. The Chancellor said that the reserve clause was not repugnant to the charter-contract doctrine because the power to repeal the bank's charter had been retained by the state. This power of repeal rested on the same legal principle that sustained state insolvency statutes: a general statute that was in force when a contract was made was part of the contract.[11] Municipal corporations were not part of this problem because, as Kent said, "They are founded by the government for public purposes and the whole interest in them belongs to the public."[12] When the whole interest remains in public hands, there can be no contract. By the mid-1830s, almost all states had placed reserve clauses in their constitutions or revised statutes. The reserve clause converted all charter-contracts into enabling acts. All regulatory statutes passed after an organization was incorporated became general amendments to its charter, and even a repealing statute was a type of amendment. Business corporations existed at the pleasure of the state. After the New York legislature passed a reserve clause, it took some time for the state to recover the corporate powers it had granted without reservation, but the state was saved any real embarrassment because almost all charters had time limits.

The final method of state regulation of business corporations was through independent commissions or special departments within state governments. Commissions had had a long development before they were applied to business corporations. In the colonial period, special commissions were erected for such important purposes as settling boundary disputes with neighboring colonies, and during the early national period, special commissions were frequently used for revising the statutes or gathering information about the tax and school laws of other states.

Permanent regulatory commissions are apparently derived from quasi-municipal corporations. The first permanent municipal commission was the Board of County Commissioners (made up of one representative from each township and incorporated village within a county) but the County Highway Commission is more directly related to the permanently established regulatory commissions for banks and railroads. Soon after the Revolution, provisions were made for building and maintaining public highways by requiring each county to have a commission that would allocate and expend local and state highway monies. The County Highway Commission was used as the model to regulate turnpikes when the state authorized each county to form a turnpike commission.

The earliest statewide regulatory bodies were chartered societies of private individuals like the Regents of the University and the New York Medical Society. Although these were private corporations, in fact they operated as state regulatory commissions to supervise professions that were vital to the public welfare, and to advise the legislature on beneficial regulations or policies. The state Agricultural Society performed a similar function. So did the state Supreme Court by exercising the power to admit or reject lawyers who could practice before it, which enforced a statewide standard of legal competence in a similar way that the New York Medical Society attempted to enforce statewide medical competence.

The intimate connection of banking to the currency made it a business that was as closely connnected with public welfare as education, highway and turnpike construction, medicine, and law. The first independent statewide regulatory commission over business corporations was the Bank Commission set up by the Safety Fund statute of 1829. Its major purposes were to detect bank frauds and gather information. It was not granted the power to regulate the supply of credit. At an earlier date, however, the first and second Banks of the United States had acted as de facto national credit-regulating commissions, and the Suffolk Bank in Boston performed the same function for New England. However, none of these credit-regulating agencies ever received official recognition for their public services; thus, the idea of a commission to regulate business corporations could have been borrowed from several sources.

When regulatory commissions for business corporations were established, they came in response to a changed social and economic situation. By 1830, the possession of a charter by a business was no longer an indication of economic privilege. Corporations had become major instruments in achieving economic democracy in the industrial sector of the economy. Furthermore, the increased transportation facilities meant that markets were no longer local. They had become statewide or regional, and a major contributor to this expansion had been certain types of corporate businesses, especially banking and transportation companies. If a state was to retain its economic health, these businesses had to be supervised by day-to-day regulation that courts could not give. When the commission device proved successful for banks, it was applied to insurance corporations and then railroads.

Regulatory agencies for banks and insurance corporations were firmly established in New York in the 1850s, but a railroad commission was tried and rejected. Other states, however, did establish permanent railroad commissions, but they possessed only limited powers: to enforce safety regulations, gather information for the legislature, and facilitate traffic interchange. They did not possess rate-making powers. After the states stopped direct or indirect guidance of railroad financial policies through partial ownership, or control of the railroad's sources of credit, commissions were the only tested regulatory device left, except chartering competing lines. When New York's Railroad Commission was dissolved, only the chartering of competing lines remained as a means of control. At a later date, however, the Railroad Commission was revived, and thereafter, it was applied to different industries as their products found a statewide and national market, and a minimum standard of performance had to be maintained.

REGULATION OF INTERSTATE BUSINESS CORPORATIONS BY THE FEDERAL COURTS

During the first decade of the nineteenth century, banks and insurance companies became the first business corporations engaged in interstate business transactions, and the volume of this business grew rapidly. In suits that attempted to enforce contracts between individuals and corporations and between corporations chartered by different states, the question arose whether business corporations could be construed as citizens of the state where they were chartered. If they were a species of citizen, they could take their interstate litigation into the federal courts on the basis of the diversity of citizenship clause of the United States Constitution.

The first federal case touching this issue was the *Bank of the United States* v. *Deveaux* in 1809. Chief Justice John Marshall's opinion refused to recognize a corporation as a single legal entity so that it could be considered as a citizen and thus sue in a federal court. He held that the diversity of citizenship clause did not apply to corporations because corporations were not citizens in a constitutional sense. Only under two circumstances were the federal courts open to corporations: (1) if Congress authorized it (especially the Bank of the United States); or (2) if all the stockholders of a corporation were, in fact, citizens of the same state and the opposing party was a citizen of another state.

Probably, in 1809, most stockholders of most business corporations were residents of the state in which the corporation was chartered, but the opinion showed little insight into the growth of a major economic force that would strongly contribute to the commercial integration of the nation. If corporations doing interstate business could not sue in a federal court, they would have to litigate in state courts, which in the early years might be very sympathetic to local interests, especially the courts of the state where a corporation was chartered. Later, however, when interstate corporate business had increased in volume and complexity, its business activities in other states might be jeopardized by adverse decisions, which would hinder the development of regional markets.[13] Marshall's lack of insight in bringing the potentially powerful political-economic interest of interstate business corporations under national protection is particularly noticeable because he was always willing to support other interests that would help weld the Union into a strong national state.

This lack of insight is particularly glaring because Marshall had made an extremely strained interpretation of the Constitution in order to protect contracts made by unincorporated syndicates that had invested in vacant lands. He understood how the interests of land speculators could be brought to support nationalizing policies because he himself was a land speculator, but he seems to have shared the business shortcomings common to most Virginians (particularly Thomas Jefferson).[14] He failed to anticipate the increased participation of corporations, particularly manufacturing corporations, in interstate business and how this new form of business needed national protection. Marshall was unwilling to allow contracts made by business corporations to be enforced in the same manner as contracts made by individual businessmen, even when his colleagues recognized this as a commercial necessity.[15]

There may have been another reason for not seizing this opportunity to expand the jurisdiction of the federal courts. The reason for bringing the *Bank of the United States* v. *Deveaux* before the Court in 1809 was to test the constitutionality of the Bank of the United States. The substantive issue involved the right of a state to tax a branch of the Bank, an issue that was not settled until ten years later in *McCulloch* v. *Maryland*. The Court had had its hands full in the previous years with the state of Pennsylvania, as an aftermath of the decision in *Huidekoper's Lessee* v. *Douglass* and other cases. In one of these cases, a general in the state militia had been brought to trial before a federal circuit court for resisting the laws of the United States, and had been convicted. The Pennsylvania legislature violently objected and solicited other states to help amend the constitution to erect an impartial tribunal to settle disputes between the general government and the states. Instead of further irritating federal-state relations by siding with the Bank of the United States, Marshall avoided the taxation issue. This left the Court free to further champion the interests of land speculators in *Fletcher* v. *Peck*, which was decided shortly afterwards.[16]

One scholar gives another explanation for the *Deveaux* opinion. Gerard C. Henderson believed that Marshall feared to ascribe even a limited status of citizenship to business corporations because a citizenship status might be interpreted as bringing them under the protection of the privileges and immunities clause of the Constitution and seem to place them beyond state control.[17] There could be much truth in this interpretation, and it is especially plausible since the corporation involved was the Bank of the United States, which was feared as a political instrument in much of the South; and other chartered business corporations were looked upon with strong suspicions, a suspicion Marshall seemed to share. Even in the North, business corporations had not yet reached a safe degree of social acceptance, although Chancellor Kent was willing to grant them the status of citizenship in 1807 for purposes of interstate commerce.

The lacuna in the Court's thinking, in harnessing the interests of interstate corporate business to the growth of nationalism did not end with the *Deveaux* decision. In 1825, Justice Story delivered the opinion of the Court in the case of the *Steamboat Thomas Jefferson*, that the admiralty jurisdiction of the federal courts was limited to where the tide ebbs and flows and did not comprehend other interstate bodies of navigable water. This decision seriously curtailed the jurisdiction of the federal courts in the rapidly growing volume of Great Lakes and inland river traffic where many steamboat transportation enterprises were organized as corporations. In a short period of time, the Court came to regret this opinion as harmful to the commercial development of the nation, but the Marshall Court did not reverse it.[18]

By the mid-1830s, the volume of interstate corporate business had become very large, and in the near absence of Congressional regulation, the problem arose as to how much power each state had to regulate out-of-state corporations doing business within its borders. This was a touchy political question in banking, particularly in regard to the interstate transfer of credit. It was an especially sensitive issue in the South where marketing the annual cotton crop was largely financed by the Bank of the United States and the profits of the cotton export trade were largely in the hands of northern businessmen. After the destruction of the second Bank, all southern states tried to secure as much of the cotton marketing business as possible. They did this by using the state's credit to borrow capital (sell bonds) that was used to establish state banking systems. What the northern states borrowed to build internal improvement projects like canals and turnpikes, the southern states borrowed to establish commercial banking systems that could finance the marketing of the cotton crop. The southern states clearly saw that banks were public service corporations that would help keep at home some of the profits of commercial agriculture.[19]

This states' rights position was defined by Justice John McKinley of the United States Supreme Court while on circuit court duty in his native state of Alabama. In a case involving the legality of contracts made by an out-of-state bank, he held that a corporation created in one state had no power to make a legal contract in another state, either directly or by its agents. This decision, if upheld by the Supreme Court, would seriously impair the very rapidly growing volume of corporate interstate business. In the *Bank of Augusta* v. *Earle*, Chief Justice Taney conceded that a corporation had no legal existence outside the boundaries of the state that created it, but like natural persons, its agents could make contracts outside of its home state unless a state prohibited this.[20] However, a state would not be presumed to exclude the agents of out-of-state corporations unless there was clear statute evidence of such intent. It was, however, legal for a state to prescribe the conditions under which out-of-state corporations could do business within its boundaries. Finally, the privileges and immunities clause of the United States Constitution applied only to United States citizens and not to corporations.

This decision allowed the southern states to regulate out-of-state banks doing business within their borders in the interest of building their own banking systems. Alabama immediately passed legislation that excluded all non-Alabama banks from selling bills of exchange or discounting notes within its borders; however, the less controversial varieties of interstate business corporations continued to expand their operations under the permissive policies adopted by most states until the 1850s when the volume of interstate insurance business and railroad traffic forced most states to regulate these corporations.

The *Bank of Augusta* decision was a workable compromise between those advocates of a highly restrictive interpretation of the powers of interstate business corporations and those who looked upon corporations as the normal business organization for large-scale enterprises. The policy the Court defined allowed the continued growth of most large-scale commercial and industrial businesses, which could take advantage of the economies of distribution afforded by railroads and which contributed to the rapid expansion of regional markets.

Finally, in 1844, the Taney Court unanimously overruled the *Deveaux* decision after hearing a complete reargument of the nature of corporations. For purposes of jurisdiction, the Court in *Louisville, Cincinnati and Charleston Railroad* v. *Letson* presumed that business corporations were citizens of the state where they were chartered. It was a realistic decision that recognized the vast expansion of interstate business transactions in the United States. It allowed business corporations with widespread ownership or possessing franchises in more than one state, like trunkline railroads, to have access to the federal courts. Admitting these corporations to the federal courts contributed to the formation of a uniform body of national commercial law, a process the Court had clumsily begun in *Swift* v. *Tyson* in 1842, and it rescued them from potentially hostile state courts. It also guaranteed the federal courts an immense increase in future business. Finally, seven years later in *Genesee Chief* v. *Fitzhugh*, the Court extended its jurisdiction over inland navigation, on the basis of an 1845 Congressional statute, by overturning Story's restrictive opinion in the case of the *Steamboat Thomas Jefferson*.[21]

More business corporations were organized in the decade of the 1850s than during the whole previous history of business corporations in the United States, and an increasing percentage of them were engaged in interstate commerce. Railroads became the most visible form of interstate business corporation, followed by banks and textile manufactories, and the decisions of the Court, in conjunction with the multiplication of general incorporation statutes in most states, laid the foundation for the vast increase in corporate interstate business. Even so, most businesses continued to meet local needs and continued to be organized as single proprietorships and partnerships.

The idea of corporate citizenship enunciated in the *Letson Case* was not popular with southerners. The South feared that if the Court could define corporations as "artificial persons" or "capable of being treated as citizens," it could also make this fiction for slaves or free Negroes. If the commerce power could be interpreted to regulate the movement of persons (*New York* v. *Miln*, 1837; *Passenger Cases*, 1849, or potentially *Groves* v. *Slaughter*, 1841) it could also be construed to regulate the interstate slave trade. The South wanted the narrowest possible definition of the commerce power to prevent any check upon the expansion of slavery. This issue nearly became an obsession in the South.

New York v. *Miln* was the first case that seemed to threaten complete state control of slavery. In 1824, the New York legislature had passed a statute that required all ship captains entering the port of

New York to report the names, ages, occupations, and other data of all passengers and take bond that none of them would become welfare cases. The law was designed to keep New York City from being overwhelmed with indigent immigrants because the city did not have the financial resources to care for them. New York argued that this law was a legitimate exercise of its power to protect the health and welfare of its citizens, while the opponents said that the law encroached on the national government's exclusive power to regulate foreign and interstate commerce. The Court's opinion, written by Justice Philip P. Barbour of Virginia, agreed with New York. His opinion upheld New York on what he considered the "impregnable position" that every state possessed "the same undeniable and unlimited jurisdiction over all persons and things within its territorial limits"; and furthermore persons were not comprehended by the commerce clause.[22] Four concurring opinions, however, recognized immigrants as coming under the commerce clause and five opinions held that a state could exercise a concurrent authority over interstate commerce whenever the national government had not acted, which was the same principle that had been defined in *Sturgis* v. *Crowninshield* in 1819.

The *Passenger Cases* of 1849 resuscitated the major issues of the *Miln* case, which were: did the commerce power comprehend the interstate transportation of persons, and could Massachusetts and New York constitutionally tax immigrants. The cases were argued three times before a fragmented court decided five to four that the state laws were unconstitutional.

The South was concerned about these laws because if the court declared them unconstitutional, such a decision would cast doubts on the constitutionality of laws in numerous southern states that prohibited the entry of free Negroes and restricted the movement of free Negro sailors when their ships were in southern ports. Taney's opinion supported these laws. He believed that each state possessed the power to exclude undesirable persons whenever the state deemed them injurious to the state's welfare and that each state could quarantine these persons at its borders and exclude them. The majority, however, believed that the federal government had exclusive control over this matter because these state laws imposed an import tax, which was expressly prohibited to the states by the Constitution. This decision seemed to indicate that southern laws controlling the movement of free Negroes were unconstitutional and that the federal government had the power to regulate the interstate slave trade. The South was deeply concerned.[23]

In the same year the *Passenger Cases* were decided, the South unsuccessfully opposed the establishment of the Department of Interior. It was opposed because it would increase the power of the federal government, and many believed it would be an instrument for bringing the internal affairs of the states under the scrutiny of the federal government. John C. Calhoun believed it would be the greatest step heretofore made in attempting to absorb the remaining powers of the states into a consolidated government.

Three years later, in 1852, the South's fears were allayed by the Court's clearly written opinion in *Cooley* v. *Board of Wardens*. At issue was a law of the state of Pennsylvania that required ships entering the port of Philadelphia to hire a pilot or pay a fee. Congress had provided for regulation of pilotage, but the national law contained nothing that was in conflict with the Pennsylvania statute. At issue was the extent of federal regulation over interstate and international commerce. The Court's majority held that the federal power to regulate commerce did not deprive the states of such power if the federal government had not acted. There were some aspects of commerce that required a single uniform rule within the nation and other aspects that required diverse regulations because of local hazards. The Pennsylvania law governing pilotage was of this category. Presumably, control of slavery was also a local situation that demanded local regulation.

In 1853, in *Marshall* v. *Baltimore and Ohio Railroad*, the South won their point when the Court shifted the grounds on which interstate business corporations could sue in federal courts.[24] The Court permitted a citizen of Virginia to sue a Maryland corporation on the presumption that all of the corporation's stockholders were citizens of Maryland. This opinion shifted the basis of diversity of citizenship from corporations themselves to the corporation's stockholders, which implicitly denied the opinion of the *Letson Case*. In practice, this reversal in no way hindered interstate business corporations from using the federal courts. This shift reassured the South that the opinion in *Bank of Augusta* v. *Earle* was still in effect—that corporations were not citizens within the meaning of the Constitution.

Even though the number of interstate business corporations grew substantially in the 1850s and the volume of interstate commerce increased even more rapidly, the slavery issue increasingly paralyzed attempts by the federal government to provide a uniform system of national rules to promote the orderly growth of interstate commerce. Congressional regulation of interstate commerce was almost wholly prevented by the slavery controversy, and the Court's efforts were substantially hindered because there were too few federal commercial statutes on which to base its opinions. The Court had to interpret contested state laws by directly interpreting the Constitution. By necessity, the Court's opinions were cast in negative terms, forbidding state action by declaring state statutes unconstitutional whenever nationalists could substantiate a claim that a state law infringed upon a purely national power. Increasingly, corporation regulation meant state regulation or no regulation at all. The states' rights agrarians wanted this national weakness as a means of protecting slavery, and northern industrial capitalists were not yet excessively penalized by a jungle of conflicting state laws.[25]

NOTES

1.   Alfred B. Street, ed., *The Council of Revision of the State of New York*, 328.

2.   Edwin M. Dodd, *American Business Corporations Until 1860*, 23–25. *Wales* v. *Stetson*, 1806, 2 Mass. 146.

3.   *Messages from the Governors of New York*, Vol. 2, Jan. 25, 1803, George Clinton.

4.   Alfred B. Streed, ed., *The Council of Revision of the State of New York*, 345.

5.   Alfred B. Street, ed., *The Council of Revision of the State of New York*, 346.

6.   Mark D. Howe, "A Footnote on the Conspiracy Theory," *Yale Law Review*, Vol. 48, 1939, 1001–1013. Oscar Handlin, Mary F. Handlin, *Commonwealth Massachusetts, 1774-1861*, 274–275; from James Sullivan, "On the Life of Corporations." In 1802, James Sullivan was Attorney General of Massachusetts (a Republican) and leaned toward the opinion that corporation charters were not repealable by the legislature.

7.   *Head* v. *Providence Insurance Company*, 1804, 2 Cranch 167. James Kent, *Commentaries on American Law* (1827), Vol. 1, 239–240. Joseph K. Angell, Samuel Ames, *A Treatise on the Law of Private Corporations Aggregate* (1832), 60. Edwin M. Dodd, *American Business Corporations Until 1860*, 41–43. Simeon E. Baldwin, *Modern Political Institutions*, 206–207, 252–253.

8.   *Dartmouth College* v. *Woodward*, 1819, 4 Wheaton 712. Story had said as much as four years earlier in *Terrett* v. *Taylor*, 1815, 9 Cranch 52.

9.   Hiram E. Sickels, ed., *Opinions of the Attorneys-General of the State of New York*, 45. *Legislative Documents* 1825, Assembly No. 108. *Senate Documents 1832*, No. 8.

10.   *Revised Statutes 1828*, Vol. 1, Ch. 18, Title 2, Sec. 8, 609. James Kent, *Commentaries on American Law* (1827), Vol. 2, 246–247.

11.   *McLaren* v. *Pennington*, 1828, 1 Paige Chancery 108–109. See also *Sturgis* v. *Crowninshield*, 1819, 4 Wheaton 122; *Ogden* v. *Saunders*, 1827, 12 Wheaton 213.

12.   James Kent, *Commentaries on American Law* (1827), Vol. 2, 222.

13.   Mitchell Wendell, *Relations Between the Federal and State Courts*, 78–79. John P. Roche, ed., *John Marshall: Major Opinions and Other Writings*, 115. *Bank of the United States* v. *Deveaux*, 1809, 5 Cranch 61.

14.   *Huidekoper's Lessee* v. *Douglass*, 1805, 3 Cranch 1. *Fletcher* v. *Peck*, 1810, 6 Cranch 87. *Fairfax* v. *Hunter's Lessee*, 1813, 7 Cranch 603. *Martin* v. *Hunter's Lessee*, 1816, 1 Wheaton 304. *Green* v. *Biddle*, 1823, 8 Wheaton 1.

15.   Edwin M. Dodd, *American Business Corporations Until 1860*, 98–100. Charles Warren, *The Supreme Court in United States History*, Vol. 1, 697–699. Marshall's opinion was all the more reactionary because Justice Story had held in *Bank of Columbia* v. *Patterson*, 1813, 7 Cranch 299, that an oral contract made by the authorized agent of a corporation was legally binding, and New York courts had speedily followed this reasoning (*Danforth* v. *Schoharie Turnpike Company*, 1815, 12 Johnson 227 and *Dunn* v. *St. Andrews Church*, 1817, 14 Johnson 118).

16.   Charles Warren, *The Supreme Court in United States History*, Vol. 1, 369–391.

17.   Gerard C. Henderson, *The Position of Foreign Corporations in American Constitutional Law*, 51–57. R. Kent Newmyer, *The Supreme Court under Marshall and Taney*, 61–71.

18.   *Steamboat Thomas Jefferson*, 1825, 10 Wheaton 428. Charles Warren, *The Supreme Court in United States History*, Vol. 2, 121–122.

19.   A. James Heins, *Constitutional Restrictions Against State Debt*, 5–6. George D. Green, "Louisiana, 1804–1861," in Rondo Cameron, ed., *Banking and Economic Development: Some Lessons of History*, 200.

20.   Charles Warren, *The Supreme Court in United States History*, Vol. 2, 50–52, 62. Gerard C. Henderson, *The Position of Foreign Corporations in American Constitutional Law*, 48. *Bank of Augusta* v. *Earle*, 1839, 13 Peters 519.

21.   Mitchell Wendell, *Relations Between the Federal and State Courts*, 122–123. *Louisville, Cincinnati and Charleston Railroad* v. *Letson*, 1844, 2 Howard 497. *Swift* v. *Tyson*, 1842, 16 Peters 1. *Genesee Chief* v. *Fitzhugh*, 1851, 12 Howard 558.

22.   *New York* v. *Miln*, 1837, 11 Peters 139. *Passenger Cases*, 1849, 7 Howard 283. *Groves* v. *Slaughter*, 1841, 15 Peters 449. See also, Carl B. Swisher, *American Constitutional Development*, 195–198.

23.   Carl B. Swisher, *American Constitutional Development*, 202–204. Charles Warren, *The Supreme Court in United States History*, Vol. 2, 181–182. Charles G. Haines, Foster H. Sherwood, *The Role of the Supreme Court in American Government and Politics, 1835-1864*, 144–148, 157–172. *Passenger Cases*, 1849, 7 Howard 283.

24.   *Cooley* v. *Board of Wardens*, 1852, 12 Howard 299. *Marshall* v. *Baltimore and Ohio Railroad*, 1853, 16 Howard 314.

25.   Carl B. Swisher, *American Constitutional Development*, 204–207, 299.

11

Conclusion

PUBLIC SERVICE: THE GUIDELINE TO NEW YORK'S CORPORATION POLICY

From the beginning of national existence, most states adopted the policy of actively encouraging the organization of private associations that performed vital public services such as religious and secular education, or undertook the construction of internal improvement projects. In New York, incorporation was readily granted to increasing numbers and varieties of these associations because incorporation was the most effective means of protecting their investments in real property. The passage of general incorporation statutes encouraged the organization of associations that performed public services because these laws provided a cheap legal process that was available at the local level. However, it soon became apparent that different classes of public service corporations required varying degrees of state regulation. Benevolent corporations received little further attention once general incorporation statutes were passed, but business corporations that were closely related to the public welfare, like banks, required extensive regulation. This was particularly true in New York where banking became closely linked to partisan politics.

When a state finally adopted a policy of granting charters of incorporation for any legitimate business enterprise (as Connecticut did in 1837 and New York did after 1846), the policy sprang from this earlier relationship: the close identity of interest between state governments and private organizations performing socially beneficial services. These business corporations did not need to have a direct relationship to public welfare, as in the case of railroads, but their formation was encouraged on broader grounds: they increased taxable wealth, they tended to slow the westward emigration of citizens by providing employment at home, or they facilitated the growth of a viable urban democracy by allowing a wide participation in businesses that could most advantageously be organized as corporations. More importantly, they helped equalize the opportunities to get rich. The passage of general incorporation laws for business corporations was the economic aspect of the policital and social forces that democratized the United States during the Age of Jackson, 1825-1855.

THE TRANSFER OF THE PUBLIC SERVICE DOCTRINE TO BUSINESS CORPORATIONS

There were several classes of corporate business that conferred social benefits on the community in much the same way as benevolent corporations. Two of these business corporations were turnpikes, which improved overland transportation, and banks, which provided the paper currency that was the normal medium of exchange. Turnpikes were financed by private investments, which made them into business franchises and in order to encourage their organization, the legislature passed a general regulatory statute for them in 1807. This statute did not have a general incorporation provision because the state felt that each petition for incorporation should be individually investigated to see that the proposed improvement was actually needed and would do what it promised. This information had to be a matter of public record before a company was granted a charter that included the powers of eminent domain, limited liability, and the right to collect a public toll.

The distinction between benevolent corporations and franchise corporations was only one of degree, even though one of them earned a private profit and the other did not. Both performed vital, visible, and noncontroversial public services that the state wished to encourage. The distinction between franchise corporations and business corporations that exploited an anonymous market was also one of degree. Both were business corporations undertaken for private profits, but one was obviously a franchise because the real estate it required for its operation (and caused its operations to be localized) could only be secured with the full cooperation of the state. Before 1820, most business corporations were thought of as franchises because most of them were. The readiness with which the legislature granted incorporation to promoters of franchise businesses, and their success in achieving their objective, constantly reminded the public of the benefits produced by business corporations.

The 1811 general incorporation statute for manufacturing companies also originated as a public service measure. It was essentially an emergency act passed on the eve of the War of 1812, when textile production became a business closely connected with public welfare because trade disruptions cut off the supply of European cloth and other manufactured products. The statute was a means of encouraging the organization of these businesses. Later, manufacturing became less directly related to public welfare because manufacturers were nonfranchise businesses that exploited an anonymous market; but the 1811 statute remained in operation because it was found convenient and because it produced little political controversy.

In those highly competitive businesses where personal liability was the accepted standard of integrity, a corporation with legal continuity and limited liability for its members would have been looked on as unfair competition. The competitive businesses, like retail and wholesale merchants, export-import brokers, ship builders, stage, canal, and river freight lines, and real estate developers, were seldom or never incorporated until the middle 1850s or later. They were invariably organized as single proprietors, partnerships (limited partnerships after 1822), or joint-stock associations. These businesses were often governed by private articles of agreement and had transferable shares, but legally they were only expanded partnerships because all the associates possessed personal liability.

Corporations were the legal and moral exception to the accepted standard of business ethics, which required personal liability, but everyone recognized that they had their place in the community because of the public services they performed. Limited liability was the price the public willingly paid to get internal improvements

built without the expenditure of public funds or to encourage entrepreneurs to manufacture products not previously made in New
York. Such an exception as limited liability could only be justified
by the public service a business performed.

Sometime between 1815 and 1825, the economic thinking of New
York's citizens underwent a significant shift in emphasis toward all
business corporations except banks. Their concern shifted from an
emphasis on personal liablity, as in partnerships, to equality of opportunity to participate in business corporations possessing limited
liability. An index of this shift in thinking was the permanent enactment in 1821 of the 1811 general incorporation statute for manufacturing enterprises. The same shift in economic attitude did not take
place in Massachusetts until 1830, and only after an arduous campaign of political and economic education led by Governor Levi
Lincoln. New York probably led the nation in this shift of attitude
toward private debts.

It is highly significant that this shift in thinking took place when
New York was undergoing extremely rapid expansion in two widely separate areas. New York City was growing in size and wealth,
while the western part of the state was being brought into
agricultural production. The completion of the Erie Canal and the
application of steamboats to inland waterways enormously accelerated commercial activity and expanded the markets tributary
to New York. As a result, there was a very rapid growth in opportunities to get rich quickly by investing in new industrial
technologies, particularly textiles and metalworking skills; or purchasing high-pressure steam engines that could be used to expand
an existing business at a rural water power site, or establish new
manufacturing operations in New York City. Abundant credit
facilities were needed to exploit these industrial and commercial opportunities, whether in New York City or in the west. In this at-
mosphere of business optimism, the public favored (or at least did
not actively oppose) policies that encouraged corporate entrepreneurs.

In the early nineteenth century, the United States appeared to be
one of the least likely nations to industrialize. It was land rich,
technologically backward, and capital deficient, and its population
was highly dispersed compared to the compact, centralized, and

technologically advanced nations of Europe. There were neither great landed or commercial magnates to supply capital, nor an efficient centralized government that could accumulate capital through taxation, nor a vigorous national policy to encourage industrialization, nor any external threat to national survival that dictated a policy of rapid industrialization. In spite of these deficiencies, the United States did industrialize. The seed capital had to be contributed voluntarily from numerous small savers, and a means had to be found to mobilize and magnify it. The means of voluntary mobilization was the business corporation and the means of magnification was banks. Industrialization developed in a social and political climate that had three major assets that more than compensated for the other deficiencies: a stable government, an energetic people experienced in voluntary corporate self-help, and responsive state legislatures that framed laws that encouraged individuals to save and invest.

From the beginning, the corporate form of organization preempted those new classes of business, such as internal improvement projects, where no single proprietors or partnerships had existed. These enterprises were the socially acceptable uses for business corporations. The corporation could better raise the capital these projects required and better provide for their efficient management. The political controversy over corporations was not between single proprietors and partnerships being driven into bankruptcy by corporations. It centered on whether it was desirable or sound policy to open the privilege of incorporation to all entrepreneurs in those types of enterprises where the corporation was the usual form of organization. In New York, this controversy first arose and was settled over banks.

BANKS AND NEW YORK POLITICS

The first banks were public service corporations to supply a region with a reliable paper currency because specie was perpetually in short supply, and to supply merchants and state governments with credit. The public service function of banks was soon obscured because the banknotes issued by several banks did not retain a uniform value. The early banks were also highly profitable and many persons of doubtful skills and character wanted to enter the business. The political controversy over banking began in New York in 1804 when the legislature passed a statute restricting banking to chartered corporations. The restraining statute was an attempt to secure a uniform value for all banknotes circulated within the state by limiting the authority to issue notes to corporations. It had the effect of making each bank a franchise to create local credit and issue the paper currency in the region it served. Three events cemented the marriage of banks and politics in New York: the passage of the second restraining law in 1818; the emergence, after 1819, of the Albany Regency as the Democratic-Republican party's policymaking body; and the inclusion of the two-thirds clause in the Constitution of 1821. The two-thirds clause required all charters of incorporation to be passed by a two-thirds majority of the legislature. It was an ill-conceived attempt by agrarians to curb banking abuses by drastically reducing the number of banks in order to increase the reliability of the currency they issued and limit the influence of banks in state politics.

It had the opposite effect. The Regency-directed legislature passed bank charters on a highly partisan basis, often giving them to persons who lacked capital or who were devoid of the necessary management skills. The main criterion was to put banking profits into the hands of deserving party members. The partisanship in granting charters made banking controversial, but the major source of controversy was banking's intimate connection with the currency. Political banks frequently supplied an excess of banknote credit, which caused inflation; or they supplied a currency that was nearly impossible to redeem for specie and thus was highly discounted; or, if one of these banks became insolvent, it left a large volume of depreciated or worthless banknotes in the hands of an unsuspecting public. These were genuine political grievances. The close link between banking and the political party that controlled the legislature also hindered the orderly development of credit facilities needed by businessmen, as well as preventing competitive banking.

The three leading principles of Regency leadership were collective legislative leadership, party discipline, and a ruthless use of patronage. When the Regency approved a bank charter, only the party's disciplined caucus could mobilize sufficient votes to pass it. After the adoption of the 1821 Constitution, the banking-corporation controversy centered around use of the restraining statutes and the two-thirds clause. It was the Regency's political use of these laws, from 1821 to 1838, that raised the broader issue of the proper relationship of all business corporations to the state.

On the other hand, the two-thirds clause was not intended to curb the incorporation of noncontroversial businesses and benevolent corporations, although its inclusive wording indicated that this would be the result. The testimony of several convention delegates and the continued operation of the pre-1821 general incorporation statutes, in spite of the two-thirds clause, amply demonstrate the clause's real intent. By 1825, the business corporation was an integral part of New York's commercial, legal, and political structure and was essentially noncontroversial. Banks were the great exception to this generalization because the public wanted the full redemption of banknotes of insolvent banks from the assets of stockholders; however, the Regency defeated every attempt to impose personal liability on bank stockholders.

The Regency's political use of the two-thirds clause to apportion bank charters to Democratic-Republican businessmen caused many ambitious entrepreneurs to oppose the Regency. They wanted to participate in the steady profits of banking or wanted to use the credit banks supplied, but they lacked sufficient political influence to secure a charter. They were denied an equal opportunity to enter the banking business. The agrarians, who feared the inflationary tendencies of unrestrained banknote credit, also opposed the Regency's banking policy because it tended to charter banks in areas remote from commercial activity where the bank's major purpose was to exercise political influence, rather than provide useful commercial credit or a reliable currency.

Discovering a satisfactory mode of regulating banks was a difficult job, but in 1829, under the leadership of Governor Van Buren, the legislature passed the Safety Fund statute, which levied a low tax on the capital of all chartered banks. The tax monies were deposited in the state-administered Safety Fund, which was designed to redeem the banknotes of all insolvent banks. It gave some degree of noteholder protection but did nothing to restrain the creation of banknote credit or satisfy the ambitions of capitalist investors and entrepreneurs who sought bank charters for the credit they could provide.

To supervise the Safety Fund banks, an independent Bank Commission was erected, but its primary concern was with bookkeeping practices and not credit policies. Restraining the credit practices of all state banks was a job performed by the second Bank of the United States, and as long as it performed this central banking function, the Safety Fund system worked quite well. The second Bank ceased its regulatory functions in 1834, but neither of New York's two potential regulatory agencies filled the void. Neither the Bank Commission nor the Mechanics and Farmers Bank, where the state kept substantial deposits, assumed the responsibility of regulating the credit policies of the state's banks. The Mechanics and Farmers Bank could have acted as a central bank, as the Suffolk Bank did in Massachusetts. It did not.

In contrast, in Massachusetts, the legislature granted bank charters whenever asked, if the petitioners were men of good character. Massachusetts also levied a one percent tax on bank capital; thus an increase in bank capital meant an increase in general revenue, which by the 1830s was the state's largest source of income. Massachusetts banks, however, were restrained in credit expansion by a regional regulatory system controlled by the Suffolk Bank of Boston. Its restraints were greatly resented by the country banks which, like those in New York, provided most of the state's currency, but it had the full support of the state government.

The 1830s was a decade of extremely rapid economic growth in which New York led the nation. It was a decade of massive investments in transportation facilities (canals and steamboats), in basic manufacturing skills, and in the creation of greatly enlarged regional markets. During the decade, the city of New York came to overshadow all other financial and commercial centers in the nation. By the end of the decade, railroads were also being built in large numbers, and the telegraph had demonstrated its success in long-distance communications. Entrepreneurs and capitalists who wanted to exploit the profit potentials of these technologies needed abundant credit, which banks could supply.

New York's banking policy was not closely geared to the broader aspects of economic development. With the tremendous increase in business opportunities in the 1830s, which depended on abundant credit for rapid exploitation, the political management of New York's banking system failed to provide enough credit for the right people. The caucus system of politically apportioning bank charters and distributing shares (largely among themselves) automatically created a majority of party members who supported the restrictive system. The minority, who doubted the political wisdom of this policy but who believed in party regularity, was extremely reluctant to break party discipline and overturn it. If this generalization is correct, it lends support to Lee Benson's thesis that the Regency was not a leading force in the rapid political, social, or economic democratization of New York society. The Regency appears to have always been in favor of keeping more than minimal restraining powers in the hands of the state, primarily for political purposes rather than for economic or social ends.[1]

Jackson's veto of the Bank satisfied four of New York's principal economic-political interests. The largest group was the anti-inflationists, composed of small urban tradesmen and agrarians. The most articulate were the urban tradesmen who opposed the Bank because it issued the largest volume of paper money in the nation and they believed that all paper money was inflationary. The Safety Fund bankers objected to the Bank because of the restraints it imposed on the expansion of banknote credit and many Wall Street bankers opposed rechartering it because they wanted the funds that were collected at the New York customs house deposited in their banks and not in Philadelphia. Entrepreneurs, if they had an opinion, disliked the Bank's restraints on the credit practices of state banks.

In the inflationary years from 1834 to 1837, following the destruction of the Bank, circulating and discounting banknotes became a very profitable business. The New York legislature was deluged with applications for additional charters. However, bank charters continued to be rationed in an attempt to satisfy two opposing factions within the Democratic party: influential Regency supporters who sought semimonopolistic bank charters as a means of becoming wealthy, and anti-inflationists who wanted to eliminate most state banks of issue now that the Monster Bank was dead. When the Regency failed to take any steps against the Safety Fund banks in 1835, the anti-inflationists joined the entrepreneurs to form the Locofocos, and break with the Democratic party.

Many Locofocos considered specie as the only safe currency because it was the most obvious check on inflation. They wanted no more banks of issue. On the other hand, many entrepreneurs and small tradesmen wanted as many banks as there were businessmen who possessed enough capital to enter the business, provided the paper currency they circulated was fully secured. These small businessmen wanted a free access to banking credit, which the restrictive policies of the Regency thwarted. They wanted free competition in banking, so they would have equal access to commercial credit. They believed that a viable urban democracy depended on this because a person could only be free if he possessed property. The democracy's ownership of property in an urban environment would be facilitated by a credit policy free from political management, coupled with a secured currency.

The destruction of the Safety Fund was made easy by the disrepute that befell it after the suspension of specie payments in May 1837. The suspension strongly contributed to the overwhelming Whig election victory in the fall of 1837. The Whigs were handed a popular mandate to change the state's banking system. The time was right for such legislation. President Van Buren's national administration had forced the New York Democracy into favoring a policy of separating banking from government because the Sub-Treasury bill, introduced in September 1837, would have radically separated the federal government from all banks. Thus, by 1838, both parties favored the principle of separating banking and government, which could only be accomplished in New York by passing a general incorporation statute for banks.

The first order of business of the 1838 legislative session was to overthrow the Safety Fund system. It was accomplished by passing a general incorporation statute for banks, or a free banking statute. The free banking statute allowed the creation of an unlimited number of banks, and thus opened the opportunities for credit creation to the speculating democracy. It also provided a paper currency that was 100 percent backed by negotiable securities held by the state. The noteholders of an insolvent bank were better protected from loss than under the Safety Fund.

Furthermore, the free banking statute left deposit credit completely unregulated, and in the 1840s and 1850s, the use of deposit credit (essentially modern bank credit) rapidly expanded while the use of banknote credit was restricted by the free banking statute's requirement that all banknotes had to have 100 percent backing. The passage of the free banking statute marked the adoption of a laissez-faire business policy by New York. It was the ultimate expression of laissez faire because it opened the politically sensitive business of creating credit to general entrepreneural participation.

The free banking statute was passed in spite of the two-thirds clause in the state constitution. In order to circumvent it, the free banks were called associations. This legal fiction was immediately challenged in the courts, but the courts refused to declare the statute unconstitutional. It was too popular. For over five years, the free banking statute was repeatedly challenged in the state courts, but it was not voided until 1845, on the eve of a referendum calling for a constitutional convention. The court's decision in *De Bow* v. *The People* was highly political. It enlisted a powerful free banking interest on the side of calling a convention, and when the convention was held, the free banking statute was embedded in the constitution. Constitutionalizing the free banking statute committed New York to the policy of passing general incorporation statutes for all other classes of business corporation and had the effect of constitutionalizing the doctrines of laissez-faire economics.

After the adoption of the Constitution of 1846, the state pursued a policy of passing general incorporation statutes for all classes of businesses that public opinion approved of being organized as corporations. General incorporation statutes transformed the corporation from an instrument of business privilege into an instrument of democratic enterprise. This transformation could only have taken place after the Regency's bank policy was overthrown and New York found a means of guaranteeing the value of the state's banknotes.

THE DEVELOPMENT OF LAISSEZ-FAIRE BUSINESS POLICY

A laissez-faire business policy meant the widest practical separation of partisan politics from the opportunites for private profits. This policy was cast in terms of corporation creation in New York because the issue was decided over the state's corporate banking policy. Banks were the most efficient means of creating credit and directing this credit into profitable investments. The Regency had limited the number of banks below the state's business needs in order to gain partisan political advantages. New York's rapid economic growth depended on an abundance of credit to finance a wide variety of manufacturing skills and numerous large-scale internal improvement projects. A laissez-faire policy prevented venal legislatures from passing laws (like New York's restraining laws) that hindered entrepreneurs from maximizing credit creation to take full advantage of legitimate profit–making opportunities. After laissez-faire policies were adopted by the various states, they helped achieve rapid exploitation of the nation's natural resources during a period of extremely rapid technological innovation and market expansion.

After the depression of 1838-1844, New York's corporation policy had to be compatible with the pervasive fear of a large public debt. From 1835 to 1842, New York had accumulated a huge bonded debt when it began enlarging the Erie Canal, building a system of feeder canals, and subsidizing the construction of several railroads. During the depths of the depression, the revenue from these projects was inadequate to sustain interest payments, and the state was forced to raise land taxes to maintain its solvency. The public reaction was an overwhelming desire to limit the debt-contracting powers of the state, which was the major reason for calling the Convention of 1846. The Constitution of 1846 prohibited the state from lending its credit to any private corporation or contracting any new debts above a very low figure. These provisions effectively excluded the state from further participation in large-scale internal improvement projects at a time when highly profitable trunkline railroads became technologically possible.

Prior to the depression in 1838, the New York legislature had been extremely generous in subsidizing internal improvement projects, beginning with canals, but including bridge construction, rivers and harbors work, and then railroads. The distinction between public and private improvement projects was not a matter of ideology but a matter of scale. The capital needed to build the larger projects could only be raised by using the state's credit.[2] After the depression ended in 1844, the public attitude toward entrepreneurship did not change: the public still wanted improvement projects built. The change was the public's insistence that the state's credit be radically restricted in subsidizing construction costs; however, public authorities were not prohibited from subsidizing projects by other means. State assets were given to entrepreneurs, and municipalities were allowed to use their credit resources to subsidize the construction of projects (mostly railroads) that would be of immediate commercial benefit to them. State aid continued to be substantial but its form changed. Increasingly, the aid was favorable statutes that equalized the opportunities of individuals and geographic areas to mobilize capital and credit in a society composed of a large number of small capitalists.

One of the most effective legal means of achieving this end was general incorporation statutes. They were politically popular because the opportunities for corporate profits were equally opened to all individuals with initiative, capital, energy, or technical skills; and capital contributions could be made in small quantities, were voluntary, and were made on the investor's own judgment. They allowed the democratic formation of business corporations with all the legal favors state governments could bestow: perpetual succession and concentration of management, single legal entity, easy access to the courts, competitive access to sources of credit, limited liability for investors, and incorporation at any time without the intermediary agency of the legislature. The most orderly and politically acceptable way to regulate business corporations was to place the necessary restraints in general incorporation statutes, with the state's experience from regulating banks serving as a model.

In fact, after the adoption of the 1846 Constitution, the state had little choice except to pass general incorporation statutes for business corporations if it expected socially useful projects to be built in the shortest possible time. The statutes were a political necessity after the depression when both the state and federal governments abdicated creative economic leadership. The national government had ceased supporting internal improvement projects by 1830, as the Maysville Road veto emphatically confirmed, and in a broader sense it had forfeited its power to give economic direction to the economy when it destroyed the Bank of the United States. The state governments also abdicated positive economic leadership after the depression when they got out of the internal improvement business.

General incorporation statutes had the effect of separating business corporations from the state in the same way general incorporation statutes for religious congregations had radically separated the state from all religious denominations. To the Jacksonian, whether Whig or Democrat, this meant that there should be free trade in capital and free access to business opportunities without governmental interference because interference had always given an unfair advantage to one group at the expense of another. This had been the result of the Regency's banking policy and it was not to be repeated.

LAISSEZ-FAIRE POLICY AND NEW YORK'S INDUSTRIAL GROWTH

According to Walt W. Rostow, the construction of turnpikes and canals and the multiplication of steamboats was a necessary preconditional investment that accelerated commercial activity to the point of take-off into self-sustaining industrial growth. These enterprises radically lowered long-distance transportation costs, expanded the size of regional markets, and encouraged the development of new technical skills. The savings they produced made it possible to rapidly build a railroad network within the state and into the interior.

After 1845, in Rostow's opinion, it was the rapid extension of trunkline railroad systems that was crucial in accelerating economic growth to the point of take-off. Railroads promoted investments in larger units of manufacturing that could take advantage of the larger markets they created, and they stimulated the development of successive manufacturing technologies that sustained overall industrial growth. Railroads also accelerated the expansion of regional markets to the point of creating a national market. They were far more effective than canals and steamboats in overcoming the great internal distances of the nation, and they could efficiently serve much larger areas that the lack of water routes excluded from full participation in a commercial economy.[3]

The various trunkline railroad networks would not have been completed so quickly had not some men had a vision of the commercial potential of huge regional markets. This vision could partially be seen by observing the explosive growth of commerce and industry in the one region in the United States that had the most complete pre-railroad transportation network. New York was the center of this region and the means of integration was the Erie Canal and steamboats on the Great Lakes, the Hudson River, Long Island Sound, and across New York Bay into New Jersey. Not until 1847 did the Erie Canal carry more goods produced in the western states than were produced in New York, but thereafter, western goods dominated the traffic. The vision of trunkline arteries of transportation integrating the huge western market into the New York market and into the commercial institutions that served the port of New York was a broader vision than was possessed by most contemporary state and national political leaders. Had this vision been left in public hands for exploitation, following the depression, it would have languished indefinitely.

Capitalist investors began making large purchases of stock in the shortline railroads of upper New York after 1845 because the increase in volume of western traffic and improvements in railroad technology made railroads a business that had an enormous profit potential. The initial, local stockholders were bought out and new managers installed. The new owners undertook extensive physical improvements with the intention of merging the shortlines of upper New York into an east-west trunkline route to tap the interior markets. These men were satisfied with the clause in the 1846 Constitution that prevented the state from underwriting bonds or purchasing shares in private corporations. The new owners did not want competition from state-built or state-controlled railroads for the potential profits of the railroad business. They wanted to exclude the state from railroad construction and management in order to build routes across state boundaries and compete with the state-owned canals for the available traffic.

Trunkline railroads under private ownership were more easily extended across state lines because they were built to satisfy an economic need and not to satisfy geographical-political considerations. They were in a position to favor through traffic at the expense of local traffic, a policy that produced a rate structure unfavorable to many local business interests. Particularly, private railroad managers fought New York's policy of protecting its canal revenues from railroad competition at a time when trunkline railroads gave every indication of repeating, on a larger scale, the catalyzing effect that the Erie Canal had had earlier on the state's economic growth. In an era when states' rights was the nation's leading political doctrine, private ownership of trunkline railroads was one of the most effective nationalizing forces at work in the country. Railroads accelerated the volume of interstate commerce, and interstate commerce acted as a strong national binding force.

If trunkline railroad management had remained in state hands, many governors would have used state control to satisfy the state's local economic interests and an interstate railroad system would have been much more difficult to organize. Each state railroad system would have been forced to modify its rate structure to favor local traffic instead of favoring the growth of through traffic. Local political and economic pressures could best be circumvented by a private management that adopted the policy of maximizing profits by operating its trunkline as a regional system. The managers of New York's trunkline railroad corporations thought in larger terms than immediate state economic interests: they thought in terms of systems extending across state boundaries and serving interstate markets. Private managers were free to adopt a policy of maximizing profits (and increasing social benefits) by operating trunklines as an interstate regional system. Managers of state-owned trunkline railroads would not have had this freedom. Any kind of state regulation that identified railroad policy with the short-term interest of one state was shortsighted.

The rivalry between the several trunkline railroads to capture the growing volume of western trade involved very large economic stakes. The eastern seaboard cities wanted the cheapest possible rates for the manufactured goods they shipped west and, likewise, the food and raw material producers of the interior wanted the cheapest possible transportation for the surpluses they sent to the seaboard cities. New York City had a competitive advantage over the other seaboard cities because it was served by two trunkline railroads and the Erie Canal. Competition between these arteries of transportation secured low interstate freight rates for New York shippers. Any rate structure designed to serve the state's local economic interests would have reduced New York's position as the preferred entry into the west.

Before the Civil War, the cities and towns of New York wanted the economics of railroad transportation at almost any cost. The situation was a mirror recurrence of the feeder canal program of the late 1830s. The state pursued a policy of encouraging the building of railroads as quickly as possible in spite of the threat they posed to canal revenues and the debt structure these revenues supported. The general incorporation statutes for railroads passed in 1848 and 1850 carried this policy into effect. They were very successful. It had been thought that the Erie Canal's ability to move bulk freight over long distances at low rates would be a restraint on railroads entering the freight business, but the Canal proved to be an ineffective means of regulating railroad freight rates. When New York established a Railroad Commission in 1855, it tried to dictate a rate policy that would protect the revenues of the Erie Canal from cutthroat railroad competition by equalizing long- and short-haul freight rates within the state. The railroads united with the shippers of New York City to secure the Commission's dissolution. The problem of regulating railroad rates, in terms of short-haul versus long-haul, is distinctly a post–Civil War problem, even though the basic issues were discussed as early as 1856, the year after the New York Central Railroad system reached Chicago.

In New York, the political orientation of the Regency's banking policy had hindered the formation of credit and capital for investment in new technologies; therefore, laissez faire was the only realistic policy to exclude political jealousies that would have retarded industrial development and delayed the building of an efficient railroad network. It was the only politically acceptable economic policy that promised to fulfill the vision of ever-expanding regional markets that crossed state lines, whether the market was tributary to New York City, Philadelphia, Boston, or Baltimore; and it was the only social policy that promised an equal opportunity for small investors to participate in new business opportunities.[4] In New York, there was no alternative to a laissez faire incorporation policy if the people wanted abundant credit and the maximum number of railroads and factories built.

General incorporation statutes for banks and railroads were the ultimate expression of a laissez faire economic policy because banks and railroads were the two classes of business corporations that had an immediate and pervasive impact on public welfare. A laissez faire incorporation policy for both banks and railroads, as well as for other classes of business corporations, coming as it did on the verge of take-off into self-sustained industrial growth, was an extremely useful legal incentive to encourage industrialization. It had been recognized as early as 1837 that the large number and variety of business corporations were making a disproportionate contribution to the rapid industrial expansion of the United States.[5]

As Rostow points out, the take-off stage in United States economic development was initiated by railroads about 1855. This study concurs, but take-off must also be linked to two observations made by Schumpeter: abundant credit is a major factor in economic growth, and this credit must be put into the hands of entrepreneurs. Take-off was not possible without railroads, the large-scale creation of credit, and a society that trained large numbers of organizers in all communities, who could become adaptive entrepreneurs. This point is strongly emphasized in this book. The needed credit was best provided by a comprehensive and competitive banking system, as indicated by Cameron, and this credit had to be allocated into the hands of the most profitable industries and the most efficient entrepreneurs—those men who, in the United States, led the business revolution.[6] In New York and the United States, general incorporation statutes for banks, railroads, and manufacturing corporations strongly contributed to accomplishing this end.

The economic interaction of these three businesses, but particularly of banks and railroads in the late 1840s and 1850s yielded the greatest private and social profits by promoting the rapid expansion of regional markets so that by 1855 railroads had created the skeleton of a national market. Concomitant with the creation of a national market was the creation of a corpus of recognizably modern commercial law developed by lawyers, judges, and state legislators in active partnership with the new men of business who had been responsible for enlarging markets from local, to regional, to national.[7]

The problem of regulating business corporations, other than banks, just emerged around 1855 when a national system of overland transportation, communication, and marketing had been barely established in its modern form. By this time, most of the legal, social, and economic problems generated by the changes of the previous thirty years had already been faced in the principal commercial and industrial states and some tentative answers given. Only at the end of the Jacksonian era did the states begin to reassert their power to regulate businesses by erecting commissions and departments, but by this time many corporations were engaged in interstate commerce and not fully amenable to state regulation. If state regulatory agencies were established, they usually came with the half-hearted approval of the industries they regulated or they did not last.

Once local transportation, communication, and marketing networks were consolidated and transformed into large regional markets; and the movement of goods accelerated by railroads; and a wide variety of manufacturing skills developed; and the basic commercial law established, American economic development took a course no person could chart. This point, which corresponds to Rostow's take-off into self-sustained industrial growth, was reached about 1855.

The democratization of corporate business opportunities during the Age of Jackson did not, however, visualize a situation where consolidation would seriously hinder or eliminate competition. It is ironic that Amos Kendall, the man who said "The world is governed too much," was the leader of an attempt to consolidate the nation's telegraph companies into one national network under one corporation's management. The laissez faire doctrine that had helped democratize corporate business opportunities fitted the entrepreneurial situation up to the point where large-scale destructive competition began, in the years between 1870 and 1890. This situation called into being new policies, the most effective being governmental encouragement or acquiescence to business consolidation through trusts and holding companies in order to efficiently exploit the completed national market. When this stage was reached, laissez faire died.

NOTES

1. Lee Benson, *The Concept of Jacksonian Democracy*, 91–93.

2. Robert A. Lively, "The American System: A Review Article," *Business History Review*, Vol. 29, 1955, 85.

3. Walt W. Rostow, *The Process of Economic Growth*, 266–267, 272–281.

4. Carter Goodrich, ed., *The Government and the Economy, 1783-1861*, 390–396: Daniel Webster, "The Application of Capital to the Benefit of All" (1836).

5. Timothy Walker, *Introduction to American Law*, 206.

6. Joseph A. Schumpeter, *The Theory of Economic Development*, 63–66, 72–75, 100–102, 106–107, 132–136. Rondo Cameron, ed., *Banking and Economic Development: Some Lessons of History*, 24–25. Thomas C. Cochran, "The Business Revolution," *American Historical Review*, Vol. 79, 1974, 1458–1459. Henry G. Aubrey, "Investment Decisions in Underdeveloped Countries," in David E. Novack, Robert Lekachman, eds., *Development and Society: The Dynamics of Economic Change*, 99.

7. Roscoe Pound, *The Formative Era of American Law*, 3–5. Morton J. Horwitz, "The Rise of Legal Formalism," *American Journal of Legal History*, Vol. 19, 1975, 251–256. Leonard W. Levy, *The Law of the Commonwealth and Chief Justice Shaw*, 22–24, 305–308, 315–320, 335–336.

Glossary
of Terms

ASSOCIATION: An unincorporated society having a number of persons voluntarily united for some special purpose, who use the form of a corporation.

BANK: An organization (usually a corporation) that receives deposits of money, makes loans of money, can issue promissory notes that can circulate as money, extends credit, discounts banknotes, or facilitates the transfer of funds by issuing bills of exchange.

BANKNOTE: A promissory note issued by a bank payable to the bearer on demand at the office of the bank of issue or where that bank keeps funds on deposit.

BANKNOTE CREDIT: The ability of a bank to issue and circulate a larger volume of banknotes than its specie assets because, at any one time, only a small volume of its banknotes in circulation will be presented for redemption. The banknotes are issued on the basis of a specie reserve held in the bank's vaults.

BANKRUPTCY LAW: A law for the benefit of creditors when a corporation is unable to pay its debts. The law sets up a legal procedure to allow the recovery of what remains of the corporation's assets, and then distributes these assets among the creditors.

BENEVOLENT PUBLIC SERVICE CORPORATION: See Charitable Corporation.

BILL OF CREDIT: A promissory note issued by a state government, upon its faith and credit, that could be used to pay all public debts and circulate as a legal medium of exchange.

BONA FIDE: In good faith, without deceit or fraud.

BOND: A written promise by a corporation to pay a fixed sum plus interest at a future date. Bonds are usually long-term obligations. The money to pay the interest has first call on the corporation's net earnings.

BOTANIC PHYSICIAN: Irregularly trained doctors who treated all diseases with remedies derived from plants, particularly plants growing in America. They mainly practiced in rural areas where graduate doctors were scarce.

BUSINESS CORPORATION: A corporation organized for the purpose of carrying on a business for profit.

CAPITALIZATION TAX: A tax levied on the legal amount of money invested in a corporation by its stockholders.

CHANCELLOR: The chief presiding judge in the Court of Chancery.

CHANCERY: The court that administers equity law.

CHARITABLE CORPORATION: A corporation organized to promote the welfare of a community or some class of persons, or mankind in general, which the state recognizes as contributing to the public welfare.

CHARTER OF INCORPORATION: An act of a legislature creating a corporation.

COMMON LAW: Common law comprises the body of principles and rules of action relating to security of government, persons, and property (originally common to all of England), which derives its authority from usage, custom, and judgments of courts of law. It is distinguished from statute law, which is created by legislative enactment.

COMMON STOCK: See Share of Stock.

CONTRACT: A legally enforceable agreement between two or more persons to do something or cease doing something.

CO-PARTNERSHIP: See Partnership.

CORPORATION: An artificial person created under the laws of a state or nation for a specific purpose. Ordinarily, a corporation consists of an association of numerous individuals, which has a different legal existence from its several members. It usually exists for a number of years or in perpetuity, irrespective of changes in number or composition of its members.

CORPORATIONS AFFECTED WITH PUBLIC INTEREST: A large class of private corporations which, on account of their special franchise charter, owes a duty to the public to perform their legal duties.

CORPORATION SOLE: A corporation sole consists of one person and his successor who is the incumbent of some particular office. This individual is incorporated to give him and his successor the legal advantages of perpetuity, which natural persons do not possess. It is usually an ecclesiastical office. A bishop is a corporation sole.

COURT: A government tribunal established by law for the administration of justice.

CREDIT: A substitute for cash money. The ability of a businessman to borrow money or obtain goods on the basis of his promise to pay later, because a person or a bank has a good opinion of his integrity and technical ability.

CURRENCY: Coined money, banknotes, or other forms of paper that circulate as money and are used as a medium of exchange. Most forms of currency are authorized by law.

DE FACTO: In fact, in actuality.

DEPOSIT CREDIT: Credit that banks transfer to the accounts of persons or corporations by a bookkeeping transaction which the borrowers then expend by check. The basis for the credit is deposits of money from many savers that are left in the custody of a bank for safety, convenience, or income.

DIRECTOR: A person appointed or elected according to law to manage or guide the policies of a corporation. The whole number of directors is called a board of directors.

DOUBLE LIABILITY: A limitation on the debts of a stockholder in a business corporation to the amount of the original investment plus a duplicate amount, in case of the bankruptcy of that corporation.

EMINENT DOMAIN: The power to take private property for public use without the consent of the owner if compensation is given at a fair valuation.

EQUITY LAW: Laws of remedial justice that are administered by the Court of Chancery, which is separate from common law courts. Chancery has the power to decree justice in situations not covered by the common law.

ESTABLISHED CHURCH: A Christian denomination that had a privileged legal status. This usually means that the public authority collects a tax from all citizens (unless specifically exempted) to be used by that denomination.

In the late colonial and early republican periods, established churches were operating in most states, although these states also had complete toleration for all other religious denominations.

FAIR VALUATION: The present market value of a property if it was put on the market and there was a buyer.

FOREIGN CORPORATION: A corporation doing business in a different legal jurisdiction from which its charter was secured. A foreign corporation can either be chartered in another state or another nation.

FRANCHISE CORPORATION: A corporation on which a government confers special privileges, like collecting a public toll or circulating banknotes as a medium of exchange. In return, the corporation constructs a public improvement or performs a valuable public service. Usually, these corporations are regulated by public authorities (in regard to their tolls and standard of service) and are free from most forms of competition. These powers are not usually possessed by individual persons under general laws.

FREE BANK: A bank chartered under New York's general incorporation law passed in 1838. It was free from the necessity of having an individual charter of incorporation passed by the state legislature. All persons who could raise the necessary capital could freely enter the banking business.

FULL LIABILITY: See Unlimited Liability.

GENERAL INCORPORATION STATUTE: A law that makes the advantages of incorporation available to all persons who qualify. The qualifications are contained in the law and are the same for all persons who seek it. Incorporation does not require a special act of the legislature that names specific persons, a specific location, and a specific capitalization.

GENERAL REGULATORY LAW: A statute that defines all of the powers possessed by one class of corporation, but requires the legislature to pass each charter of incorporation on an individual basis. General regulatory laws were usually passed for franchise corporations. They allowed the legislature to examine each petition individually and grant it only after a public hearing.

HERBAL DOCTOR: See Botanic Physician.

JOINT-STOCK COMPANY: An unincorporated business

company that is legally a partnership but has the same plan of organization as incorporated businesses except its stockholders do not possess limited liability.

JURISDICTION: The authority by which courts and judicial officers recognize and exercise their legal authority over a class of cases.

LAISSEZ FAIRE: A philosophy of political economy that believed that there should be the greatest practical separation of politics from the opportunities for business profits. Its purpose was to achieve the most rapid industrialization by excluding interference by state legislatures.

LIABLE: Bound or obliged by law; responsible by law for certain obligation such as the full payment of business debts.

LIMITED LIABILITY: A limit set by law on the debts of a shareholder in a business corporation to the amount of his investment or some stated additional fraction of this investment, if the business becomes bankrupt. See Double Liability.

LIMITED PARTNERSHIP: A partnership consisting of one or more co-partners who conduct the business, and one or more special partners who

contribute investment capital but who are not liable beyond this capital contribution.

MANDAMUS: An order issued from a court of superior jurisdiction to an inferior court, or to a private or municipal corporation commanding the performance of some duty.

MASTER IN CHANCERY: An assistant to a Judge of Chancery who attempts to resolve the conflicting legal claims of a large number of persons. He reports his findings to the judge so that a decree can be made.

MECHANIC'S LIEN: A claim created by law that secures priority of payment for work performed by employees of businesses that become bankrupt.

MORTMAIN: Laws to prevent the accumulation of land in the hands of corporations (usually religious or charitable corporations) except under certain conditions. They aimed to prevent land from being withdrawn from commercial development at a time when land was the chief form of wealth.

MUNICIPAL CORPORATION: A corporation organized for governmental purposes. A unit of government created by a superior political authority to administer local civil government, which is usually vested with subordinate powers of legislation.

MUNICIPALITY: See Municipal Corporation.

NONUSER CLAUSE: The neglect of a franchise corporation to exercise its legal right within a specified time, in which case the franchise privilege reverts to the state that originally granted it.

OBITER DICTA: An opinion or general statement by a court which is not necessary for the decision of the case being decided.

OUT-OF-STATE CORPORATION: See Foreign Corporation.

PAID-IN: Shares of a corporation in which the face value of each share has been wholly or partially invested in the corporation. This device was used in the early days of business corporations when the capital requirements of a business could not be accurately estimated, nor immediately raised.

PARTNERSHIP: A voluntary contract between two or more persons to jointly place their money and skills in some lawful business venture, with the understanding that there will be a proportional division of profit between them.

PERSONAL LIABILITY: See Unlimited Liability.

PERSONAL PROPERTY TAX: A tax levied on the moveable property owned by a person or a corporation.

PREFERRED STOCK: A separate class of stock in a corporation which has a priority in the payment of dividends over the rest of the stock.

PREMIUM: The sum paid by the assured to the underwriter as the cost for being insured.

PRIVATE CORPORATION: A corporation that has been voluntarily formed by private persons for private purposes, having no direct franchise responsibilities.

PRIVATEER: A sailing vessel owned and armed by private persons that is commissioned by a government to make war upon the enemy's commerce.

PRO FORMA: A matter of form or habitual legal action.

PRO RATA: In proportion; proportionately.

PROXY VOTING: A person who substitutes for another in order to vote his interest at a meeting of corporation shareholders.

PUBLIC CORPORATION: See Municipal Corporation.

QUASI-CORPORATION: A public organization resembling a

corporation but which is not a corporation in all respects, yet is recognized by statutes or long usage as a corporation. Its duties can be enforced by law.

QUO WARRENTO: A court order requesting a corporation to state the authority for its existence after it has ceased performing the duties for which it was created.

REGRESSIVE VOTING: A provision in a charter of incorporation that penalizes large stockholders: viz. it provides that a person owning ten shares could cast only eight votes and if he owned one hundred shares, he could cast only fifty votes, and if he owned a thousand shares he could cast only two hundred and fifty votes.

REGULATORY COMMISSION: A body of persons with the power to make and enforce such rules as the government delegates to it over any industry or branch of commerce which the state defines as being affected with the public interest.

RESERVE CLAUSE: The power the state reserves to itself to alter or repeal any corporation charter at any time for any reason. When embodied in a general law, this power automatically becomes part of the corporation's charter. This power negated the obligation of contract clause of the United States Constitution which the Supreme Court in the *Dartmouth College Case* interpreted to mean that corporation charters were contracts. The reserve clause converts all corporation charters into enabling acts.

SCIRE FACIAS: A judicial order that enforces some matter of judicial record. It allows a court to enforce a continuing legal action or enforce a judgment that has remained dormant for a number of years.

SHARE OF STOCK: The legal title to a definite portion of capital invested in a business enterprise and to a definite share of the profits, if there are any profits that are distributed.

SOCIETY: An association or company, generally unincorporated, of persons voluntarily united to act for some common purpose. See Association.

SPECIE: Gold or silver coins.

STARE DECISIS: The principle by which a court adheres to a general rule laid down in a previous case. To follow the precedent of a legal case already decided by the court and not disturb a settled point.

STATUTE: An act of the legislature declaring, commanding or prohibiting something. It is always a written law.

SUB-MODO CORPORATION: A corporation that exists under qualification or restriction and is not a full corporation. See Quasi-corporation.

THOMPSONITE PHYSICIAN: A variety of herbal doctor that flourished from about 1815 to 1860 in the United States. They believed that the best cure for diseases was to restore body heat by steam baths or by herbs that promoted body heat by violent body movements, like vomiting.

TRUST: A right of property, real or personal, held by one party for the benefit of another.

TRUSTEE: The person appointed or required by law to administer a trust by either a specific or implied agreement.

UNEARNED PREMIUM FUND: A fund maintained by insurance corporations that will guarantee the payment of a person's risks if the company becomes bankrupt.

UNLIMITED LIABILITY: The responsibility of a shareholder in a corporation or a partner in a partnership for all of the debts of the business upon its bankruptcy. The payment of these debts is guaranteed by a legal claim upon the total assets of all of the corporation's shareholders or all the members of the partnership.

VOLUNTARY BANKRUPTCY: Bankruptcy initiated on the petition of the debtor to be adjudged insolvent in order to get out from under a load of debt. It can be initiated without the consent of the creditors.

APPENDIX 2

Chronology
of General Incorporation
and General Regulatory
Statutes of New York, 1784–1855

1784 Trustees of Religious Congregations—general incorporation

1786 County Loan Officers—general incorporation

1787 Colleges and Academies—general incorporation (delegated to the Regents of the University)

1788 Municipal Corporations—de facto general regulatory

1788 Overseers of the Poor—de facto general regulatory

1792 County Loan Officers—general incorporation

1796 Library Companies—general incorporation

1801 **Constitutional Convention**

1801 **Compiled Statutes**

1806 Medical Societies—general incorporation limited to counties

1807 Turnpike Corporations—general regulatory

1808 County Loan Commissions—general incorporation

1811 Manufacturing Corporations—general incorporation

1811 Bible Societies—general incorporation

1813 **Compiled Statutes**

1814 Privateering Associations—general incorporation with license from the United States government

1814 Banks—general incorporation: **Lost**

1815 Trustees of School Districts and Township Common School Commissioners—general incorporation

1817 Bible Societies and Common Prayer Book Societies—general incorporation

1819 Agricultural Societies—general organizational for county societies

1820 Charitable Societies—general incorporation: **Lost**

1821 Lancaster and Bell Schools—general incorporation

1821 **Constitutional Convention**

1822 Limited Partnerships

1825   Banks—general regulatory: **Lost**

1828   Obituary Societies—general incorporation: **Lost**

1828   **Revised Statutes**

1829   Banks—general regulatory (Safety Fund Statute)

1832   Rural Fire Companies—general organizational

1835   Banks—general incorporation: **Lost**

1836   Mutual Insurance Companies—general incorporation: **Lost**

1837   Banks—general incorporation: **Lost**

1838   Banks—general incorporation (Free Banking Statute)

1839   Military Associations—general incorporation: **Lost**

1846   Constitutional Convention

1846   Savings Banks—general incorporation: **Lost**

1847   Plank Roads and Turnpikes—general incorporation

1847   Cemetery Associations—general incorporation

1847   Villages—general incorporation

1847   Village Fire Companies—general organizational

1847   Manufacturing Companies—general incorporation: **Lost**

1847   Railroads—general incorporation: **Lost**

1848   Toll Bridges—general incorporation

1848   Gas Light Companies—general incorporation

1848   Railroads—general incorporation

1848   Manufacturing, Mechanical, and Chemical Companies—general incorporation

1848   Telegraphs—general incorporation

1848   Benevolent, Charitable, Scientific, and Missionary Societies—general incorporation

1848   Savings banks—general incorporation: **Lost**

1849   Insurance—general incorporation

1850   Railroads—general incorporation (repeal of 1848 statute)

1850   Savings banks—general incorporation: **Lost**

1851   Building, Mutual Loan, and Accumulating Fund Associations—general incorporation

1851   Proprietary Academies or High Schools—general incorporation

1851   Savings banks—general incorporation: **Lost**

1852   Ocean Steam Navigation Companies—general incorporation

1852   **Compiled Statutes**

1853   Life and Health Insurance Companies—general incorporation

1853   Fire Insurance Companies—general incorporation

1853   Agricultural and Horticultural Societies—general incorporation

1853   Medical Schools—general incorporation

1853   Proprietary Reference and Circulating Libraries—general incorporation

1853   Building Erection Companies—general incorporation

1853   Ferries—general incorporation

1853   Union School Districts—general incorporation

1854   Societies to Establish Free Churches—general incorporation

1854   Private and Family Cemeteries—general incorporation

1854   Associations for Improving the Breed of Horses—general incorporation

1854   Stage Companies in the City of New York— general incorporation

1854   Navigation Companies on Lake George—general incorporation

1854   Lake and River Navigation Companies—general incorporation

1855   Agricultural and Horticultural Societies—general incorporation

Table
of Cases

Attorney General v. *Utica Insurance Company*, 1817, 2 Johns Chancery 370; 86.

Bank of Augusta v. *Earle*, 1839, 13 Peters 519; 248, 251.
Bank of Columbia v. *Patterson*, 1813, 7 Cranch 299; 253.
Bank of Poughkeepsie v. *Ibbotson*, 1840, 24 Wendell 479; 115.
Bank of the United States v. *Deveaux*, 1809, 5 Cranch 61; 245, 246, 247, 248.
Bank of the United States v. *Planters Bank of Georgia*, 1824, 9 Wheaton 904; 147.
Bank of Utica v. *The City of Utica*, 1834, 4 Paige Chancery 399; 115.
Beekman v. *Saratoga and Schenectady Railroad Corporation*, 1831, 3 Paige Chancery 75; 226.
Bolander v. *Stevens*, 1840, 23 Wendell 103; 160.
Briggs v. *Penniman*, 1826, 8 Cowen 392; 72, 115, 190.
Briscoe v. *Bank of Kentucky*, 1837, 11 Peters 257; 58, 134, 160.
Bristol v. *Barker*, 1817, 14 Johns 204; 87, 112.
Brooks v. Hill, 1848, 1 Mich. 118; 174.

Charles River Bridge Company v. *Warren Bridge Company*, 1837, 11 Peters 420; 205.
Clinton Woollen and Cotton Manufacturing Company v. *Morse*, 1817 (unreported), cited in *The People* v. *Utica Insurance Company*, 1818, 15 Johns 382; 114.
Columbian Manufacturing Company v. *Vanderpoel*, 1825, 4 Cowen 556; 114.
Cooley v. *Board of Wardens*, 1852, 12 Howard 299; 251.
Corning v. *Greene*, 1856, 23 Barbour 33; 229.
Craig v. *Missouri*, 1830, 4 Peters 410; 133.

Danforth v. *Schoharie Turnpike Company*, 1815, 12 Johnson 227; 253.
Dartmouth College v. *Woodward*, 1819, 4 Wheaton 518; 96, 238, 240.
DeBow v. *The People*, 1845, 1 Denio 12; 168, 169, 170, 171, 265.
Delafield v. *Kinney*, 1840, 24 Wendell 347; 162.
Denton v. *Jackson*, 1817, 2 Johns Chancery 325; 36.
Deraismes v. *Merchants Mutual Insurance Company*, 1848, 1 Comstock 371; 228.
Dunn v. *St. Andrews Church*, 1817, 14 Johnson 118; 253.
Dutchess Cotton Manufactory v. *Davis*, 1817, 14 Johns 238; 70.

Fairfax v. *Hunter's Lessee*, 1813, 7 Cranch 603; 253.
Falconer v. *Campbell*, 1840, 8 McLean 195, West Publishing Co., Vol. 8, Case 4620, 963; 174.
Fletcher v. *Peck*, 1810, 6 Cranch 87; 246, 253.

Gardner v. *Village of Newburgh*, 1816, 2 Johnson Chancery 162; 226.
Genesee Chief v. *Fitzhugh*, 1851, 12 Howard 443; 249.
Gibbons v. *Ogden*, 1824, 9 Wheaton 1; 44.
Gifford v. *Livingston*, 1845, 2 Denio 336; 171.
Gillet v. *Moody*, 1850, 3 Comstock 385; 172.
Grant v. *Fancher*, 1826, 5 Cowen 309; 36.
Green v. *Biddle*, 1823, 8 Wheaton 1; 253.
Green v. *Graves*, 1844, 1 Douglass 351; 174.
Groves v. *Slaughter*, 1841, 15 Peters 449; 249.

Head v. *Providence Insurance Company*, 1804, 2 Cranch 127; 112, 253.
Huidekoper's Lessee v. *Douglass*, 1805, 3 Cranch 1; 246, 253.

Jackson v. *Cory*, 1811, 8 Johns 385; 36.
Jackson v. *Hartwell*, 1811, 8 Johns 422; 36.

Louisville, Cincinnati and Charleston Railroad v. *Letson*, 1844, 2 Howard 497; 248, 249, 251.

McCulloch v. *Maryland*, 1819, 4 Wheaton 316; 113, 246.
McLaren v. *Pennington*, 1828, 1 Paige Chancery 108; 253.
Marcy v. *Clark*, 1821, 17 Mass. 334; 115.
Marshall v. *Baltimore and Ohio Railroad*, 1853, 16 Howard 314; 251.
Martin v. *Hunter's Lessee*, 1816, 1 Wheaton 304; 253.
The Matter of the Bank of Danville, 1844, 6 Hill 370; 174.
The Matter of Oliver Lee and Company's Bank, 1860, 21 N.Y. 13; 190.
Mohawk and Hudson Railroad Company v. *Clute*, 1834, 4 Paige Chancery 395; 114, 214.

The Supervisors of Niagara v. *The People*, 1844, 7 Hill 506; 167, 171, 172.
Swift v. *Tyson*, 1842, 16 Peters 1; 249.

Terrett v. *Taylor*, 1815, 9 Cranch 43; 32, 253.
Thomas v. *Dakin*, 1839, 22 Wendell 81; 158, 165, 171, 174.
Todd v. *Birdsall*, 1823, 1 Cowen 260; 36.

U.S. Trust Company v. *U.S. Fire Insurance Company*, 1858, 18 N.Y. 199; 190.

Wales v. *Stetson*, 1806, 2 Mass. 146; 238.
Warner v. *Beers*, 1840, 23 Wendell 103; 160, 161, 162, 163, 166, 167, 169, 170, 171, 172.
Williams v. *Michigan Bank*, 1831, 7 Wendell 542; 229.
Williams v. *Williams*, 1853, 8 N.Y. 525; 11.
Willoughby v. *Comstock*, 1842, 3 Hill 389, 174.

Bibliography

STATUTES

The Colonial Laws of New York, 1664–1774, Charles Z. Collin, Issac H. Maynard, Eli C. Belknap, Daniel Magone, John J. Linson, Robert C. Cumming, eds.; Albany, 1894.

The Laws of the State of New York Comprising the Constitution and Acts of the Legislature since the Revolution, from the First to the Twentieth Session Inclusive, 1778–1799; Thomas Greenleaf, ed.; Thomas Greenleaf Printer, New York, 1799.

Laws of the State of New York, 1777–1801; Weed, Parsons, Albany, 1886–1887.

Laws of the State of New York, 1798–1807; Albany, 1798–1807.

Public Laws of the State of New York, 1808-1810; Albany, 1808-1810.

Private Laws of the State of the New York, 1808–1810; Albany, 1808–1810.

Laws of the State of New York, 1807–1809; Albany, 1809.

Laws of the State of New York, 1811–1856; Albany, 1811–1856.

Laws of the State of New York, James Kent, Jacob Radcliff, eds; Charles R. Webster and George Webster Printer, Albany, 1802.

Laws of the State of New York Revised and Passed at the Thirty-sixth Session of the Legislature; H. C. Southwick, Albany, 1813.

The Revised Statutes of New York, 1828, John Duer, Benjamin F. Butler, John C. Spencer, eds.; Packard and Van Benthuysen, Printer, Albany, 1829.

The Revised Statutes of the State of New York, 1852, Hiram Denio, ed.; Gould, Banks, Albany, 1852.

The Acts and Resolves, Public and Private of the Province of Massachusetts Bay; Wright and Potter, Boston, 1869–1922.

The Perpetual Laws of the Commonwealth of Massachusetts, 1780–1800; I. Thomas and E. T. Andrews, Boston, 1801.

Private and Special Statutes of the Commonwealth of Massachusetts, 1780-1805; Manning and Loring, Boston, 1805.

The Laws of the Commonwealth of Massachusetts, 1780-1807; Boston, 1808.

Laws of the Commonwealth of Massachusetts, 1806-1838; Boston, 1806-1838.

Acts and Resolves Passed by the Legislature of Massachusetts, 1839-1855; Boston, 1839-1855.

LEGISLATIVE DOCUMENTS AND JOURNALS

Before 1820, the legislative documents are irregularly preserved and only partially bound. They are frequently duplicated by being included within the journals of the Assembly and Senate. The numbering of the documents is usually consecutive with a heading indicating whether the Assembly or Senate ordered its printing. From 1820 through 1830, the documents are usually bound but not all have been preserved. After 1831, legislative documents are divided into two series, one for the Assembly and the other for the Senate. The best collection of early documents is at the New York State Library in Albany.

Legislative Documents of the State of New York, 1815-1830; Albany, 1815-1830.

Documents of the Assembly of the State of New York, 1831-1856; Albany, 1831-1856.

Documents of the Senate of the State of New York, 1831-1856; Albany, 1831-1856.

Journal of the Assembly of the State of New York, 1784-1830; Albany, 1784-1830.

Journal of the Senate of the State of New York, 1784-1830; Albany, 1784-1830.

JUDICIAL RECORDS

Reports of the Cases of Practice Determined in the Supreme Court of Judicature of the State of New York, from April Term 1794, to November Term 1805, to which is Prefixed all the Rules and Orders of the Court; Coleman and Caines Reports, New York, 1808.

Reports of Cases Argued and Determined in the Supreme Judicature, and in the Court for the Trial of Impeachments and Correction of Errors in the State of New York, 1806-1846; Albany, 1806-1846.

Reports of Cases Argued and Determined in the Court of Appeals of the State of New York, 1847-1855; Albany, 1847-1855.

Reports of Cases Argued and Determined in the Court of Chancery of the State of New York, 1814–1848; Albany, 1814–1848.

An Analytical and Practical Synopsis of all the Cases Argued and Reversed in Law and Equity in the Court for the Correction of Errors of the State of New York from 1788 to 1847, Ralph Lockwood, ed.; Banks, Gould, New York, 1848.

CONSTITUTIONAL CONVENTIONS

Reports of the Proceedings and Debates of the Convention of 1821, Assembled for the Purpose of Amending the Constitution of the State of New York, Nathaniel H. Carter, William L. Stone, Marcus T. C. Gould, reporters; E. and E. Hosford Printer, Albany, 1821.

Report of the Debates and Proceedings of the Convention of the State of New York Held at the Capital in the City of Albany, August 28, 1821, L. H. Clarke, reporter; J. Seymour Printer, New York, 1821.

Journal of the Convention of the State of New York; Cantine and Leake Printers, Albany, 1821.

Debates and Proceedings in the New York State Convention for the Revision of the Constitution, S. Croswell, R. Sutton, reporters; *Albany Argus*, Albany, 1846.

Report of the Debates and Proceedings of the Convention for the Revision of the Constitution of New York, 1846, William G. Bishop, William H. Attree, reporters; *Evening Atlas*, Albany, 1846.

Journal of the Convention of the State of New York, Begun and Held at the Capital in the City of Albany on the First Day of June, 1846, W. H. Hill, F. S. Rew, reporters; Carroll and Cook Printer, Albany, 1846.

Documents of the Convention of the State of New York, 1846, Carroll and Cook Printer, Albany, 1846.

The Constitution of the State of New York Adopted November 3, 1846, Together with Marginal Notes and a Copious Index, I. R. Elwood, ed.; C. Van Benthuysen, Albany, 1847.

Manual for the Use of the Convention to Revise the Constitution of the State of New York, Convened at Albany, June 1, 1846; Walker and Creighead Printers, New York, 1846.

New York Convention Manual Prepared in Pursuance of Chapters 194 and 458, of the Laws of 1867, Part II, Statistics, Franklin B. Hough, ed.; Weed, Parsons, Albany, 1867.

The Federal and State Constitutions, Colonial Charters and Other Organic Laws of the United States, Benjamin P. Poore, ed.; United States Government Printing Office, Washington, D.C., 1877.

BIBLIOGRAPHIES, INDEXES, AND TREATISES
(Consulted but not usually cited)

Angell, Joseph K. *A Treatise on the Law of Fire and Life Insurance*, Little, Brown, Boston, 1854 (reprinted, Arno Press, New York, 1972).

————, Samuel Ames. *A Treatise on the Law of Private Corporations Aggregate*, Hilliard, Gray, Little, and Wilkins, Boston, 1832 (1st ed.); Boston 1855 (5th ed.).

Brever, Ernest H., ed. *Constitutional Developments in New York, 1777–1958: A Bibliography of Conventions and Constitutions with Selected References for Constitutional Research*, New York State Library Bibliography Bulletin, 82, Albany, 1958.

Clark, Aaron, ed. *A List of All Incorporations in New York*, Assembly Journal, 1819, Appendix.

Cleveland, John. *The Banking System of the State of New York with Notes and References to Adjudged Cases*, John S. Voorhies, New York, 1857.

Corwin, Edward S. *The Commerce Power versus States Rights*, Princeton University Press, Princeton, 1936.

Dillon, John F. *A Treatise on the Law of Municipal Corporations*, James Cockcroft, Chicago, 1872.

Dougherty, John H. *The Constitutional History of the State of New York*, Neale Publishing, New York, 1925.

Endlich, Gustav A. *The Law of Building Associations*, Frederick D. Linn, Jersey City, 1895.

Evans, George H. *Business Incorporation in the United States, 1800–1943*, National Bureau of Economic Research, New York, 1948.

General Index of the Documents and Laws of the State of New York, Thurlow Weed Printer, Albany, 1842.

General Index of the Legislative Documents of the State of New York, 1777–1888, James B. Lyon, Albany, 1891.

Gillet, T. S., ed. *General Index of the Laws of the State of New York*, Weed, Parsons, Albany, 1859.

Hasse, Adelaide, ed. *Index of Economic Material in Documents of the States of the United States: New York, 1789–1904*, Carnegie Institute of Washington, New York, 1907.

Hough, Franklin B., David Murray. *Historical and Statistical Record of the University of the State of New York, 1784–1884*, Weed, Parsons, Albany, 1885.

Keitt, Lawrence, ed. *An Annotated Bibliography of Bibliographies of Statutory Materials of the United States*, Harvard University Press, Cambridge, 1934.

Keyes, Emerson W., ed. *Special Report on Savings Banks*, Van Benthuysen, Albany, 1868.

Lincoln, Charles Z., ed. *Messages from the Governors of New York*, J. B. Lyon, Albany, 1909.

McMaster, Robert B. *Railroad Laws of the State of New York*, Baker, Voorhis, New York, 1872.

Phillips, Willard. *A Treatise on the Law of Insurance*, Wells and Lilly Publisher, Boston, 1823 (1st ed.); Boston, 1840 (2nd ed.); Boston, 1854 (4th ed.).

Pierce, Edward L. *A Treatise on American Railroad Law*, John S. Voorhies, New York, 1857.

Scott, Henry W. *The Courts of the State of New York*, Wilson Publishing, New York, 1909.

Story, Joseph. *Commentaries on the Constitution of the United States*, Hilliard, Gray, Boston, 1833.

Sundheim, Joseph H. *Law of Building and Loan Associations*, Callaghan, Chicago, 1833.

Transactions of the Medical Society of the State of New York, 1807–1856, Charles Van Benthuysen, Albany, 1868.

Troubat, Francis J. *The Law of Commandatary and Limited Partnerships in the United States*, James Kay, Philadelphia, 1853.

Walker, Timothy. *Introduction to American Law*, P. H. Nicklin and T. Johnson, Law Booksellers, Philadelphia, 1837.

Zollman, Carl F. *American Law of Charities*, Bruce Publishing, Milwaukee, 1924.

UNPUBLISHED WORKS

Butler, Benjamin F. New York State Library, Albany.

Flagg, Azariah C. New York Public Library, New York City.

McFaul, John M. The Politics of Jacksonian Finance, University of California Doctoral Dissertation, 1963.

Remini, Robert V. The Early Political Career of Martin Van Buren, 1782–1828, Columbia University Doctoral Dissertation, 1951.

Reubens, Beatrice G. State Financing of Private Enterprises in Early New York, Columbia University Doctoral Dissertation, 1960.

Spencer, Ivor D. William L. Marcy and the Albany Regency, Brown University Doctoral Dissertation, 1940.

NEWSPAPERS

Albany Argus.

BOOKS AND ARTICLES

Abbot, Frank C. *Government Policy and Higher Education, A Study of the Regents of the University of the State of New York, 1784–1949*, Cornell University Press, Ithaca, 1958.

Akagi, Roy H. *The Town Proprietors of the New England Colonies, 1620–1770*, University of Pennsylvania Press, Philadelphia, 1924.

Albion, Robert G. *The Rise of New York Port, 1815–1860*, Scribner, New York, 1939.

Angell, Joseph K. *A Treatise on the Law of Fire and Life Insurance*, Little, Brown, Boston, 1854 (reprinted, Arno Press, New York, 1972).

_____. Samuel Ames. *A Treatise on the Law of Private Corporations Aggregate*, Hilliard, Gray, Little, and Wilkins, Boston, 1832 (1st ed.); Boston, 1843 (2nd ed); Boston, 1846 (3rd ed.); Boston, 1852 (4th ed.); Boston, 1855 (5th ed.).

Aubrey, Henry G. "Investment Decisions in Underdeveloped Countries," in *Development and Society: The Dynamics of Economic Change*, David F. Novack, Robert Lekachman, eds., St. Martin's Press, New York, 1968.

Bailyn, Bernard. *Education in the Forming of American Society*, University of North Carolina Press, Chapel Hill, 1960.

Bainbridge, John. *Biography of an Idea: The Story of Mutual Fire and Casualty Insurance*, Doubleday, New York, 1952.

Baldwin, Simeon E. "American Business Corporations Before 1789," *American Historical Review*, Vol. 8, 1903.

_____. *Modern Political Institutions*, Little, Brown, Boston, 1908.

Bayles, Ernest E., Bruce L. Hood. *Growth of American Educational Thought and Practice*, Harper and Row, New York, 1966.

Benson, Lee. *Merchants, Farmers, and Railroads: Railroad Regulation and New York Politics, 1850–1887*, Harvard University Press, Cambridge, 1955.

_____. *The Concept of Jacksonian Democracy*, Princeton University Press, Princeton, 1961.

Blackstone, William. *Commentaries on the Laws of England* (8th ed., 1778), William G. Hammond, ed., Bancroft-Whitney, San Francisco, 1890.

Blandi, Joseph G. *Maryland Business Corporations, 1783–1852*, Johns Hopkins Press, Baltimore, 1934.

Blau, Joseph L., ed. *Social Theories of Jacksonian Democracy*, Hafner Publishing, New York, 1954.

Bodfish, Henry M., ed. *History of Building and Loan in the United States*, United States Building and Loan League, Chicago, 1931.

Bolles, Albert S. *Industrial History of the United States*, Henry Publishing, Norwich, Ct., 1881.

Bourne, William O. *History of the Public School Society of New York*, William Wood, New York, 1870.

Bruchey, Stuart. *The Roots of American Economic Growth, 1607–1861: An Essay in Social Causation*, Harper and Row, New York, 1965.

Burn, D. L. "The Genesis of American Engineering Competition, 1850–1870," *Economic History*, Vol. 2, 1931.

Byrdsall, Fitzwilliam. *The History of the Loco-Foco or Equal Rights Party*, Burt Franklin, New York, 1967 (reprint of 1842 edition).

Cadman, John W. *The Corporation in New Jersey, 1791–1875*, Harvard University Press, Cambridge, 1949.

Callender, Guy S. "The Early Transportation and Banking Enterprises of the States in Relation to the Growth of Corporations," *Quarterly Journal of Economics*, Vol. 17, 1902.

Cameron, Rondo. *Banking in the Early Stages of Industrialization*, Oxford University Press, New York, 1967.

_____, ed. *Banking and Economic Development: Some Lessons of History*, Oxford University Press, New York, 1972.

Chaddock, Robert E. *The Safety-Fund Banking System in New York, 1829–1866*, U.S. Government Printing Office, Washington, D.C., 1910.

Chandler, Alfred, D., Jr., ed. *The Railroads, the Nation's First Big Business*, Harcourt, Brace and World, New York, 1965.

_____. "The Railroads: Pioneers in Modern Corporate Management," *Business History Review*, Vol. 39, 1965.

Chroust, Anton-Hermann. *The Rise of the Legal Profession in America*, University of Oklahoma Press, Norman, 1965.

Clark, Victor S. *History of Manufactures in the United States*, Carnegie Institution of Washington, McGraw-Hill, New York, 1929.

Clough, Shepard B. *A Century of American Life Insurance: A History of the Mutual Life Insurance Company of New York, 1843–1943*, Columbia University Press, New York, 1946.

Cochran, Thomas C. *Railroad Leaders, 1845–1890*, Harvard University Press, Cambridge, 1953.

_____. "The Entrepreneur in American Capital Formation," in *Capital Formation and Economic Growth*, Moses Abramovitz, ed., Princeton University Press, Princeton, 1955.

_____. "The Business Revolution," *American Historical Review*, Vol. 79, 1974.

Cole, Arthur H. *The American Wool Manufacture*, Harvard University Press, Cambridge, 1926.

Cremin, Lawrence A. *American Education: The Colonial Experience, 1607–1783*, Harper and Row, New York, 1970.

Cross, Whitney R. *The Burned-Over District: The Social and Intellectual History of Enthusiastic Religion in Western New York, 1800–1850*, Cornell University Press, Ithaca, N.Y., 1950.

Davis, Joseph S. *Essays in the Earlier History of American Corporations*, Harvard University Press, Cambridge, 1917.

Davis, Lance E. "Stock Ownership in the Early New England Textile Industry," *Business History Review*, Vol. 32, 1958.

_____. "New England Textile Mills and the Capital Markets: A Study of Industrial Borrowing 1850–1860," *Journal of Economic History*, Vol. 20, 1960.

_____, Peter L. Payne. "From Benevolence to Business: The Story of Two Savings Banks," *Business History Review*, Vol. 32, 1958.

Degler, Carl N. "The Locofocos: Urban Agrarians," *Journal of Economic History*, Vol. 16, 1956.

Dewey, Davis R. *State Banking Before the Civil War*, U.S. Government Printing Office, Washington, D.C., 1910.

_____. *Financial History of the United States*, Longmans, Green, New York, 1915.

Dignan, Patrick J. *A History of the Legal Incorporation of Catholic Church Property in the United States, 1784–1932*, Catholic University of America, Washington, D.C., 1933.

Dillon, John F. *Treatise on the Law of Municipal Corporations*, James Cockcroft, Chicago, 1872.

Dodd, Edwin M. "The Evolution of Limited Liability in American Industry: Massachusetts," *Harvard Law Review*, Vol. 61, 1948.

_____. *American Business Corporations Until 1860: With Special Reference to Massachusetts*, Harvard University Press, Cambridge, 1954.

Domett, Henry W. *A History of the Bank of New York, 1784–1884*, Riverside Press, Cambridge, Mass., 1884.

Donovan, Herbert D. A. *The Barnburners, 1832–1852*, New York University Press, New York, 1925.

Dorfman, Joseph. "The Jackson Wage-Earner Thesis," *American Historical Review*, Vol. 54, 1949.

_____. "Chancellor Kent and the Developing American Economy," *Columbia Law Review*, Vol. 61, 1961.

Durrenburger, Joseph A. *Turnpikes: A Study of the Toll Road Movement in the Middle Atlantic States and Maryland*, Southern Stationery and Printing, Valadosta, Ga., 1931.

Ellis, David M. *Land Lords and Farmers in the Hudson-Mohawk Region,* *1790-1850,* Cornell University Press, Ithaca, 1946.

Erickson, Erling A. *Banking in Frontier Iowa, 1836-1865,* Iowa State University Press, Ames, 1971.

Fenstermaker, J. Van. *The Development of American Commercial Banking 1782-1837,* Bureau of Economic and Business Research, Kent State University, Kent, Ohio, 1965.

Fishlow, Albert. *American Railroads and the Transformation of the Ante-Bellum Economy,* Harvard University Press, Cambridge, 1965.

Flagg, Azariah C. *Banks and Banking in the State of New York from the Adoption of the Constitution in 1777 to 1864,* Rome Brothers, Brooklyn, 1868.

Flick, Alexander C., ed. *The History of the State of New York,* New York State Historical Association, Columbia University Press, New York, 1934.

Foulke, Roy A. *The Sinews of American Commerce,* Dun and Bradstreet, New York, 1941.

Fox, Dixon R. *The Decline of Aristocracy in the Politics of New York,* *1801-1840,* Columbia University Press, New York, 1919.

Gabel, Richard J. *Public Funds for Church and Private Schools,* Catholic University of America, Washington, D.C., 1937.

Gatell, Frank O. "Spoils of the Bank War: Political Bias in the Selection of Pet Banks," *American Historical Review,* Vol. 70, 1964.

_____. "Sober Second Thoughts on Van Buren, the Albany Regency, and the Wall Street Conspiracy," *Journal of American History,* Vol. 53, 1966.

_____. "Money and Party in Jacksonian America: A Quantitative Look at New York City's Men of Quality," *Political Science Quarterly,* Vol. 82, 1967.

Gibb, George S. *The Saco-Lowell Shops,* Harvard University Press, Cambridge, 1950.

Goodrich, Carter. "The Revulsion Against Internal Improvements," *Journal of Economic History,* Vol. 10, 1950.

_____. *Government Promotion of American Canals and Railroads, 1800-1890,* Columbia University Press, New York, 1960.

_____, ed. *The Government and the Economy, 1783-1861,* Bobbs-Merrill, Indianapolis, 1967.

Green, George D. "Louisiana, 1804-1861," in *Banking and Economic Development: Some Lessons of History,* Rondo Cameron, ed., Oxford University Press, New York, 1972.

Gunn, L. Ray. "Political Implications of General Incorporation Laws in New York to 1860," *Mid-America,* Vol. 59, 1977.

Haar, Charles M. "Legislative Regulations of New York Industrial Corporations, 1800–1850," *New York History Magazine*, Vol. 22, 1941.

Habakkuk, H. J. *American and British Technology in the Nineteenth Century: The Search for Labour-Saving Inventions*, Cambridge University Press, Cambridge, 1962.

Haines, Charles G., Foster H. Sherwood. *The Role of the Supreme Court in American Government and Politics, 1835–1864*, University of California Press, Berkeley, 1957.

Hammond, Bray. "Long and Short Term Credit in Early American Banking," *Quarterly Journal of Economics*, Vol. 49, 1934.

_____. "Free Banks and Corporations: The New York Free Banking Act of 1838," *Journal of Political Economy*, Vol. 44, 1936.

_____. *Banks and Politics in America from the Revolution to the Civil War*, Princeton University Press, Princeton, 1957.

Hammond, Jabez D. *Life and Times of Silas Wright*, Hall and Dickson Publishers, Syracuse, New York, 1848.

_____. *The History of Political Parties in the State of New York*, Phinney and Company, Buffalo, 1850.

Handlin, Oscar, Mary F. Handlin. "Origins of the American Business Corporation," *Journal of Economic History*, Vol. 5, 1945.

_____. *Commonwealth Massachusetts, 1774–1861*, New York University Press, New York, 1947.

Harlow, Alvin E. *The Road of the Century: The Story of the New York Central*, Creative Age Press, New York, 1947.

Hartz, Louis. *Economic Policy and Democratic Thought: Pennsylvania, 1776–1860*, Harvard University Press, Cambridge, 1948.

Hedrick, Ulysses P. *A History of Agriculture in the State of New York*, New York Agricultural Society, J. B. Lyon, Albany, 1933.

Heins, A. James, *Constitutional Restrictions Against State Debt*, University of Wisconsin Press, Madison, 1963.

Henderson, Gerard C. *The Position of Foreign Corporations in American Constitutional Law*, Harvard University Press, Cambridge, 1918.

Hepburn, Alonzo B. *A History of Currency in the United States*, Augustus M. Kelley Publishers, New York, 1967 (reprint of 1903 ed.).

Hildreth, Richard. *The History of Banks: To Which is Added a Demonstration of the Advantages and Necessity of Free Competition in the Business of Banking*, Hilliard, Gray, Boston, 1837.

Hinsdale, Burke A. *Horace Mann and the Common School Revival in the United States*, Scribner, New York, 1898.

Hobson, Elsie G. *Educational Legislation and Administration in the State of New York, 1777–1850*, University of Chicago Press, Chicago, 1918.

Hofstadter, Richard. "William Leggett, Spokesman of Jacksonian Democracy," *Political Science Quarterly*, Vol. 58, 1943.

Horne, H. Oliver. *A History of Savings Banks*, Oxford University Press, London, 1947.

Horton, John T. *James Kent, A Study in Conservatism, 1763–1847*, Appleton-Century, New York, 1939.

Horwitz, Morton J. "The Transformation in the Conception of Property in American Law, 1780–1860," *University of Chicago Law Review*, Vol. 40, 1973.

_____. "The Rise of Legal Formalism," *American Journal of Legal History*, Vol. 19, 1975.

Hough, Franklin B. *New York Convention Manual Prepared in Pursuance of Chapters 194 and 458 of the Laws of 1867*, Part II, Statistics, Weed, Parsons, Albany, 1867.

Howard, Stanley E. "The Limited Partnership in New Jersey," *Journal of Business of the University of Chicago*, Vol. 7, 1934.

_____. "Stockholders' Liability under the New York Act of March 22, 1811," *Journal of Political Economy*, Vol. 46, 1938.

Howe, Mark D. "A Footnote on the Conspiracy Theory," *Yale Law Review*, Vol. 48, 1939.

Hugins, Walter. *Jacksonian Democracy and the Working Class*, Stanford University Press, Stanford, Calif., 1960.

Hurst, James W. *Law and the Conditions of Freedom in Nineteenth Century United States*, University of Wisconsin Press, Madison, 1956.

_____. *The Legitimacy of the Business Corporation in the Law of the United States, 1780–1970*, University of Virginia Press, Charlottesville, 1970.

James, Marquis. *Biography of a Business, 1792–1942: The Insurance Company of North America*, Bobbs-Merrill, New York, 1942.

Jenkins, John S. *History of Political Parties in the State of New York*, Alden and Markham Publishers, Auburn, N.Y., 1846.

Jenks, Leland H. "Railroads as an Economic Force in American Development," *Journal of Economic History*, Vol. 4, 1944.

Jeremy, David J. "Innovation in American Textile Technology during the Early 19th Century," *Technology and Culture*, Vol. 14, 1973.

Johnson, A. B. "The Legislative History of Corporations in the State of New York, or, The Progress of Liberal Sentiments," *Hunt's Merchants Magazine*, Vol. 23, December 1850 in *The Government and the Economy: 1783–1861*, Carter Goodrich, ed., Bobbs-Merrill, Indianapolis, 1967.

Kaestle, Carl F. "Common Schools Before the Common School Revival:

New York Schooling in the 1790's," *History of Education Quarterly*, Vol. 12, 1972.

_____. *The Evolution of an Urban School System: New York City, 1750–1850*, Harvard University Press, Cambridge, 1973.

Kent, James. *Commentaries on American Laws*, O. Halsted Publisher, New York, 1827 (1st ed.); New York, 1832 (2nd ed.); New York, 1851 (7th ed.).

Kessler, William C. "A Statistical Study of the New York General Incorporation Act of 1811," *Journal of Political Economy*, Vol. 48, 1940.

_____. "Incorporation in New England: A Statistical Study, 1800–1875," *Journal of Economic History*, Vol. 8, 1948.

Kett, Joseph F. *The Formation of the American Medical Profession*, Yale University Press, New Haven, 1968.

Keyes, Emerson W. *A History of Savings Banks in the United States*, Bradford Rhodes, New York, 1876.

King, Charles R., ed. *Life and Correspondence of Rufus King*, G. P. Putnam, New York, 1900.

Kirkland, Edward C. *Men Cities and Transportation: A Study in New England History, 1820–1900*, Harvard University Press, Cambridge, 1948.

Klebaner, Benjamin J. "State-Chartered American Commercial Banks, 1781–1801," *Business History Review*, Vol. 53, 1979.

Klein, Milton M. *The Politics of Diversity: Essays in the History of Colonial New York*, Kennikat Press, Port Washington, N.Y., 1974.

Knox, John J. *A History of Banking in the United States*, Augustus M. Kelley, New York, 1969 (reprint of 1903 ed.).

Kolko, Gabriel. *Railroads and Regulations, 1877–1916*, Princeton University Press, Princeton, 1965.

Lamb, Robert K. "The Entrepreneur and the Community," in *Men in Business: Essays on the Historical Role of the Entrepreneur*, William Miller, ed., Harper and Row, New York 1962.

Lamberton, E. V. "Colonial Libraries of Pennsylvania," *Pennsylvania Magazine of History and Biography*, Vol. 42, 1918.

Lebergott, Stanley. "United States Transport Advance and Externalities," *Journal of Economic History*, Vol. 26, 1966.

Levy, Leonard W. *The Law of the Commonwealth and Chief Justice Shaw*, Harper and Row, New York, 1967.

Lincoln, Charles Z. *The Constitutional History of New York from the Beginning of the Colonial Period to the Year 1905*, New York Lawyers Cooperative Publishing Company, Rochester, N.Y., 1906.

Lively, Robert A. "The American System: A Review Article," *Business History Review*, Vol. 29, 1955.

Lockridge, Kenneth A. *Literacy in Colonial New England: An Enquiry into the Social Context of Literacy in the Early Modern West*, Norton, New York, 1974.

Lynch, Denis T. *An Epoch and a Man: Martin Van Buren and His Times*, Horace Liveright, New York, 1929.

McAnear, Beverly. "College Founding in the American Colonies, 1745–1775," *Mississippi Valley Historical Review*, Vol. 42, 1955.

McBain, Howard L. *DeWitt Clinton and the Origin of the Spoils System in New York*, AMS Press, New York, 1967.

McCluggage, Robert W. *A History of the American Dental Association*, American Dental Association, Chicago, 1959.

McDonald, Forrest. *We the People, The Economic Origins of the Constitution*, University of Chicago Press, Chicago, 1958.

MacGill, Caroline E. *History of Transportation in the United States Before 1860*, Carnegie Institution, Peter Smith, Publisher, Washington, D.C., 1948.

MacKenzie, William L. *The Lives and Opinions of Benjamin F. Butler and Jesse Hoyt*, Cook Publishers, Boston, 1845.

———. *The Life and Times of Martin Van Buren and the Letters and Correspondence of Martin Van Buren*, Cooke Publishers, Boston, 1846.

McLoughlin, William G. "The Role of Religion in the Revolution: Liberty of Conscience and Cultural Cohesion in the New Nation," in *Essays on the American Revolution*, Stephen G. Kurtz, James H. Hutson, eds., University of North Carolina Press, Chapel Hill, 1973.

Manning, James H. *Century of American Savings Banks*, B. F. Buck, New York, 1917.

Marti, Donald B. "Early Agricultural Societies in New York, The Foundations of Improvement," *New York History*, Vol. 48, 1967.

Meyers, Marvin. *The Jacksonian Persuasion: Politics and Belief*, Stanford University Press, Stanford, Calif., 1957.

Miller, Douglas T. *Jacksonian Aristocracy: Class and Democracy in New York, 1830–1860*, Oxford University Press, New York, 1967.

Miller, George F. *The Academy System of the State of New York*, J. B. Lyon, Albany, 1922.

Miller, Nathan. *The Enterprise of a Free People: Aspects of Economic Development in New York State During the Canal Period, 1792–1838*, Cornell University Press, Ithaca, 1962.

Muscalus, John A. *The Use of Banking Enterprises in the Financing of Public Education, 1796–1866*, University of Pennsylvania Press, Philadelphia, 1945.

Newmyer, R. Kent. *The Supreme Court under Marshall and Taney*, Thomas Y. Crowell, New York, 1968.

North, Douglass C. *The Economic Growth of the United States, 1790–1860*, Norton, New York, 1966.

Olmstead, Alan L. *New York City Mutual Savings Banks, 1819–1861*, University of North Carolina Press, Chapel Hill, 1976.

Payne, Peter L., Lance E. Davis. *The Savings Bank of Baltimore, 1818–1866*, Johns Hopkins Press, Baltimore, 1956.

Pessen, Edward. "The Workingmen's Movement of the Jacksonian Era," *Mississippi Valley Historical Review*, Vol. 43, 1956.

Peterson, Merrill D., ed. *Democracy, Liberty, and Property: The State Constitutional Conventions of the 1820's*, Bobbs-Merrill, Indianapolis, 1966.

Pierce, Edward L. *A Treatise on American Railroad Law*, John S. Voorhies, New York, 1857.

Pierce, Harry H. *Railroads of New York: A Study of Government Aid, 1826–1875*, Harvard University Press, Cambridge, 1953.

Poor, Henry V. *Sketch of the Rise and Progress of the Internal Improvement of the Internal Commerce of the United States*, Manual of the Railroads of the United States, New York, 1881.

Pound, Roscoe. *The Formative Era of American Law*, Peter Smith, New York, 1950.

Pratt, John W. *Religion, Politics and Diversity: The Church-State Theme in New York*, Cornell University Press, Ithaca, 1967.

Pred, Allan. "Manufacturing in the American Mercantile City, 1800–1840," *Annals of the Association of American Geographers*, Vol. 56, 1966.

Pursell, Carroll W. *Early Stationary Steam Engines in America: A Study in the Migration of a Technology*, Smithsonian Institution Press, Washington, D.C., 1969.

Raguet, Condy. *A Treatise on Currency and Banking*, Augustus M. Kelley Publishers, New York, 1967 (reprint of 1840 ed.).

Rammelkamp, C. H. "The Campaign of 1824 in New York," *Annual Report of the American Historical Association, 1904*, U.S. Government Printing Office, Washington, D.C., 1905.

Redlich, Fritz. *The Molding of American Banking: Men and Ideas*, Hafner Publishing, New York, Part I, 1947; Part II, 1951.

Reid, James D. *The Telegraph in America*, Derby Brothers, New York, 1879.

Remini, Robert V. "The Albany Regency," *New York History*, Vol. 39, 1958.

Ringwalt, John L. *Development of Transportation Systems in the United States*, Railway World Office, Philadelphia, 1888.

Roche, John P., ed. *John Marshall: Major Opinions and Other Writings*, Bobbs-Merrill, Indianapolis, 1967.

Rockoff, Hugh. "The Free Banking Era: A Reexamination," *Journal of Money, Credit, and Banking*, Vol. 6, 1974.

Rogers, Henry W. "Municipal Corporations, 1701–1901," in *Two Centuries Growth of American Law, 1701–1901*, Yale Bicentennial Publications, Scribner, New York, 1902.

Rosenberg, Nathan. "Technological Change in the Machine Tool Industry, 1840–1910," *Journal of Economic History*, Vol. 23, 1963.

Rostow, Walt W. "The Take-off into Self-Sustained Growth," *Economic Journal*, Vol. 66, 1956.

_____. *The Process of Economic Growth*, Norton, New York, 1962.

Rudolph, Frederick, ed. *Essays on Education in the Early Republic*, Harvard University Press, Cambridge, 1965.

Sawyer, John E. "The Social Basis of the American System of Manufacturing," *Journal of Economic History*, Vol. 14, 1954.

Scheiber, Harry N. "Property Law, Expropriation, and Resource Allocation by Government: The United States, 1789–1910," *Journal of Economic History*, Vol. 33, 1973.

Schlesinger, Arthur M., Jr. *The Age of Jackson*, Little, Brown, Boston, 1945.

Schmidt, Louis B. "Internal Commerce and the Development of National Economy," *Journal of Political Economy*, Vol. 47, 1939.

Schumpeter, Joseph A. *The Theory of Economic Development*, Harvard University Press, Cambridge, 1936.

_____. *Business Cycles*, McGraw-Hill, New York, 1939.

_____. *Capitalism, Socialism, and Democracy*, Harper and Brothers Publishers, New York, 1942.

Seavoy, Ronald E. "Laws to Encourage Manufacturing: New York Policy and the 1811 General Incorporation Statute," *Business History Review*, Vol. 46, 1972.

_____. "Borrowed Laws to Speed Development: Michigan, 1835–1863," *Michigan History*, Vol. 59, 1975.

_____. "The Public Service Origins of the American Business Corporation," *Business History Review*, Vol. 52, 1978.

Shannon, H. A. "The Coming of General Limited Liability," *Economic History Review*, Vol. 2, 1931.

Sharp, James R. *The Jacksonians versus the Banks: Politics in the States After the Panic of 1837*, Columbia University Press, New York, 1970.

Shaw, Ronald E. *Erie Water West, A History of the Erie Canal, 1792–1854*, University of Kentucky Press, Lexington, 1966.

Shera, Jesse H. *Foundations of the Public Library: The Origins of the Public Library Movement in New England, 1629–1855*, University of Chicago Press, Chicago, 1949.

Sherwood, Sidney. *The University of the State of New York: History of Higher Education in the State of New York*, U.S. Government Printing Office, Washington, D.C., 1900.

Shryock, Richard H. *Medical Licensing in America, 1650–1965*, Johns Hopkins Press, Baltimore, 1967.

Sickels, Hiram E., ed. *Opinions of the Attorneys-General of the State of New York from the Formation of the State Government to February 1872*, Banks, Albany, 1872.

Smelser, Marshall. *The Democratic Republic, 1801–1815*, Harper and Row, New York, 1968.

Smith, Merritt R. *Harpers Ferry Armory and the New Technology: The Challenge of Change*, Cornell University Press, Ithaca, 1977.

Smith, Timothy L. "Protestant Schooling and American Nationality," *Journal of American History*, Vol. 53, 1967.

_____. "Congregation, State and Denomination: The Forming of the American Religious Structure," *William and Mary Quarterly*, Vol. 25, 1968.

Smith, Walter B. *Economic Aspects of the Second Bank of the United States*, Harvard University Press, Cambridge, 1953.

Sowers, Don C. *The Financial History of New York State from 1789 to 1912*, Columbia University Press, New York, 1914.

Spencer, Ivor D. "William L. Marcy Goes Conservative," *Mississippi Valley Historical Review*, Vol. 31, 1944.

_____. *The Victor and the Spoils, A Life of William L. Marcy*, Brown University Press, Providence, 1959.

Stevens, Frank W. *The Beginnings of the New York Central Railroad: A History*, G. P. Putnam and The Knickerbocker Press, New York, 1926.

Story, Joseph. *Commentaries on the Constitution of the United States*, Hilliard, Gray, Boston, 1833.

Strassmann, Wolfgang P. *Risk and Technological Innovation: American Manufacturing Methods During the Nineteenth Century*, Cornell University Press, Ithaca, 1959.

Street, Alfred B., ed. *The Council of Revision of New York*, William Gould Publishers, Albany, 1859.

Sumner, William G. *A History of Banking in the United States*, Journal of Commerce and Commercial Bulletin, New York, 1896.

Sundheim, Joseph H. *Law of Building and Loan Associations*, Callaghan, Chicago, 1933.

Swisher, Carl B. *American Constitutional Development*, Houghton Mifflin and The Riverside Press, Cambridge, Mass., 1954.

Taylor, George R., ed. *The Early Development of the American Cotton Textile Industry*, Harper and Row, New York, 1969 (especially Nathan Appleton, "Introduction of the Power Loom and Origin of Lowell," and Samuel Batchelder, "Introduction and Early Progress of the Cotton Manufacture in the United States").

Temin, Peter. *Iron and Steel in Nineteenth-Century America: An Economic Inquiry*, MIT Press, Cambridge, Mass., 1964.

_____. "Steam and Waterpower in the Early Nineteenth Century," *Journal of Economic History*, Vol. 26, 1966.

Thayer, Theodore. "The Land-Bank System in the American Colonies," *Journal of Economic History*, Vol. 13, 1953.

Thompson, Robert L. *Wiring a Continent, 1832–1866*, Princeton University Press, Princeton, 1947.

Timberlake, Richard H. "Denominational Factors in Nineteenth-Century Currency Experience," *Journal of Economic History*, Vol. 34, 1974.

Trescott, Paul B. *Financing American Enterprise: The Story of Commercial Banking*, Harper and Row, New York, 1963.

Trimble, William. "Diverging Tendencies in the New York Democracy in the Period of the Locofocos," *American Historical Review*, Vol. 24, 1919.

Troubat, Francis J. *The Law of Commandatary and Limited Partnerships in the United States*, James Kay, Philadelphia, 1853.

Van Ingen, Philip. *The New York Academy of Medicine: Its First Hundred Years*, Columbia University Press, New York, 1949.

Vatter, Barbara. "Industrial Borrowing by the New England Textile Mills, 1840–1860, A Comment," *Journal of Economic History*, Vol. 21, 1961.

Walker, Timothy. *Introduction to American Law*, P. H. Nicklin and T. Johnson Law Booksellers, Philadelphia, 1837.

Wallace, Michael. "Changing Concepts of Party in the United States: New York, 1814–1828," *American Historical Review*, Vol. 74, 1968.

Ware, Caroline F. *The Early New England Cotton Manufacture: A Study in Industrial Beginnings*, Houghton Mifflin, Boston, 1931.

Warren, Charles. *The Supreme Court in United States History*, Little, Brown, Boston, 1932.

_____. *Bankruptcy in United States History*, Harvard University Press, Cambridge, 1935.

Welfling, Weldon. *Savings Banking in New York State: A Study of*

Changes in Savings Bank Practice and Policy Occasioned by Important Economic Changes, Duke University Press, Durham, N.C., 1939.

Wells, Guy F. *Parish Education in Colonial Virginia*, Columbia University Press, New York, 1923.

Wendell, Mitchell. *Relations Between the Federal and State Courts*, Columbia University Press, New York, 1949.

Wilburn, Jean A. *Biddle's Bank: The Crucial Years*, Columbia University Press, New York, 1967.

Williamson, Harold F. "Money and Commercial Banking, 1789–1865," in *The Growth of the American Economy*, Harold F. Williamson, ed., Prentice-Hall, Englewood Cliffs, N.J., 1958.

Wilson, Charles. "The Entrepreneur in the Industrial Revolution in Britain," in *Europe and the Industrial Revolution*, Sima Liberman, ed., Schenkman Publishers, Cambridge, Mass., 1972.

Wyllie, Irvin G. "The Search for an American Law of Charity, 1776–1844," *Mississippi Valley Historical Review*, Vol. 46, 1959.

Young, James H. *The Toadstool Millionaires*, Princeton University Press, Princeton, 1961.

Zartman, Lester W., ed. *Yale Readings in Insurance*, Yale University Press, New Haven, 1919.

Zollman, Carl F. *American Law of Charities*, Bruce Publishing, Milwaukee, 1924.

Anon., "Banking as it Ought to Be," *The United States Magazine and Democratic Review*, Vol. 12, 1843.

Anon., "Railroad Legislation in New York in 1849," *The Merchant's Magazine and Commercial Review*, Vol. 21, July-Dec. 1849.

Index

About the Author

RONALD E. SEAVOY is Associate Professor of History at Bowling Green State University, Bowling Green, Ohio. His articles have appeared in *Business History Review*, *Michigan History*, and other journals.